THE UNKNOWN
RUSSIAN
THEATER
AN ANTHOLOGY

TRANSLATED & EDITED BY

MICHAEL GREEN

AND

JEROME KATSELL

Ardis, Ann Arbor

Copyright © 1991 by Ardis Publishers
All rights reserved under International and
Pan-American Copyright Conventions
Printed in the United States of America

Ardis Publishers
2901 Heatherway
Ann Arbor, Michigan 48104

 # 22275376

Library of Congress Cataloging-in-Publication Data

The unknown Russian theater / edited & translated by Michael Green &
Jerome Katsell.
v.   cm.
Translated from the Russian.
ISBN 0-88233-554-5 (v. 1) : $39.95
1. Russian drama—19th century—Translations into English.
2. English drama—Translations from Russian.   I. Green, Michael.
II. Katsell, Jerome.
PG3245.U55   1990
891.72'308—dc20   90-45667
CIP

110442

CONTENTS

INTRODUCTION

The aim of this volume is a modest one, to serve as a bypath rather than a main road. It is an anthology of prerevolutionary Russian drama, but not of the works that predictably find their way into collections of this kind. Instead of the acknowledged "masterpieces" and "classics," the reader will here discover works that have, somewhat mysteriously, remained virtually unknown in the English-speaking world. And for a simple reason—they are, for the most part, previously untranslated. This volume does contain two plays that have already appeared in English: Ivan Turgenev's *The Weakest Link*, in a 1924 version, and Alexei Pisemsky's *Baal* (in the translation here included) in a literary journal. It is our hope that the plays that follow will serve as a supplement to the orthodox and traditional anthologies which it does not aim to rival or supersede.

But let us not be over-modest. If the five-act *Month in the Country* is incontestably Turgenev's dramatic *chef d'oeuvre*, a one-acter such as *The Weakest Link* is not at all its inferior in the finesse and subtlety which are the distinguishing marks of Turgenev the playwright. Alexander Ostrovsky, that staple of the Russian theatrical repertoire, has not been an exportable commodity, probably because of the intensely national nature of his subject matter. (One thinks of the narrowly oppressive life of the merchant class on the upper Volga depicted in *The Thunderstorm*, an earlier play than *Larisa*, which usually serves to represent him in anthologies.)

Nikolai Gogol's *Inspector General* has been called "perhaps Russia's greatest play, and one of the greatest comedies of the world repertoire." However, it is a play that centers on Russian provincial life, and before writing it Gogol had already been working on another drama that could be seen as a prelude to the cycle of stories that imaged forth the "unreal city" that was Gogol's St. Petersburg. If the central figure of *The Order of Vladimir, Third Class* is a bureaucrat obsessed with gaining a government decoration, the world of Pisemsky's *Baal* is that of the rampant capitalism of the 1870s in Russia. Though rated by many critics as inferior to Pisemsky's "anthology" play *A Bitter Fate* (1859), *Baal*, first produced in 1873, was held by a French critic to be not unworthy of Balzac himself.

Alone among the writers of this collection, Fyodor Sologub's work belongs to the immediate prerevolutionary period. He was important to such movements as Decadence and Symbolism, which dominated the literary stage at the beginning of this century. Although, according to D. S. Mirsky, his was "the most refined and most delicate of all modern Russian poetry," Sologub is best remembered for his brilliant novel, *The Petty Demon*, whose hero, the odious Peredonov, seems to embody the ignorance, malice, servility and paranoia of Russian minor officialdom. While Sologub's dramatic work hardly reaches the level of his best fiction and poetry, it exhibits an impressive mastery of the theater and a hard,

ironic brilliance. *Vanka the Steward and the Page Jehan*, included here, has a dual-
ity of construction that is characteristic of Symbolism.

This introduction, then, will not attempt a potted history of the Russian nine-
teenth-century theater, of which full-scale studies exist to provide a broad
overview; rather it will content itself with specifics—an illuminating detail here, a
significant connection there.

Peter's new capital and his Table of Ranks had given a local habitation and a
name to a bureaucracy that has remained a fixture of Russian life. The central action of *The Order of Vladimir, Third Class* is built around the obsession of a petty
official with the attainment by hook or by crook of an honor awarded only to
government servants of the highest rank. It is clear from the surviving fragments
of this comedy that Gogol's first dramatic foray, had he not lost creative impetus,
would hardly have been unworthy of the author of *The Inspector General*, which
was soon to follow.

"Fragments"—yes; but each of them sufficiently complete to be deserving of
the subtitle "Little Comedy," as Pushkin's dramatic miniatures had been given
that of "Little Tragedies" by their author. It is worth asking why Gogol left unfinished a play which might have preceded *Inspector General* as a triumphant comedy of Russian life. It was left to Meyerhold's fabled 1926 version of *Inspector
General* to transform it into what *Vladimir* could have been—not a comedy of the
Russian imperial boondocks, but of the glamorized capital city of the mayoral
couple's social-climbing dreams.

One reason for *Vladimir*'s unfinished state is the complexity of its action.
Apart from the central theme of Barsukov's obsession with the government
award into which, surrealistically, he ultimately imagines himself transformed,
there were to be a number of subplots. These subplots comprise the surviving
fragments that are offered here. One such subplot involves the lawsuit brought
by Barsukov's brother, a provincial landowner, concerning the alleged forgery of
a rich aunt's will. A second subplot features Barsukov's widowed sister and her
attempts to tyrannize her son into matrimony. There is also the obsessive petty
snobbery of the servants, reflecting the "high society" of their betters in a distort-
ing mirror.

The last of these subplots, originally entitled *High Society Scenes*, shows Gogol
at his most masterly. He manipulates domineering mother, smothered thirty-
year-old son, and shameless scoundrel in his most adroit manner. Like his best-
known work, this "fragment" has a simple structure that provides an excuse for a
series of encounters that allow for the creation of "proverbial" grotesques in the
best Gogolian style. However, *Sobachkin (Mr. Dog)*, as we have entitled this
piece, is but one of a series of a diversity that Gogol, never a deviser of ingenious
plots, found impossible to weld into an effective unity. And, as we shall see, fear
of the censorship also played a part in Gogol's failure to complete this work.

On the subject of censorship, Gogol's fear was vividly expressed in early
1833, at the time he was working on *Vladimir*:

> There's a comedy I'm dying to write. When I was in Moscow [in 1832], when I was on the
> road, and when I arrived here too, I couldn't get it out of my head; but I haven't written any-
> thing down yet. I began to put a plot together the other day, and a title has already written it-
> self on a fat white notebook: *Vladimir, Third Class*. And how much malice, laughter, salt

there is in it: But suddenly I pulled up sharply, having realized that my pen was running up
against such things as the censorship couldn't possibly let through.

Turgenev began a short obituary of Gogol published in the *Moscow Gazette*
(Moskovskie vedomosti) in 1852 with these words: "Gogol is dead! What
Russian soul will not be shaken by these three words?" (In Russian there are two
words.) This notice, in which Turgenev had the temerity to apply the epithet
"great" to the dead writer, was published in Moscow after having been forbidden
by the St. Petersburg censorship. Such apparent flouting of law, which seems to
have been the result of chance rather than ingenuity, brought down upon
Turgenev's head the wrath of no less a personage than Nicholas I, on whose orders Turgenev was placed under arrest and forced to endure a month on his estate under police supervision.

By the time of this indiscretion, Turgenev had decided to abandon the career
of dramatist on which he had been set. From the mid-1840s to the early 1850s,
Turgenev's central preoccupation had been to reform the Russian stage, to create
a new repertoire for the impoverished Russian theater of his day: "We do not yet
possess a dramatic literature and are still without dramatists; that vein in our na-
tive soil has yet to produce abundant ore." Turgenev's notebooks from this period reveal that in addition to his ten published plays, he had plans and sketches
for an additional nine.

Alfred de Musset was the writer whose work most profoundly influenced
Turgenev the dramatist. The Russians had been the first to appreciate the origi-
nality of de Musset as a dramatist, and it has been suggested that an anonymous
review that appeared in *The Contemporary* (No. 12, 1841, apparently by I.I.
Panaev) offers such a perceptive understanding of the special qualities shared by
de Musset's little *Proverbes* and Turgenev's one-act "Proverb," *The Weakest Link*
(1848), that even though it makes no mention of Turgenev, it deserves to be
quoted:

> M. de Musset has created a new genre of brief dramatic conversations, to which he has given
> the name of proverb. What marks this new kind of play? It is almost totally devoid of scenic
> action: its chief merit consists of the manner in which it succeeds in conveying what is subtle
> and refined in the sort of conversation to be heard in a *salon*.

The critic's regret that "the lack of style for *salon* conversation in our country
renders difficult the translation of de Musset's *Proverbes* into Russian" is puzzling
if he did know, as he surely must have, *The Weakest Link*. Turgenev's little play
clearly demonstrates the opposite to be true: that the language of sophisticated
society can be made to express the most delicate subtleties of "psychological action." It should be noted that a literal translation of the title of Turgenev's play,
"Where It is Thin, There It Breaks," has the proverbial ring characteristic of de
Musset's *Proverbes (Il faut qu'une porte soit ouverte ou fermée*, for example).

If there was ever a play in which "nothing happens," then it is surely *The
Weakest Link*. This is another drama on the favorite Russian theme of a marriage
proposal that somehow doesn't get made, and the "action" of the play is in fact a
psychological duel between the male and female protagonists. Card games, billiards, tea-drinking are made to serve a choric function very much in the manner

of Chekhov. How prematurely Chekhovian is the scene where Vera, who of course plays the piano, produces a musical commentary on the progress of her conversation with Gorsky, who comes to the brink of surrendering his treasured bachelor freedom. *The Weakest Link* is an early example of psychological drama in a Russian setting, and in it Turgenev, as only he could, combined psychological insight with lyric grace.

A great admirer and devoted friend of Turgenev, Pisemsky, is best remembered for two works written in successive years: the novel *A Thousand Souls* of 1858, and the drama *A Bitter Fate* of 1859. Both these compositions are fine examples of critical realism. The last decade of Pisemsky's life was dedicated to the theater. During these years the main object of his attack was the relentless capitalist expansionism characteristic of Russia of the time. Pisemsky now revealed a heightened sense of social responsibility that had been less evident in his earlier work. Rebuked for betraying the cause of pure art, Pisemsky responded angrily that it was a writer's duty "to expose all exploiters, concessionaires, speculators...."

Pisemsky does not appear to have taken umbrage at a friend's definition of the plays of these years as "dramatic pamphlets." These anti-capitalist "pamphlets" include: *The Plunderers* and *Baal* (1873), *An Enlightened Time* (1875), and *The Financial Genius* (1876). In the increasingly reactionary political atmosphere of the period, Pisemsky encountered difficulties with both performance and publication of these dramas. When, in desperation, he conferred with the head of the censorship committee and asked that gentleman's advice as to what he should write, he was informed that "it is better not to write at all."

The play of Pisemsky included here, however, does not attempt to describe government bureaucracy, and, consequently, did not encounter censorship difficulties. In Pisemsky's own words, describing the theme of the play:

> Nowadays everyone is worshipping Baal, that God of money and material success, which, like that Fate of the Greeks in days of yore, hovers over the world and prophesies everything that is to come... Under his pressure men work abomination and perform great deeds, they suffer and they triumph.

Though these plays have been described as "pamphlets," it would not be just to dismiss *Baal* as a one-dimensional work. As the passage quoted above makes clear, under the influence of Baal it is possible to perform "great deeds" as well as to "work abomination." In *Baal* lust for gold is the dominant theme, but it does not easily overwhelm the power of the emotions. Mirovich, the play's hero, a bureaucrat with a conscience, is hopelessly torn between his love for a capitalist's wife and material survival. It is Mirovich who pronounces the play's bitter coda:

> Great God Baal, accept two more sacrifices for your altar. Torture them, bloodthirsty God, tear out their hearts and souls with your fiery claws. Soon all will bow down to you, in this century stripped of ideals, aspirations and hopes, this century of the brazen ruble, the forged papers, the phony evidence.

Pisemsky's sponsor in Moscow literary circles and a longtime source of practical support was Alexander Ostrovsky. Ostrovsky's fifty or so plays are the first great corpus of Russian national drama and still form the backbone of the repertoire of the Russian theater. Perhaps it is the strong national flavor of Ostrovsky's drama which has been a barrier to its universal acceptance.

The only one of Ostrovsky's plays to become widely known in the West is *The Thunderstorm* (1859), the heroine of which is driven to suicide by her tyrannical mother-in-law. Yet surely no less deserving of a place in the international repertoire is *Larisa*, written some twenty years later. The textbook title of this play is *The Dowerless Bride*. Since this title is somewhat maladroit in English, we replace it with the name of the heroine, who, no less than Katerina in *The Thunderstorm*, provides the Russian actress with one of her great tragic roles—perhaps the closest she has to a Desdemona.

Ostrovsky wrote comedies for the most part, and only four of his plays are designated "drama"; both *Larisa (1879)* and *The Thunderstorm* belong to this small group. *Larisa* is not only a tragedy of character, but also a subtle and penetrating study of the Russian social structure of the late nineteenth century. No Marxist sociologist could make a more perceptive analysis of the embourgeoisement of the landed aristocracy than that embodied in the figure of Paratov. The manipulative and scheming mother of the play's heroine Larisa is intent on exploiting her daughter's beauty to restore the prestige of an impoverished noble family. The newly powerful merchant class is represented primarily by the wealthy Knurov, who does everything in his power to make Larisa his mistress. Desperate to escape an unbearable situation, Larisa consents to marry the pathetic but respectable government official Karandyshev. Although a social tragedy, the play is not without its comic element. Ostrovsky's comedy *The Forest* had been a great popular success, and one of its characters, the traveling actor Neschastlivtsev ("Mr. Unfortunate"), makes a reappearance here.

In these days of women's liberation, Larisa's plight will surely strike a chord, especially her bitter response to Karandyshev's remark: "They look on you like a thing." "A thing—yes, that's it, a thing... at last a word has been found to fit me." Larisa has long been contemplating suicide, and the tone of her response to Karandyshev when, mad with jealousy, he puts a bullet through her breast, must be a challenge to any actress: "Ah, thank you for that." Melodrama? Irony? Pathos? A combination of all three? Such is the stuff of this remarkable play.

Fyodor Sologub was born into a poor St. Petersburg family and made his living as a schoolteacher in the provinces. With such a background, he might have been expected to have gone the way of social protest, as the "plebeians" of the 1860s had done before him. Sologub's protest, however, was of a different kind: he became the most thoroughgoing decadent of the Decadents (at least on paper), tirelessly reiterating the supremacy of art and the artist's creative will. A private mythology strongly tinged with fin-de-siècle diabolism pervades Sologub's work. His central myth is of a world ruled by the malevolent dragon of the sun; thus life is seen as an evil, darkness and death as a longed-for good.

Vanka the Steward and the Page Jehan had its first performance at Komissarzhevskaya's theater, the only theater willing to put on Symbolist drama. More rigorously than any other drama of the period, *Vanka* formalizes the dual-

ity of vision central to the Symbolist theater by means of an ingenious construc-
tive device: a simple tale of adultery is subjected to contrasting treatment in a series of alternating scenes; those set in ancient Russia strike a note of coarse lech-
ery, while those set in medieval France breathe an air of refined chivalry. Thus
the spectator is constantly thrust from one plane to another, exactly in the manner prescribed by Meyerhold's "grotesque theater." Curiously enough, only the
play's "Russian" scenes were well received by contemporary audiences. For a
later (1915) production, Sologub added a third, modern variant of the adultery
theme and gave the play a new title that might be rendered in English as *Hanky-
Panky through the Ages*. Most regrettably, this version has remained unpublished.

A kind of pendant to *Vanka*, and another playful excursion into *style russe*,
was the parodistic fairytale play *Night Dances*, which bristles with facetious
anachronisms and literary "in" jokes. Evreinov's 1909 production of this play
was a lighthearted amateur affair that seems to have included in its cast half of literary and artistic St. Petersburg—among the writers, Voloshin, A. Tolstoi,
Remizov and Gorodetsky, and among the painters, Bakst and Somov; the
dances of the title were choreographed by Fokine.

The variety of style in this collection gives some idea of the rich legacy of prerevolutionary Russian theater that still awaits discovery in the English-speaking
world. Apart from Ostrovsky, the writers selected here were not primarily or ex-
clusively dramatists. Perhaps this selection of plays will offer new insights into
the achievement of these men.

NIKOLAI GOGOL

THE ORDER OF VLADIMIR, THIRD CLASS
FOUR SCENES IN SEARCH OF A PLAY

SCENE I
THE MORNING OF A GOVERNMENT OFFICIAL

CHARACTERS

Pavel Petrovich, a government official
Katerina Ivanovna, his wife
Alexander Ivanovich, another government official
Schreider, head clerk in Pavel Petrovich's office
First Servant
Second Servant

I

An office. Several shelves with books. Papers scattered about a table. Pavel Petrovich, a government official comes out in his dressing gown, stretches and rings for a servant. Voice from the anteroom, "Coming!" Pavel Petrovich rings a second time. Again the same voice, "Coming!" Pavel Petrovich impatiently rings a third time. Enter servant.

PAVEL PETROVICH. Have you gone deaf or something?
FIRST SERVANT. Not in the least.
PAVEL PETROVICH. Then why didn't you condescend to put in an appearance before my third ring?
FIRST SERVANT. What did you want me to do? I couldn't just throw everything aside when I was polishing boots.
PAVEL PETROVICH. And what was Ivan doing?
FIRST SERVANT. He was sweeping up, then went out to the stable.
PAVEL PETROVICH. Let me have the dog. *(Servant carries in dog.)* Tippy-Tippler! Tippy-Tippler! Hey, Tippy! Let me put on your little ribbon. *(Hooks ribbon to the dog's tail.)*
Second Servant comes running in.
SECOND SERVANT. Alexander Ivanovich!
PAVEL PETROVICH. Show him in. *(Hurriedly shoves the dog to one side and unrolls a legal code.)*

II

Pavel Petrovich and Alexander Ivanovich, also a government official.

ALEXANDER IVANOVICH. Good morning to you, Pavel Petrovich!
PAVEL PETROVICH. And how are you today, Alexander Ivanovich?
ALEXANDER IVANOVICH. Thank you for asking. I haven't disturbed you, have I?

PAVEL PETROVICH. How can you ask such a thing? You know I'm always busy with something. Well, so what time did you get home then?

ALEXANDER IVANOVICH. Sometime after five in the morning. As soon as I turned off Officer Street, just when I was approaching the baker's shop, I asked a passerby, "Tell me brother, did you hear the clock strike?" "It has struck five already," he says. And that's how I found out it was past five.

PAVEL PETROVICH. Just imagine, I arrived at almost the same time myself. So how did your little game of whist go, hee-hee-hee?

ALEXANDER IVANOVICH. Hee-hee-hee! I have to admit, yes, I even saw it in my dreams.

PAVEL PETROVICH. Hee-hee-hee! What's he doing playing a king? I can't help thinking. And I've got three clubs in my hand and one of them a queen; and Luke Fedoseyevich, I noticed, hasn't got a bidding hand.

ALEXANDER IVANOVICH. The eighth rubber lasted the longest.

PAVEL PETROVICH. Yes. *(Falls silent.)* I'm just giving Luke Fedoseyevich a wink so he'd trump—nothing doing. All he had to do was trump, and my jack of spades would take the trick.

ALEXANDER IVANOVICH. Come on now, Pavel Petrovich, the jack doesn't take the trick.

PAVEL PETROVICH. Yes, he does.

ALEXANDER IVANOVICH. He does not—there's no way you could fit one into your hand.

PAVEL PETROVICH. But Luke Fedoseyevich's seven of spades? Surely you haven't forgotten that?

ALEXANDER IVANOVICH. Did he have a spade? Slipped my mind somehow.

PAVEL PETROVICH. Of course, he had two spades: the four—he covered the queen with it—and the seven.

ALEXANDER IVANOVICH. No, Pavel Petrovich, begging your pardon, he couldn't have had more than one spade.

PAVEL PETROVICH. Gracious heavens, Alexander Ivanovich, who are you telling this? Two spades! I can see them now, a four and a seven.

ALEXANDER IVANOVICH. A four that's so, but there was no seven. Surely you can see that in that case he'd have trumped.

PAVEL PETROVICH. I'll be damned if he didn't, Alexander Ivanovich. I'll be damned if he didn't!

ALEXANDER IVANOVICH. No, Pavel Petrovich. That would be a completely impossible set of circumstances.

PAVEL PETROVICH. Very well, Alexander Ivanovich! Here's the solution. Let's go see Luke Fedoseyevich tomorrow. What do you say to that?

ALEXANDER IVANOVICH. Very well.

PAVEL PETROVICH. And we'll put it to him personally. Did he have a seven of spades in his hand or not?

ALEXANDER IVANOVICH. Fine, I've nothing against it. But if you consider the matter, it's strange that Luke Fedoseyevich played so badly. You wouldn't say he's devoid of intelligence. After all, he conducts himself with finesse....

PAVEL PETROVICH. To that you can add he's an extremely well informed man. A type, between the two of us, you don't come across often in Russia. Were you at His Excellency's?

ALEXANDER IVANOVICH. Yes, I was. I've just come from his place. It was a bit on the cold side this morning. You know, I think, that I've taken to wearing an elk-lined undercoat, much better than flannel and doesn't make you too hot. So on this occasion I ordered my fur coat. When I got to His Excellency's—His Excellency is still asleep. I waited patiently. Well, and then we got to talking about this and that.

PAVEL PETROVICH. And did my name make an appearance?

ALEXANDER IVANOVICH. How could you doubt it? Yes, it turned out to be an exceedingly interesting conversation.

PAVEL PETROVICH (brightening). How? In what way?

ALEXANDER IVANOVICH. Let me give you a detailed account. There's one particularly interesting thing. Among other things, His Excellency asked where I'd been keeping myself and why he hadn't seen me for such a long time, and expressed an interest in last night's little party and who was there. So I said, "Your Excellency, there were Pavel Grigorovich Borshchov, Ilya Vladimirovich Bubunitsyn." After each word his Excellency said "hm!" And I said, "and there was also someone known to Your Excellency...."

PAVEL PETROVICH. And who would that be?

ALEXANDER IVANOVICH. Just a moment. And what do you think his Excellency said to that?

PAVEL PETROVICH. I don't know.

ALEXANDER IVANOVICH. He said, "And who would that be?" "Pavel Petrovich Barsukov," I answered. "Hm!" said His Excellency, "he's an official, and at the same time..." (Raises his eyes.) Your ceilings are rather well decorated— at your expense or the landlord's?

PAVEL PETROVICH. This is a government apartment you know.

ALEXANDER IVANOVICH. Not bad, not bad at all. Baskets, a lyre, bread and tambourines all around. Very, very life-like!

PAVEL PETROVICH (impatiently). But what exactly did His Excellency say?

ALEXANDER IVANOVICH. Oh yes, I'd forgotten. What was it he said any- way?

PAVEL PETROVICH. He said, "hm!" His Excellency said, "hm!... An offi- cial, I believe...."

ALEXANDER IVANOVICH. Yes, yes that's what he said, "...an official... well, and... works in my office...." After that the conversation wasn't so interest- ing and turned to everyday matters.

PAVEL PETROVICH. And the conversation didn't get around to me again?

ALEXANDER IVANOVICH. No.

PAVEL PETROVICH (to himself). Well, not much so far. Oh heavens above! What if he had said, "...a certain Barsukov, in respect of this, that and the other of his services, I hereby present him with...."

III

The same and Schreider (who peers through the door).

PAVEL PETROVICH. Come in, come in. It's all right; please come over here. Is it about the report?

SCHREIDER. Your signature is needed. This is a memorandum for the board, and this report goes to the Director.

PAVEL PETROVICH *(reading meanwhile)*. "Attention: Director..." What's the meaning of this? The margins are uneven. How can that be? Did you know you could be put under arrest? *(Directs a meaningful look at Schreider.)*

SCHREIDER. I spoke to Ivan Ivanovich about that. He told me the Minister wouldn't pay any attention to such a trifle.

PAVEL PETROVICH. Trifle! It's fine for Ivan Ivanovich to talk that way. Yes. I think the same way myself: the Minister certainly wouldn't bother about it. But what if he did bother?

SCHREIDER. It can be rewritten, but then it will be late. However, since you've been kind enough to say that the Minister isn't likely...

PAVEL PETROVICH. Yes! That's all true. I completely agree with you—he won't bother with such trifles. But what happens if he were to say, "Let's have a look, is there enough room here for the margins?"

SCHREIDER. In that case, I'll immediately rewrite it.

PAVEL PETROVICH. Exactly—"in that case." I'm talking to you and explaining this, you see, because you've received a university education. Otherwise, I wouldn't waste my breath.

SCHREIDER. I made so bold only because the Minister himself...

PAVEL PETROVICH. I don't disagree in the slightest. That's how it is—the Minister wouldn't even bother to look at it, it wouldn't even enter his head. But what if suddenly...? What then?

SCHREIDER. I'll rewrite it. *(Exits.)*

IV

PAVEL PETROVICH *(shrugs and turns to Alexander Ivanovich)*. Just as addle-brained as ever. A decent enough young fellow. Not long since he graduated the university, but here *(points to his forehead)* zero. You can't imagine, my dear Alexander Ivanovich, how much hard work it took me to get everything straightened out around here. You should have seen the shape things were in when I took on the job: just imagine, not a single clerk could write the letters of the alphabet correctly. You'd take a look and someone would have put a "to" in the wrong place. Then someone else would write "Ex" on one line and "cellency" on the next. In a word, it was a terrible mess—a regular Tower of Babel. But now, if you pick up any document, why it's just beautiful! Perfection! The heart rejoices, the spirit is triumphant. Have we put things in order? Everything!

ALEXANDER IVANOVICH. You've achieved rank through sweat and blood.

PAVEL PETROVICH *(with a sigh)*. That's it exactly, sweat and blood. What's to be done about it, it's my nature after all. Just think where I'd be today if I'd blown my own horn. There wouldn't be room on my chest for all the awards. But what do you expect of me? That's just not the way I am. I may often drop a hint, let slip the odd reminder, but to say it straight out, to request something for myself directly..., no, that's not my style! Others may constantly win the prizes... But that just isn't my nature... I can lower myself to anything, but never to the contemptible! *(Sighs.)* I have only one desire... to get a medal around my neck. Not because it would attract interest, but simply so people could see I was respected by the powers that be. I want to ask of you, my most good-hearted Alexander Ivanovich, well, if the occasion should arise, just naturally in passing— to drop his Excellency a hint, that Barsukov has established such order in his office, order rarely encountered anywhere—something along those lines.

ALEXANDER IVANOVICH. With the greatest pleasure, if the occasion should arise.

V

The same and Katerina Alexandrovna, wife of Pavel Petrovich.

KATERINA ALEXANDROVNA *(catching sight of Alexander Ivanovich)*. Well, if it isn't Alexander Ivanovich! My goodness, it's been a long time since we've seen each other! You must have quite forgotten me. How is Natalya Fominishna?

ALEXANDER IVANOVICH. Thank God she's in good health. But she was almost taken ill a week ago.

KATERINA ALEXANDROVNA. Oh?

ALEXANDER IVANOVICH. She had some colic and shortness of breath in her chest and the pit of her stomach. The doctor prescribed a purgative and a poultice of camomile and salammoniac.

KATERINA ALEXANDROVNA. You should try homeopathic remedies.

PAVEL PETROVICH. Really, it's amazing when you think of it—the spread of enlightenment. Here you are, Katerina Alexandrovna, talking homeopathics. Not long ago I was at the circus. And guess what? A little fellow about, how can I give you an idea, about so big *(indicates with his hand)* not more than three years old. You should have seen how he could dance a jig on the thinnest of tightropes! I'm serious when I assure you that one is breathless with fright.

ALEXANDRA IVANOVNA. Melas sings very well.

PAVEL PETROVICH *(meaningfully)*. Melas? Yes indeed!—with great feeling!

ALEXANDER IVANOVICH. Yes, very well.

PAVEL PETROVICH. Did you notice how skillfully she hits a note right up here? *(Twiddles his fingers in front of his eyes.)*

ALEXANDER IVANOVICH. Exactly, she hits it with amazing precision. But it's almost two o'clock.

PAVEL PETROVICH. And where are you off to, Alexander Ivanovich?

ALEXANDER IVANOVICH. Time to go! I've still got to stop by three more places before lunch.

PAVEL PETROVICH. Well, good-bye then. When will we see each other again? Oh, yes, I forgot—tomorrow we'll be at Luke Fedoseyevich's, won't we?

ALEXANDER IVANOVICH. To be sure. *(Bows.)*

KATERINA ALEXANDROVNA. Farewell, Alexander Ivanovich!

ALEXANDER IVANOVICH *(in the hallway, putting on his fur coat)*. I can't stand that sort. Doesn't do a thing, just puts on weight and pretends he's the one who knows what's what, and did this and took care of that. Now I see what he's after! Decorations! He'll get them, the scoundrel: He'll get them! That kind always makes it. And me? I'm five years his senior in the service and have yet to be put forward. What a revolting physiognomy! And how he played the coy innocent! He has no desire for honors, he'd only like the powers that be to take some notice of him. Even asked me to put in a word. You've certainly found the right fellow for that, old boy! I'll do you such a good turn that you'll never get an award! Won't get it! *(Punches his hand several times for emphasis and exits.)*

SCENE II
THE LAWSUIT

CHARACTERS

Alexander Ivanovich Prolyotov, Senate Departmental Chief
Chrysanth Petrovich Burdyukov, landowner
Andrei, servant

I

A study. Prolyotov, a Senate Departmental Secretary, sits by himself in an armchair and hiccups repeatedly.

PROLYOTOV. What's the matter with me? A regular belching session! Yesterday's lunch has lodged in my gullet. Those button mushrooms and that fish soup. You just eat and eat; ugh, the devil alone knows what you stuff yourself with! *(Hiccups.)* Here we go *(hiccups)*, again! *(Hiccups.)* One more time *(hiccups)*. Well, let's try for a fourth! *(Hiccups.)* The hell with it, why not a fourth. Shall I read the *Northern Bee* again and see what's up? I'm sick of this *Northern Bee*, it's just like a woman who's been an old maid too long. *(Reads and suddenly shrieks.)* An award for Krakhmanov! Eh? Petrushka Krakhmanov! He was just a little kid like that. *(Indicates with his hand.)* I got him into the Cadet Corps myself. What do you think of that? *(Continues to read and shriek, eyes popping.)* What's this? What's this? Surely it can't be Burdyukov? Yes, it is, Pavel Petrovich Burdyukov, promoted! What's the world coming to? A bribe taker, hauled twice before the court; his father was a thief, robbed the treasury, as loathsome a creature as you can imagine. What's the world coming to? But then all the world takes him for a decent fellow. The scoundrel! He says, "The Bukhtelev affair hasn't been properly settled, the Senate hasn't looked into it." What do you think of that? It's just that the scoundrel found out my share was twenty thousand, so why shouldn't he get some too? Like a dog in his den, if he can't have it, no one else can. Well I know your kind; you can pull your act on someone else! I've heard a few things about you. It's maddening when you pick up a newspaper, take a glance and all you feel is sickness at heart and disgust. Hey there, Andrei!

II

SERVANT *(entering)*. What can I do for you, sir?
PROLYOTOV. Get rid of this paper. What put it into your head to bring it anyway? Fool that you are! *(Andrei takes away the paper.)* How about that Burdyukov, eh? That's someone, not to mince words, I'd like to see deported to Kamchatka. I have to admit it would be the greatest pleasure to play him a nasty trick. I'd do it this very moment, but so far the opportunity hasn't presented itself. May I ask your advice? God is wrath. And I'd like to treat you sweet and gentle and dab your lips with scented ointment. And what a pair of lips the scoundrel has on him. Lips like an ox, like a son-of-a-bitch!

SERVANT. Burdyukov has arrived.

PROLYOTOV. Who?

SERVANT. Burdyukov has arrived, just now.

PROLYOTOV. What's this nonsense you're blathering!

SERVANT. It's just as I say, Sir.

PROLYOTOV. You're lying, you idiot! Burdyukov visiting me? Pavel Petrovich Burdyukov!

SERVANT. No, not Pavel Petrovich, but some other Burdyukov.

PROLYOTOV. What do you mean, some other Burdyukov?

SERVANT. See for yourself, Sir. He's right here.

PROLYOTOV. Show him in.

III

Prolyotov and Chrysanth Petrovich Burdyukov.

BURDYUKOV. Excuse me for disturbing you. Circumstances and certain business affairs compelled me to leave my home town. I've come to request your personal assistance, your patronage.

PROLYOTOV *(aside).* Yes, certainly a different one, although there is a certain resemblance. *(Aloud.)* What is it you wish, and how can I be of service?

BURDYUKOV *(with a shake of his shoulders).* Legal action, a lawsuit!

PROLYOTOV. A lawsuit? Against whom?

BURDYUKOV. My own brother.

PROLYOTOV. First tell me your surname, and then explain the whole business. Please, take a seat here.

BURDYUKOV. My surname is Burdyukov, the son of Pyotr Khristoforovich, and this action is against my own brother, Pavel Petrovich Burdyukov.

PROLYOTOV. What are you saying! What? No, it can't be!

BURDYUKOV. Why are you staring at me like that? Do you think I'd leave Tambov and come galloping by post chaise for nothing?

PROLYOTOV. God be praised that you've taken up such a good cause. Let's get to know each other better. There isn't a more intelligent action you could have thought up. Just tell me now there isn't any justice or greatness of spirit. Why here it is. Here's a brother bound by blood, family ties, but no weakness is shown! Legal proceedings against his own brother! Let me embrace you.

BURDYUKOV. By all means! I'll embrace you myself for your readiness to help. *(They embrace.)* At first, I must confess, looking at your countenance, I couldn't believe that you are a sound man.

PROLYOTOV. How do you like that! Why so?

BURDYUKOV. I'm serious. Allow me to ask; is it true that when your departed mother was expecting you, she was frightened by something?

PROLYOTOV. What kind of nonsense is that?

BURDYUKOV. No, I'm telling you, don't be offended, such things happen very often. Our assessor, for example, has a lower jaw like a ram, as if it had been cut off, all overgrown with wool, just like a ram. And it all came about by an insignificant circumstance, when his dear departed mother was giving birth, a ram comes trotting up to the window and the evil one himself makes it start bleating.

PROLYOTOV. Well, let's leave the assessor and the ram in peace. How glad I am to see you!

BURDYUKOV. And I'm so glad to have acquired such protection. Only now that I'm beginning to get a better look at you, I see that your face is somehow familiar. We had a lieutenant in the carbineer division who was the spitting image of you. A terrible drunk! I can tell you a day didn't go by without him getting his face smashed.

PROLYOTOV *(aside)*. This provincial bear clearly hasn't acquired the habit of holding his tongue. All the rubbish he has in his heart is immediately on his lips. *(Aloud.)* I don't have much time; let's, please, get to the matter at hand.

BURDYUKOV. Very well, but it's not something easily told. It's quite a tangled business. Did you ever know Evdokiya Malafeyevna Zherbtsova, a landowner of the Ustyug district? You didn't—very well. Her relationship to me, as well as that beast my brother, is that of aunt. Her closest heirs are my brother and myself—as you can see things have come to a pretty pass. And there's our sister too—the one who married General Pavlishchev. There's nothing to be said about her, she's already gotten her share. But that scoundrel, my brother, he's fit to be the devil's uncle. So he went to our aunt's place. "You, auntie," says he, "have already lived seventy years, glory be to God. Why should you have to worry about business affairs at such an advanced age? It'd be better if I took care of things and looked after you." There you have it! Mark well, mark well. He came and installed himself at her place, like the lord of the manor. Do you hear what I'm saying?

PROLYOTOV. Yes, I do.

BURDYUKOV. See what I'm saying! Yes. And auntie takes to her bed. God only knows why; maybe he slipped her something. I've been getting word indirectly. Mark well! I go there and I'm greeted in the hallway by the beast, I mean my brother. He's positively dissolved in tears, and overcome with grief: "Well," he says, "little brother, we are eternally unfortunate, our benefactress..." What, has she given up the ghost? "No, but she is on the brink of death," he says. I enter her room and it's like he said, auntie lying with arms and legs askew and rolling her eyes. Well, what should I do? Cry? Wouldn't help. Wouldn't help at all, would it?

PROLYOTOV. No, it wouldn't.

BURDYUKOV. Well, there was nothing to be done. Such, apparently, was the will of God. I moved in closer: "Well," I say, "Auntie, we're all of us mortal; only God, as they say, is all-powerful in our life, if not today then tomorrow. Wouldn't it be proper for you to make some sort of arrangement in good time?" But what's up with Auntie? I see that she can't even twist her tongue, all she says is: "eh...eh...eh." And that rascal who was standing by her bed, that brother of mine, says, "That's Auntie explaining that she has already made arrangements." Do you hear that, do you hear that!

PROLYOTOV. All right, did she really say that?

BURDYUKOV. The hell she did! All she said was: "Eh... eh... eh." I moved closer still: "Permit me to inquire, then, Auntie, what arrangements?" And Auntie? Auntie again answers, "eh, eh, eh." And that villain, my brother, again comes out with, "Auntie says that all the details of the disposition are to be found in her last will and testament." Do you hear that? Do you hear that? What could I do? I held my tongue and didn't say a word.

PROLYOTOV. But, if I may be allowed to observe, why didn't you expose the falsehood there and then?

BURDYUKOV. And so? *(Gesticulates.)* They began swearing that was exactly what she'd been saying. And so... I believed it.

PROLYOTOV. And did they unseal her last will and testament?

BURDYUKOV. Yes, they did.

PROLYOTOV. And what then?

BURDYUKOV. Here's what then. As soon as everything has been performed in accordance with our Christian duty, I say that it ought to be time to read the behest of the deceased. My brother can't say a thing; such a display of suffering and despair he gave that it was a wonder to behold! "Take it," he says, "and read it yourself." The witnesses gathered round and we read it. And what do you think was in this last will and testament? Here's what: "To my nephew Pavel son of Peter Burdyukov (just listen to this!), in requital of his filial care and his constant presence (mark that well! mark that well!), I leave to him my nobly acquired ancestral estate in the province of Ustyug...." There you are! There you are! See what things have come to!... "Five hundred souls according to the census, all lands and properties and so on and so forth." Well? Do you hear that! "To my niece, Maria, daughter of Pyotr Povalishchev, née Burdyukova, I leave the village of one hundred souls due to her. To my nephew (here it is! mark it well! here's the bitter pill!) Chrysanth, son of Pyotr Burdyukov (listen! just listen!) in memory of me (oho, ho-ho!) I leave: three Shtametov skirts and all the odds and ends in the barn, such as a pair of feather mattresses, some crockery, a number of sheets and nightcaps," and the devil knows what other rags and tatters! Well? How does it strike you? I ask you, what the hell do I need with Shtametov skirts?

PROLYOTOV. Oh, what a swindler he is!

BURDYUKOV. Swindling—you're right there. But I ask you, what am I to do with Shtametov skirts? Wear them on my head?

PROLYOTOV. And had the witnesses affixed their signatures?

BURDYUKOV. Naturally he managed to recruit some riffraff for the purpose.

PROLYOTOV. And the dear departed signed in her own hand?

BURDYUKOV. There's the rub, she'd signed, but only the devil could make it out.

PROLYOTOV. How come?

BURDYUKOV. Well, this is how: the deceased was called Eudoxia, but there was no making head or tail of what she'd scribbled.

PROLYOTOV. What do you mean?

BURDYUKOV. The devil knows what it is. She was supposed to write "Eudoxia," but she'd written "Dowse it."

PROLYOTOV. What's that you say!

BURDYUKOV. Oh, I tell you that brother of mine won't stop at anything: And to my nephew Chrysanth Petrov three Shtametov skirts!"

PROLYOTOV (aside). He's really got a head on his shoulders that Pavel Petrovich Burdyukov. I would have never thought him capable of such contrivance.

BURDYUKOV (gesticulating). "Dowse it!" What does that mean? There's no such name, is there: "Dowse it?"

PROLYOTOV. How do you intend to proceed?

BURDYUKOV. I've already filed a petition to have the will declared null and void because the signature is false. They'll have to tell the truth—the deceased was called Eudoxia, and not "Dowse it."

PROLYOTOV. That's how it should be. And now you can leave it all to me. I'll immediately write to a certain department secretary, and you in the meantime get me a copy of that last will and testament.

BURDYUKOV. I'm inexpressibly obliged to you. (Picks up his hat.) Which door do I go out through—this or that?

PROLYOTOV. This way, if you will be so kind.

BURDYUKOV. All right. I asked because I'll have cause to use them again. I take my leave, respected sir. What was your name? I keep forgetting everything.

PROLYOTOV. Alexander Ivanovich.

BURDYUKOV. Alexander Ivanovich! There's an Alexander Ivanovich Proldyukovsky. Are you acquainted with him?

PROLYOTOV. No.

BURDYUKOV. He still lives a few miles from my village. Farewell!

PROLYOTOV. Farewell, most respected sir, farewell!

IV

Prolyotov, then a servant.

PROLYOTOV. Well, here's a rare find! What a gift! As if the Lord himself had made a donation. Hard to explain, but you feel an ineffable joy in your soul, either as if your wife had given birth to a son or the Minister had kissed you in the presence of the entire office. There's magnetism here, I swear to God! Hey, there, Andrei! Go right over now to my secretary and tell him to come here. Do you hear? Well now, wait a second; here's something for a drop of vodka; you can get drunk as a skunk. I give you permission just for today. And here's something to get gingerbread cakes for your son. Yes, and tell my secretary to come at once—a most urgent matter. At last, at long last a bit of luck has come my way! Hold on now. I'll sit down to play you, Pavel Petrovich Burdyukov, and we'll see how you'll dance to my tune. And if I can recruit a few musicians from the Senate for my orchestra, you'll dance such a jig that your sides will never stop aching.

SCENE III
THE SERVANTS' QUARTERS

CHARACTERS

Pyotr, servant
Ivan, servant
Grigory, servant
Servant-Stranger
Fyodor Fyodorovich, master
Man in Fur Coat
Majordomo
Annushka, servant girl

I

A lobby. A door to the right leads to a stairway; on the left a door to the drawing room. The rear curtain represents a door, somewhat to one side, leading to the study. Between the doors a long bench extends the entire length of the wall.

Pyotr, Ivan and Grigory are sleeping on it, each with his head resting on the other's shoulder. A loud ringing from the stairway door. The servants awaken.

GRIGORY. Run and open the door! They're ringing!

PYOTR. And why are you just sitting there? Got water on the knees or something? Can't get up?

IVAN *(gesturing)*. I'll go, no way to avoid it, I'll open up. *(Opens the door. Yells.)* Andryushka's here!

Servant-Stranger enters wearing a cap, an overcoat, and carrying a package.

GRIGORY. Ah, you Moscow crow! Where'd you blow in from?

SERVANT-STRANGER. Ah, it's you, you son of a Finn! You should try running the distance I have. She told me *(picks up package)* to take it all the way to the flower seller on Petersburg road. She wouldn't dream of giving me five kopecks for a cab, eh? And I'm to stop at your master's too. Is he sleeping?

GRIGORY. Who? Our bear? No, he hasn't let out a growl from his lair yet.

PYOTR. Is it true your mistress gives you socks to darn? *(All laugh.)*

GRIGORY. All right, brother, you'll be the sock darner. That's what we'll call you from now on.

SERVANT-STRANGER. You're lying, I've never darned anything in my life.

PYOTR. We all know how it is. A house servant is cook before lunch; after lunch he's coachman, or lackey, or he sews slippers.

SERVANT-STRANGER. Well, what of it? A fellow should be a jack-of-all-trades. No sitting idle. Of course, I'm both lackey and ladies' tailor. I sew for the lady of the house, and for others too—earn a few kopecks that way. And what about you, seems you do nothing?

GRIGORY. No, my friend, a good master doesn't bother his footman with work, there are laborers for that. Count Bulkin over there has thirty servants alone, and you can't get by there without: "Hey, Petrushka, run a little errand for me." "No," he'll say, "that's none of my business; be so good as to tell Ivan to do it." That's how it goes! That's what it means for a landowner to live like a landowner! And your midget of a mistress comes from Moscow in her nutshell of a carriage, the horses with their tails tied with fancy ribbons. *(All laugh.)*

SERVANT-STRANGER. Well, you are a wag, a wag indeed! And what's the result of lying around all day? That is why you don't have a kopeck to your name.

GRIGORY. What do I need your kopecks for? And the master, what use is he? He'll pay me my wages whether I work or not. And why save it up for my old age? What kind of a master wouldn't give his servant a pension for all his services?

SERVANT-STRANGER. Well, I hear the folks here are giving a ball.

PYOTR. Yes, are you coming?

SERVANT-STRANGER. And what kind of a ball will it be? Maybe it's just a silly rumor.

GRIGORY. No, brother, it's the real thing. Everyone's contributing at least one ruble. The princess's cook gave five rubles and will be preparing the banquet himself. You won't be offered just a plate of nuts. There'll be pounds and pounds of candy, and ice cream too. *(A soft ring is heard from the master's study.)*

SERVANT-STRANGER. Jump to it. The master's calling.

GRIGORY. He can wait.... They'll be fireworks, too. They tried to arrange some music too, but it didn't work out; they couldn't get hold of a bass, that wouldn't have been...

A ring is heard from the study, louder this time.

SERVANT-STRANGER. Jump to it, better get going! They're ringing.

GRIGORY. He can wait a bit. Well, how much will you contribute?

SERVANT-STRANGER. But it's just a ball, nothing special about it, is there?

GRIGORY. Come on, my old socks darner, loosen your purse strings. Look after him, Pyotr. See how much he... *(Points a finger at the stranger. At this moment the door from the study opens and the master, in a dressing gown, comes in, and reach - ing out a hand, grabs Grigory by the ear. Everyone jumps up.)*

II

MASTER. So, you good-for-nothings! Three fellows, and not one of them willing to leave his place. I rang with all my might. Almost broke the cord.

GRIGORY. We couldn't hear anything, Your Honor.

MASTER. You're lying.

GRIGORY. Swear to God. Why should I lie? Pyotr was sitting here too. Swear to God. That little bell of yours, Your Honor, isn't any good. You can never hear the sound. You'll have to call the smith to repair it.

MASTER. All right, call the smith.

GRIGORY. Yes, that's just what I was saying to the butler. And what comes of it? You tell him something, and all you get for it is a scolding.

MASTER *(catching sight of the servant-stranger)*. And who is this fellow?

GRIGORY. He's from Anna Petrovna's. Came to see you for some reason.

MASTER. What do you have to say for yourself, brother?

SERVANT-STRANGER. My lady ordered me to pay my respects and to report that she's coming to see you today.

MASTER. Why? Do you have any idea?

SERVANT-STRANGER. I've no way of knowing. She just said, "Tell Fyodor Fyodorovich that I pay my respects and will be coming to see him...."

MASTER. But when? At what time?

SERVANT-STRANGER. I don't know at what time: She just said that I should inform Fyodor Fyodorovich, that I, as she put it, myself, will be paying him a visit...

MASTER. Very well. Pyotr, help me get dressed quickly—I'm going out. And the rest of you—don't receive anyone. Do you hear—tell everyone I'm not at home. *(Goes out, followed by Pyotr.)*

III

SERVANT-STRANGER *(to Grigory)*. Well, you see how you got your deserts.

GRIGORY *(gesticulating)*. Ah, that's the way this work is! No matter how hard you try, you always get hell. *(A ring is heard from the stairway door.)* Here we go again. *(To Ivan.)* Hurry up and open the door. And what are you yawning for? *(Ivan opens the door. A gentleman in a fur coat enters.)*

IV

GENTLEMAN IN FUR COAT. Is Fyodor Fyodorovich at home?

GRIGORY. Absolutely not.

GENTLEMAN IN FUR COAT. Too bad. You don't know where he's gone?

GRIGORY. That is not known. Probably went to his department. How shall I introduce you?

GENTLEMAN IN FUR COAT. Tell him that Neveleshchagin was here. Very sorry, tell him, that I didn't find him at home. Got it? You won't forget? Neveleshchagin.

GRIGORY. Lentyagin.

GENTLEMAN IN FUR COAT *(carefully)*. Neveleshchagin.

GRIGORY. You're not German, are you?

GENTLEMAN IN FUR COAT. What kind of German! Just an ordinary Russian. Ne-ve-le-shcha-gin.

GRIGORY. Hear that, Ivan, don't forget: Erdashchagin.

Exit gentleman in fur coat.

V

SERVANT-STRANGER. Good-bye, my friends, it's time I was off too.
GRIGORY. Oh all right—do you think you'll be at the ball?
SERVANT-STRANGER. I'll see about that later. Good-bye, Ivan!
IVAN. Good-bye! *(Goes to open the door.)*

VI

A servant girl rushes through the lobby.

GRIGORY. And where are we going? Let's have a look at you. *(Grabs her by the skirt of her dress.)*
SERVANT GIRL. Don't, don't, Grigory Pavlovich. Don't hold me up. There's no time at all. *(Breaks free and runs through to the stairway door.)*
GRIGORY *(looking after her)*. There she went, slipped right through! *(Laughs.)* Ha, ha, ha!
IVAN *(laughs)*. Hee, hee, hee! *(The master comes out. Grigory and Ivan's faces grow furrowed and scowling suddenly. Grigory takes a fur coat from a hanger and throws it over his master's shoulders. The master exits.)*
GRIGORY *(stands in the middle of the room picking his nose)*. Well, here's some free time for us. The master has gone out. What could be better? No, now we'll have to put up with that devil, the pot bellied majordomo.

The majordomo's shout is heard off stage. "A regular curse of God. Ten men in the house and not one lifts a finger."

VII

MAJORDOMO *(enters with sharp gestures and gesticulations)*. You should at least fear your own conscience if you don't fear God. You know the rugs have yet to be beaten. You, Grigory Pavlovich, should be an example to the others, but you sleep right from morning to night. By God, your eyes have become quite bloated from sleeping. After all, Grigory Pavlovich, you're nothing but a terrible scoundrel.
GRIGORY. That so? Not being a man, I'm not allowed to grab a couple of winks?
MAJORDOMO. Who's got anything against that? Why not nod off for awhile? But you can't sleep the whole day. There's you, for example, Pyotr Ivanovich. You—not to use bad language—have the look of a pig about you. I swear to God. How much work do you have to do? Two or three candlesticks to clean. So what's gotten into you anyway? *(Pyotr slowly exits.)* And you, Vanka, could do with a good poke in the neck.
GRIGORY *(going out)*. Oh life, life, every day there's trouble and strife!

MAJORDOMO *(alone)*. Proper behavior consists in each man knowing his duty. If you're a servant, then behave like a servant; a nobleman, then act the nobleman, a bishop, act like a bishop. And what would happen if everyone got it into his head... I would immediately say: no, I'm not a Majordomo. I'm a governor, or something to do with the infantry. If I tried it everyone would say: no, you lie, you're a Majordomo, not a general, that's what! You've got nothing to do with bone joor, commong voo fransay, but with taking care of the house and seeing that the servants behave, that's what!

VIII

Enter Annushka, a maidservant from a neighboring household.

MAJORDOMO. Ah, Anna Gavrilovna! It is with great pleasure that I behold you.

ANNUSHKA. Don't trouble yourself, Lavrenty Pavlovich. I dropped in to see you for a moment on purpose. I ran into your master's carriage and realized he wasn't going to be at home.

MAJORDOMO. You did very well. My wife and I will be more than happy to have you. Sit down, please.

ANNUSHKA *(sitting down)*. Tell me, do you know anything about the ball that's being planned in a few days time?

MAJORDOMO. Of course I know. It's been, you might say, a matter of organization. One man, then another and then, in a manner of speaking, a third. It all amounts to quite a sum as things go. My wife and I made a five ruble donation. Well, naturally, a ball, or, as they usually put it, a party. Of course, refreshments will be served, something to cool you down. There'll be dancing and such entertainment for the young folk.

ANNUSHKA. I wouldn't miss it for the world! I've only stopped by to find out if you and Agafya Ivanovna will be there.

MAJORDOMO. All I hear from Agafya Ivanovna is about you.

ANNUSHKA. The kind of people that'll be there, that's the only thing that worries me.

MAJORDOMO. Don't worry yourself, Anna Gavrilovna, it'll be a thoroughly respectable gathering. I can tell you that I've heard that Count Tolstozub's valet, and Prince Bryukhovetsky's coachman and bartender will be there, as well as some of the princess's serving maids. I think there'll be some government clerks as well.

ANNUSHKA. The one thing I don't like is that those coachmen will be there. They always smell of coarse tobacco or vodka, and they're all so uneducated; a bunch of know-nothings.

MAJORDOMO. Let me tell you, Anna Gavrilovna, that there are coachmen and coachmen. In the nature of things they find themselves attached to horses, and sometimes have to clean out, if you'll excuse the expression, manure. Of course, a simple man likes to drink a glass of vodka, or, because he can't afford better, to smoke coarse tobacco, the kind the common folk usually smoke. Well, then, it's quite natural, in a manner of speaking, that a coachman will on occasion stink of manure or vodka. That's in the nature of things. But you'll have to agree, Anna Gavrilovna, there are those coachmen who are, you might say, more stable lads than coachmen. Their responsibility, or one might say, office, consists in growing oats, or telling someone off, if, for example, the coachman or the postilion is at fault.

ANNUSHKA. How well you speak, Lavrenty Pavlovich! It's always a delight to listen to you!

MAJORDOMO (with a satisfied smile). No need for gratitude, miss. It's something not everyone has, you know, the art of speaking, that is to say the gift of words. Naturally, it sometimes happens... that, as folk put it, tongue-tiedness... Yes. Or there are other similar instances, that, however, come direct from nature... May I ask you if you'd pay a visit to my room?

Exit Annushka. Lavrenty behind her.

SCENE IV
SOBACHKIN

CHARACTERS

Marya Alexandrovna, lady of the house
Mikhail Andreyevich, her son
Servant
Sobachkin, friend of the family

A room in Marya Alexandrovna's house.

I

Marya Alexandrovna, an elderly woman, and her son Mikhail Andreyevich.

MARYA. Listen, Misha. I've been wanting to speak to you about something for a long time. You've got to have a change of work.

MISHA. By all means. As soon as you like.

MARYA. You've got to serve in the military.

MISHA *(eyes popping)*. The military?

MARYA. Yes.

MISHA. Are you serious, Mama? The military?

MARYA. Why this show of amazement?

MISHA. For heaven's sake, don't you realize that I'd have to start out as a junker?

MARYA. Well, yes, serve a year as a junker, then they'll promote you to officer rank—I'll see to that.

MISHA. But what do you see in me that's military? My build is quite unmilitary. Have a heart, mommy dear! Really, what you've said has taken me quite off guard. I, I... simply don't know what to think... I'm a bit on the plumpish side, thank goodness, and when I dress up in a junker uniform with its short tails, I'll be a laughing stock.

MARYA. Have no fear. They'll make you an officer and you'll wear a uniform with long tails that will completely conceal your portliness, so nothing will be noticed. It's even better you're on the stout side—promotion will come much faster—they'll be embarrassed to have such a stout ensign in the regiment.

MISHA. But, Mama, I've only got a year before I'm made a collegiate assessor. I've already held the rank of titular counselor for two years.

MARYA. Stop it, stop it! That word "titular" grates on my ears. God knows what comes into my head without that. I want my son to serve in the Guards. I can't stand looking at civilian mufti.

MISHA. But, Mumkins, examine me carefully, including my exterior. Already in school they were calling me bunny. In the military you've got to gallop boldly on horseback, have a ringing voice, a knightly carriage and be narrow in the waist.

MARYA. You'll manage to acquire all those things. I definitely want you to change your profession. There's an important reason behind it.

MISHA. What reason?

MARYA. An important one.

MISHA. Tell me then, what reason?

MARYA. The reason... I don't even know if you'll get the idea. That fool Gubomazova... day before yesterday she was talking so I'd overhear—it was at the Rogozhinskys'. I was sitting two armchairs away. In front of me were Sofya Vortushkova, Princess Alexandrina, and I was right behind the princess. What do you think that dreary old thing had the nerve to say? I wanted to jump, I can tell you, and if Princess Alexandrina hadn't been there. I don't know what I'd have done. She said, "I'm very glad they don't allow any civilians at the court balls. They're all, she says, so *mauvais genre*, there's something low class about them. I'm happy, she says, my Alexis doesn't wear that disgusting dress-coat." And she enunciated it all so affectedly, in such a tone, she really did.... To tell the truth, I don't know what I would have done to her. And her son is a raving idiot. The only thing he's good for is a nimble foot in a dance. What a disgusting reptile he is!

MISHA. And is that the whole reason, mama?

MARYA. Yes, to get my own back. I want my son to serve in the Guards, too, and to be at all the court balls.

MISHA. I ask you, Mommy, just because Gubomazova is a fool...

MARYA. No, I've made a firm decision. Let her shake with fury, let her go out of her mind.

MISHA. All the same...

MARYA. Oh, I'll give her what for! Let her have her way. I'll strain every nerve and my son will be in the Guards too. Even if it has its disadvantages, I'll make it happen. I'm not going to let any old harridan turn up her snub nose and puff herself up in front of me. No, I'm not going to let that happen. I'm not... have it your way, oh do, Natalya Andreyevna.

MISHA. But surely you won't vex her that way?

MARYA. I just won't let her get away with that!

MISHA. If you insist, Mommy, I'll transfer to the military. But, really, I'll find it a joke myself to see myself in uniform.

MARYA. At least it will be a lot nobler than those miserable tails. Now for the second matter. I want to marry you off.

MISHA. A change of career and marriage all at once?

MARYA. Why not? Is it against the rules to change jobs and get married?

MISHA. But I don't yet have any intention. I don't want to get married just yet.

MARYA. You'll want to as soon as you find out who the girl is. This marriage will bring you luck in your career and in your family life. To put it in a nutshell, I want to marry you off to Princess Shlyopokhostova.

MISHA. But, mama, she's a first-class idiot.

MARYA. Not first-class at all, the same class as all the others. A marvelous girl, just that she hasn't got any memory. Occasionally she forgets herself and says something that's not to the point. But that's absentmindedness, and, at the same time, she isn't at all a scandal-monger and doesn't think up anything nasty.

MISHA. For pity's sake, Mama. What kind of scandal-monger could she be! She can hardly put two words together, and when she does all you can do is throw up your hands. Mommy, dearest, you know yourself that marriage is an affair of the heart, the spirit must...

MARYA. So that's how it is—I had a premonition. Listen to me and stop playing the liberal. It doesn't suit you, doesn't suit you at all; I've told you God knows how many times. It suits some people, but it doesn't suit you at all.

MISHA. Oh, Mama, when have I ever disobeyed you? It won't be long before I'm thirty, but all the same I submit to you in everything like a child. You tell me to go somewhere I'd rather die than go, and I go there and don't give the slightest sign I'm not enjoying it. You order me to hobnob at some reception or other, and I hobnob, even though it's not at all to my fancy. You order me to dance at balls, and I dance, even though everyone laughs at the figure I cut. And, finally, you ask me to change my career, and I'm changing my career, becoming a cadet at the age of thirty—at the age of thirty I'm having a second childhood just to please you! And in spite of everything not a day goes by when you don't throw my liberalism in my face. A minute doesn't pass without you calling me a liberal. It's hard to take, Mama! Upon my life, it's hard to take! I deserve better for my true love and devotion to you...

MARYA. Please don't talk about it. As if I didn't know you're a liberal. I even know who puts you up to it; it's that disgusting Sobachkin's fault.

MISHA. No, Mama, that's too much—too much to be accused of taking advice from Sobachkin. Sobachkin is a scoundrel, a gambler, anything you like. But he's not at fault here. I'll never allow him to have the slightest influence over me.

MARYA. Heaven defend us, what a terrible man! I really got a fright when I realized what he was. He's got no principles, no virtues. What a horrible, horrible person. If only you knew what tales he's been spreading about me. I couldn't show my face for three months. He said that I serve greasy candle-ends for dinner, that my rugs don't get beaten clean for weeks at a time, that I went out for a drive with a harness of plain rope attached to the collar of a dairy horse. I turned red as a beet and was sick for more than a week. I don't know how I was able to put up with all that. Honestly, it was only my faith in Providence that sustained me.

MISHA. And you think that such a person could possibly have any influence on me? You think I'd allow it?

MARYA. I told him he musn't dare appear in my presence and that you can only make amends if you make the princess a *déclaration* this very day without beating around the bush.

MISHA. But, Mama, what if it can't be done?

MARYA. What do you mean, can't be done? How could that be?

MISHA *(aside)*. Well, here it is, the decisive moment! *(Aloud.)* Allow me at least to have a say in this, a matter on which my future happiness depends. You haven't asked me yet... Well, if there isn't a possibility of my being in love with someone else.

MARYA. I have to admit that'd be news to me. I haven't heard a word about that. And who is this "someone else"?

MISHA. Oh, Mama, I swear there's never been anyone like her! An angel, an angel in body and soul.

MARYA. What family is she from; who is her father?

MISHA. Her father is Alexander Alexandrovich Odosimov.

MARYA. Odosimov? The name's completely unknown to me. I don't know a thing about this Odosimov. Does he have any money?

MISHA. A rare individual, a marvelous man!

MARYA. And money?

MISHA. How shall I put it? You'd have to see him. You won't find such spiritual riches anywhere in the world.

MARYA. But what is he? What rank is he exactly? And what property does he have?

MISHA. I understand what you want, Mama. Allow me to express my candid thoughts on this account. In any case, the way things are now, I'll wager there isn't in the whole of Russia a single bachelor who isn't looking for a wealthy fiancée. Everyone wants to set himself up in the world with his wife's dowry. All right, that may be excusable to a certain extent. I understand that a man who is down on his luck, who hasn't been able to get on in the service, who hasn't been able to make a fortune, perhaps because of an excess of honesty—I can see that he could well be within his rights to seek a wealthy fiancée. And it might be that parents would be doing less than justice if they didn't acknowledge the attainments of such men and refused to give them their daughters in marriage. But judge for yourself, is it just for a man of wealth to look for a wealthy fiancée? What would the world come to then? It's the same thing as putting an overcoat over a fur coat when the weather's hot enough already and when the overcoat might be covering someone else's shoulders. No, Mommikins, there's no justice in that! Her father sacrificed all he had in the world to the education of his daughter.

MARYA. That'll be quite enough. I don't have the strength to listen to any more. I know it all, everything. You've fallen in love with some slut, the daughter of some supply clerk, a girl who sells her wares on the streets.

MISHA. Mama...

MARYA. The father's a drunk, the mother a cook, the rest of the clan law enforcement agents or in the saloon trade. And I've got to listen to all this, to put up with it from my own son, for whose sake I have spared nothing. No, I won't survive this!

MISHA. But, Mommy, please...

MARYA. Lord have mercy on us, the morals of young people. No, I'll never survive this. I swear, I'll never survive it... Oh, what's happening, my head has begun to spin! *(Shouts out.)* I've been stabbed in the back! Mashka, give me the medicine bottle. I don't know if I'll last out the day. Oh that cruel son of mine!

MISHA *(throws himself at her feet)*. Calm down, Mommy. You'll do yourself harm...

MARYA. All this was caused by that horrible Sobachkin. I don't know why we haven't been able to rid ourselves of that plague.

SERVANT *(in the doorway)*. Sobachkin has arrived.

MARYA. What! Sobachkin? Send him away, send him away. I don't want the slightest trace of him around here!

The same and Sobachkin.

SOBACHKIN. Marya Alexandrovna. Be so magnanimous as to forgive me for not coming to see you for such a long time. I swear to God, I couldn't get away. You wouldn't believe how busy I am. I knew you'd be angry, I just knew you would. *(Catches sight of Misha.)* Greetings, friend. How are you?

MARYA *(aside)*. I don't have the words to describe it! Who does he think he is? Has the nerve to apologize for not coming to see us for so long.

SOBACHKIN. How delighted I am that, judging from your faces, you are so fresh and healthy. And how's that little brother of yours? I thought I'd find him here for sure.

MARYA. Then you should have gone to his place and not come here.

SOBACHKIN *(chuckling)*. I came here to tell you an exceedingly interesting little story.

MARYA. I don't care much for interesting little stories.

SOBACHKIN. About Natalya Andreyevna Gubomazova?

MARYA. What's that, about Gubomazova! *(Attempting to hide her curiosity.)* So what was this, something that happened recently?

SOBACHKIN. Just the other day.

MARYA. What was it, then?

SOBACHKIN. Did you know that she beats her maids?

MARYA. No! What are you saying? What a scandal, shameful! Is it possible?

SOBACHKIN. Cross my heart and hope to die. Once she orders a guilty ser-vant girl to lie down in the proper way on a bed for a beating and goes out to another room, I don't remember what for, probably to get a whip. Meanwhile, the girl gets up and goes out of the room for something or other, and her place is taken by Natalya Andreyevna's husband who lies down and falls asleep. Natalya Andreyevna appears with the whip, orders another girl to sit on his legs, covers him with bedding and gives her husband a good beating!

MARYA *(throwing up her hands)*. Oh. my God, how shameful! Why didn't I know anything about this before? I can tell you I always felt that she could do it.

SOBACHKIN. Naturally. That's what I told the whole world. The general opinion of her is: "An exemplary wife, sits at home, concerns herself with edu-cating her children, teaches them English herself." Some education! Whips her husband daily, like a dog. Awfully sorry I won't be able to stay any longer. *(Bows to everyone.)*

MARYA. But where are you off to, Andrei Kondratevich? Aren't you ashamed not having visited me for such a long time? I've always thought of you as a friend of the family. Do stay, please! There are a few more things I'd like to talk over with you. Listen, Misha, there's a coach-maker waiting for me in the ser-vants' quarters. Please talk to him. Ask if he can give my coach a fresh coat of paint by the first of the month. I want it sky blue with a light trim, in the style of Gubomazova's.

Exit Misha.

I sent him away on purpose so I could have a word with you in private. Tell me, you're the one to ask, do you know of any Alexander Alexandrovich Odosimov?

SOBACHKIN. Odosimov? Odosimov? Odosimov... I know, there is an Odosimov—a bureau chief or head of a department... that's it, precisely...

MARYA. Just imagine, I've just heard a funny story about... There's a great favor you can do me.

SOBACHKIN. Your wish is my command. For you I'll do anything, you know that yourself.

MARYA. This is what it is: my son has fallen in love, or to be more precise, not fallen in love, but something simply got into his head. Well, he's still a youngster... In a word, he's delirious about the daughter of this Odosimov.

SOBACHKIN. Delirious? Well, he hasn't said anything of it to me. But, of course, he must be delirious about her if you say so.

MARYA. Andrei Kondratevich, I would like to ask a great service of you. I know that women are drawn to you.

SOBACHKIN. Heh, heh, heh. And what makes you think that? But, after all, I am... Just imagine, there are six girls working at the pastry shop. You probably think I ran after them, or something like that. I swear I didn't look at them. Yes, and I can tell you something even better. You know what's his name, Yermolai, Yermolai? Yermolai, the one who lived on Liteynaya Street, not far from Kirochnaya?

MARYA. Don't know anyone there.

SOBACHKIN. Dammit! Yermolai Ivanovich, I think. I can't for the life of me remember his last name. His wife got tangled in some kind of affair about five years ago. You must know her—Silfida Petrovna.

MARYA. Not in the slightest; I don't know any Yermolai Ivanovich, or any Silfida Petrovna.

SOBACHKIN. Dammit! And he lived not far from Kuropatkin.

MARYA. I don't know Kuropatkin either.

SOBACHKIN. You'll remember later. The daughter's drowning in money, a two hundred thousand dowry. And I'm not laying it on thick; cards on the table before you reach the altar.

MARYA. What are you saying! And you didn't marry her?

SOBACHKIN. No, I didn't. Her father was on his knees three days trying to talk me into it. The daughter didn't survive the blow. She's in a nunnery now.

MARYA. Why didn't you get married?

SOBACHKIN. Just didn't somehow. I thought to myself: the father's a tax collector, the family potluck. Believe me, I really felt sorry later. The devil take it, that's the way of the world. Everything is conventions and propriety. How many people have they already laid low.

MARYA. Why worry about the world? (Aside.) I beg your pardon! Nowadays every pencil pusher thinks he's an aristocrat. Take some little titular counselor and just listen to him prattling away.

SOBACHKIN. But, it can't be, Marya Alexandrovna. It really can't, it's all somehow... Don't you know... They'll start saying, "Well, he's gone and got married, the devil only knows who to..." Anyway, things like that are always happening to me. On one occasion it's true, it wasn't my fault at all, there was absolutely nothing on my part... well, what was I to do? *(In a soft voice.)* You know, when the ice melts on the Neva, they always find two or three drowned women. But I'd better be quiet; you can really get into trouble with this sort of thing. Yes, they love me, but then why should I? You couldn't tell from my face that...

MARYA. Enough of that. As if you didn't know you're good-looking.

SOBACHKIN *(chuckles)*. And just imagine, when I was a little fellow, not one lady would pass by without chucking me under the chin and saying, "What a handsome little devil!"

MARYA *(aside)*. Just listen to him. As far as beauty goes, he's as ugly as a pug dog and he imagines he's good-looking. *(Aloud.)* Listen to me, Andrei Kondratievich, you can pull it off with your looks. My son is head over heels in love and imagines she's pure sweetness and light. Isn't there some way we could—you know what I mean—put her somehow in a light that, how should I put it, takes the gilding off the lily? Let's imagine you produce such an effect that she falls madly in love with you.

SOBACHKIN. Marya Alexandrovna, she'll go out of her mind. Have no doubt, she will! I'll put my head on the block if she doesn't. I can tell you, Marya Alexandrovna, that I've never missed the mark. Why just the other day...

MARYA. Well, whatever happens, if she goes out of her mind for you or not, I want the rumors flying about town that you're having an affair... And my son to get wind of it.

SOBACHKIN. Your son?

MARYA. Yes, my son.

SOBACHKIN. Yes.

MARYA. What do you mean "yes?"

SOBACHKIN. Nothing at all, I just said, "yes."

MARYA. Surely you won't find it difficult.

SOBACHKIN. Nothing to it. But all these people in love... You wouldn't believe the absurd things they get caught up in, ridiculous infantile tomfoolery. Now it's pistols, now it's... the devil himself only knows what it is. Of course, it's not that I mean in any way, but, you know, it's improper in decent society.

MARYA. Oh! You needn't worry on that account. Rely on me. I won't let my son do anything like that.

SOBACHKIN. I just happened to mention it in passing. Believe me, Marya Alexandrovna, if it came to risking my life for your sake, I'd do it with pleasure, as God is my witness, with pleasure. My devotion is such, I admit it's positively embarrassing—Lord knows what you make of it, but it's no more than the profoundest respect. Oh, yes, it's a good thing I remembered. I beg you, Marya Alexandrovna, to make me a little loan—a mere two thousand—for the shortest while. Confound this idiotic memory of mine. As I was getting dressed today the whole time I kept thinking I mustn't forget that bank book and deliberately laid it on the table right in front of my eyes. And what do you suppose? I took everything, my snuffbox, even an extra handkerchief, but that bank book was left lying on the table.

MARYA *(aside)*. What's to be done with him? Give him money and he'll squander it and if I don't give it to him, he'll let loose such nonsense about me all over town that I won't dare show even the tip of my nose. And I like that business about forgetting his bank book. Oh, you've got a bank book all right, empty. But there's nothing to be done. I'll have to give him some. *(Aloud.)* By all means, Andrei Kondratevich, wait here a moment and I'll get some right away.

SOBACHKIN. Very good. I'll just be sitting here.

MARYA *(aside)*. He can't do a thing without money, the scoundrel.

SOBACHKIN *(alone)*. Yes, those two thousand will certainly come in handy. I won't pay off my debts though. The shoemaker can wait, and the tailor can wait, and Anna Ivanovna can wait, too. Of course she'll scream bloody murder, but what can I do? Can't go squandering on everything that comes along. She'll just have to make do with my love, and as for the dress, she's lying; she has it already. And here's what I'll do: there'll be a carnival soon; that little carriage of mine, though it's a new one, has already been on view; but they say that Joachim has just got hold of the latest model and hasn't shown it to anyone yet. If I apply those two thousand to my coach I can really spruce it up. Then you can imagine what an effect I'll produce. It could well be there will only be one or two carriages to equal mine in the whole carnival. They'll start talking about me everywhere. All the same, I've got to think about Marya Alexandrovna's little assignment. It seems to me the most sensible thing is to start with love letters. Write a letter in the girl's name, yes, and accidentally drop it when he's around or leave it accidentally on the desk in his room. It could, of course, turn out badly. Well, what of it? All they can give me are a few thwacks. Thwacks are a bit painful, of course, but not so much that I'd... I can always make myself scarce, and if it comes to that, why I'll head straight for Marya Alexandrovna's bedroom and right under her bed. Let's just see him drag me out from under there. But the main thing is how to write the letter? I hate writing worse than death! I mean, I'd sooner be cut to pieces! You think you can express yourself magnificently on paper, then when it comes to taking up your pen it's as if someone had given you a slap in the face. There's confusion worse confounded—your hand refuses to cooperate and that's it. But how about this? I've got a few letters written to me recently. What if I choose the best of them, rub out the name, and write in another one. Why not, what's wrong with that? Yes, indeed. I'll just rummage about here in my pocket and perhaps I'll have the luck to find the very thing. *(Pulls a bundle of letters from his pocket.)* This one, for instance, "I'm vary thank God hailthy but indispoged with pain. Looks like you've completely fargotten, darlin. Ivan Danilovich saw you sweethart in the theeater and you shoulda calmed me with your funnin conaisation." Doesn't seem to be any spelling here, devil take it. No, there's no pulling the wool over anyone's eyes with that one. *(Continues.)* "Darling, I have sewn some suspenders for you." There she goes, carried away with sweet nothings! A lot of what you might call bucolic; smells of Chateaubriand to me. Well, maybe this one'll have something. *(Unseals another letter and squints in the effort to decipher it.)* "Gentle friend!" Hm! *(Presses his lips together.)* No, that's not it, not "gentle friend." Could it be "most tender, dearest"? No, not "dearest", no, no. *(Reads.)* "Bla... black... blackguard." Hey! "If you, the perfidious seducer of my innocence, do not return the money I loaned you for a grocery store, money which I, in my emotional inexperience, gave you, baboon face *(gritting these last words through his teeth)* ...then I'll report you to the police." Devil knows what that is! Devil alone knows! There just isn't a thing in this letter. Of course, you can talk about anything, but do it with propriety, with the sort of expressions that won't insult a man. No, no, I see these letters aren't any good; they won't do at all. I need to come up with something strong, something that, as they say, seethes with passion. Well, let's have a look at this one. *(Reads.)* "Cruel tyrant of my soul!" Ah, here's something at last. "Be moved by my bitter lot!" And exceedingly noble, as God's my witness. You can see good upbringing in that. Right from the start it makes an impression. That's the way to write. With feeling, and at the same time a man isn't insulted. Yes, this is the letter I'll plant on him. No need to read on, no need at all. Only I don't know how to rub out the name so that you wouldn't notice. *(Looks at the signature.)* Hey, that's good, didn't even put her first name. Splendid! I'll put it in myself. This little affair is taking care of itself very nicely. And they say that appearances aren't important. If you weren't a tempting little morsel then they wouldn't fall in love with you, and without falling in love, they wouldn't write letters and if I didn't have these letters, I wouldn't know how to deal with this affair. *(Going over to the mirror.)* I must admit I wasn't quite up to scratch today, but at other times there's something in my face you might even call meaningful. Too bad I've got terrible teeth, otherwise I'd be the spitting image of Bagration. I don't know in what style to let my sideburns grow—so that they form a definite fringe all around, as if, as they say, sewn round with broadcloth, or to shave it all bare, and cultivate a little something under my lip. Eh?

IVAN TURGENEV

THE WEAKEST LINK
A Comedy in One Act

CHARACTERS

Anna Vasilyevna Libanova, landowner, 40 years old
Vera Nikolayevna, her daughter, 19 years old
Mlle. Bienaimé, live-in companion and governess, 42 years old
Varvara Ivanovna Morozova, relative of Libanova, 45 years old
Vladimir Petrovich Stanitsyn, neighbor, 28 years old
Ivan Pavlych Mukhin, neighbor, 30 years old
Yevgeny Andreyich Gorsky, neighbor, 26 years old
Captain Chukalov, 40 years old
Butler
Servants

The action takes place on Mrs. Libanova's estate.

The theater represents the entrance hall of a wealthy landowner's mansion; facing— the door to the dining room, to the left a glass door to the garden. The walls are hung with portraits; on the forestage a desk covered with journals; a piano, several arm - chairs; slightly to the rear a Chinese billiard table; large wall clocks in the corner.

GORSKY *(entering)*. No one here? So much the better..... What time is it?... Half past nine. *(Becomes thoughtful for a moment.)* Today's the decisive day.... Yes.... Yes... *(Goes over to the desk, picks up a journal.)* Le Journal des Debats of April 3, new style, but it's July now... hmm....Let's see what the news is.... *(Begins to read. Mukhin enters from the dining room. Gorsky glances round.)* Well, well, well... Mukhin! What brings you here? When did you arrive?

MUKHIN. Last night, but I left town at six o'clock the evening before. My coachman lost his way.

GORSKY. I didn't know you were acquainted with Madame de Libanoff.

MUKHIN. But this is my first visit. I was introduced to Madame de Libanoff, as you call her, at the Governor's ball; I danced with her daughter and was rewarded with an invitation. *(He looks about him.)* She certainly has a fine mansion.

GORSKY. That's putting it mildly. It's the finest mansion in the province. *(Shows him Le Journal des Debats.)* See here: "We even get the *Telegraph*." Joking apart, it's a good life they have here.... A delightful mixture of Russian pastoral and French *vie de château*. You'll see. The proprietor... well, she's a widow and well off... but the daughter....

MUKHIN *(interrupting)*. The daughter is a darling....

GORSKY. Aha! *(After a moment's silence.)* Yes.

MUKHIN. What's her name?

GORSKY *(solemnly)*. Her name is Vera Nikolayevna.... She has a splendid dowry.

MUKHIN. That's all the same to me. I'm no suitor, you know.

GORSKY. You're no suitor, but *(looking him up and down)* you're dressed like one.

MUKHIN. Surely you're not jealous.

GORSKY. What next! Why don't we sit and chat until the ladies come down to tea.

MUKHIN. I have nothing against sitting down, and we can chat later.... Tell me in a few words what sort of house this is, what the people are like.... You're an old inhabitant, after all.

GORSKY. Yes, my late mother detested Mrs. Libanova for twenty years.... We're old acquaintances. I've visited her in Petersburg and I've run into her abroad. So you want to know what sort of people live here—by all means. Madame de Libanoff (that's what's written on her visiting cards, with the addition née Salotopine).... Madame de Libanoff is a good enough woman, she lives and lets live. She doesn't belong to the highest society, but she's not totally unknown in Petersburg either; General Monplaisir stays at her house when he's passing through. Her husband died young; otherwise she would have gone into society. She keeps herself well; she's a bit of a sentimentalist, she's spoilt; the entertainment she offers is somewhere between the casual and the considerate; no real chic, you know.... But thank the Lord she doesn't get hot and bothered, doesn't talk through her nose, doesn't gossip. She keeps the house in order and manages the estate herself.... The mind of an administrator! She has a relative living here—Morozova, Varvara Ivanovna, an excellent woman, also a widow, only a poor one. I suspect she's as spiteful as a vixen, and I know for certain that she can't abide her benefactress.... But you'll come across all sorts of things here. The household boasts a French governess who pours tea, sighs for Paris, loves *le petit mot pour rire* and languidly rolls her eyes.... Surveyors and architects run after her, but since Mlle Bienamé doesn't play cards and preference calls for three players, a certain Chukhanov, a penniless, retired army captain, is retained for this purpose. He has a mustachio and a dashing air, but he's really a toady and a flatterer. All these personages are in permanent residence, but Mrs. Libanova has many other friends... easy to lose count.... Oh yes, I forgot to name one of her most constant visitors, Doctor Guttmann, Karl Karlich. He's a handsome young fellow with silky sideburns; he's hopeless as a medico but he kisses Anna Vasilyevna's hands most rapturously.... Anna Vasilyevna doesn't find this in the least unpleasant and she does have rather fine hands, a little on the pudgy side perhaps, but white and with fingertips that turn up most elegantly....

MUKHIN *(impatiently)*. But why don't you say anything about the daughter?

GORSKY. Just wait a moment. I'm saving her for last. Still, what can I tell you about Vera Nikolayevna? Really don't know. Who can make out an eighteen-year- old girl? She's still in ferment, like a young wine. But she could make a splendid woman. She has intelligence, discrimination, character; and she has a tender heart and is eager for experience. She's a great egoist too. It won't be long before she's married.

MUKHIN. To whom?

GORSKY. That I can't tell you.... But she won't be a spinster for long.

MUKHIN. Well it goes without saying a good dowry....

GORSKY. No, not for that reason.

MUKHIN. For what reason then?

GORSKY. Because she has grasped the fact that a woman's life only begins with her wedding day; and she wants to live. Listen... what time is it?

MUKHIN (glancing at his watch). Ten....

GORSKY. Ten.... So I still have time. Listen. A terrible struggle is going on between me and Vera Nikolayevna. Do you know why I came galloping here at breakneck speed yesterday morning?

MUKHIN. No, I don't know. Why?

GORSKY. Because today a young man—someone you know—intends to ask for her hand in marriage.

MUKHIN. Who can that be?

GORSKY. Stanitsyn.

MUKHIN. Vladimir Stanitsyn?

GORSKY. Vladimir Petrovich Stanitsyn, a retired lieutenant of the guards, a good friend of mine, and the nicest fellow imaginable. Judge for yourself—I was the one who brought him to the house. And why did I bring him? For the very purpose of marrying Vera Nikolayevna. He's a decent fellow, modest, not terribly bright, a bit of a lazybones and a stay-at-home. You couldn't ask for a better husband. And she understands that. And as an old friend of the family I have her best interests at heart.

MUKHIN. So you came galloping over in order to be witness to the happiness of your protégé?

GORSKY. On the contrary, I came here to break up the match.

MUKHIN. I don't understand you.

GORSKY. Hmm... But I would have thought the matter is clear enough.

MUKHIN. Do you want to marry her yourself, then?

GORSKY. No I don't; but I don't want her to get married either.

MUKHIN. You're in love with her.

GORSKY. I don't think so.

MUKHIN. You're in love with her, my friend, and afraid of giving yourself away.

GORSKY. What nonsense! I'm ready to tell you everything.

MUKHIN . All right, so you're courting her then....

GORSKY. Oh, no I'm not! In any case, I've no intention of marrying her.

MUKHIN. You're a modest one, there's no denying that.

GORSKY. Listen to me; I'm being absolutely frank with you now. This is how things stand. I know that if I asked for her hand, she would prefer me to our mutual friend, Vladimir Petrovich. As far as her mother is concerned, Stanitsyn and I are both acceptable suitors. She won't make difficulties. Vera thinks I'm in love with her, and knows that I'm terrified of marriage... she'd like to overcome this fear of mine... and so she's waiting.... But she isn't going to wait for long. And not because she's afraid of losing Stanitsyn; that poor boy burns high and low like a candle... but there's another reason she won't wait any longer! She's getting wind of me, the little rogue! She's beginning to suspect me! To put it bluntly, she's afraid of pushing me up against the wall, but on the other hand she wants at all costs to find out what I ... what my intentions are. And that's why a battle is raging between us. But I feel that today will be the decisive one. The serpent will either slip from my hands or strangle me. I haven't lost hope yet, though.... It may well be I'll escape Scylla and not fall into Charybdis. One problem: Stanitsyn is so much in love that he's incapable of jealousy and anger. So he goes about with his mouth hanging open and a gaze as sweet as sugar candy. He's terribly funny, but the way things are now, the game isn't to be won with ridicule. Tenderness is called for. I got started with that yesterday. And I didn't have to force myself, that's the amazing thing. I swear to God I don't understand myself any more.

MUKHIN. And how did you get started?

GORSKY. Like this. I already told you I arrived rather early yesterday. The day before yesterday I had learned of Stanitsyn's intentions. There's no point in going into detail about how I did.... Stanitsyn is trusting and not very discreet. I don't know whether Vera Nikolayevna has a premonition of her admirer's pro-posal—that would be just like her—only yesterday she was keeping a special eye on me. You can't imagine how hard it is, even when a man is accustomed to it, to endure the penetrating gaze of those innocent but intelligent eyes, especially when she screws them up. I suppose she must have been struck by the change in my treatment of her. I have a reputation for coldness and sarcasm, and I'm delighted with it: that kind of reputation makes living easier... but yesterday I had to put on a show tenderness and concern. What's the point of lying? I really did feel a touch of emotion, and my heart was ready to soften. You know me, Mukhin my friend; you know how incapable I am of ceasing to be an observer even in the most touching moments of human existence... but yesterday Vera presented an entrancing spectacle to our observer. She had surrendered herself to a passion, if not to the passion of love—I am unworthy of such an honor—then to that of curiosity, she was filled with apprehension, with distrust of her own feelings, didn't understand them.... All this was charmingly reflected in her fresh little face. I didn't leave her the whole day, and by the evening I felt that I was beginning to lose control of myself.... Oh Mukhin, Mukhin! The protracted nearness of a pair of youthful shoulders, of that youthful breathing—that's a very dangerous thing! In the evening we went into the garden. The weather was mar-velous. There was an inexpressible silence in the air.... Mlle. Bienaimé came out on the balcony with a candle: and the flame didn't stir. We took a long stroll along the soft, sandy path by the pond, within sight of the house. Stars softly glimmered on the water and in the sky.... Mlle. Bienaimé took care to keep a watchful eye on us from the height of her balcony... I suggested to Vera Nikolayevna that we embark. She agreed. I began rowing gently to the middle of the narrow pond. "Où allez-vous donc?" came the Frenchwoman's voice. "Nulle part." I answered loudly and rested the oars. "Nulle part," I added in an under-tone, "Nous sommes trop bien ici." Vera lowered her eyes, smiled, and began to draw the tip of her parasol across the water.... A sweet, pensive smile rounded her girlish cheeks... she was going to say something but only sighed—cheerfully somehow, in the way that children sigh. Well, what more can I tell you? I threw all my caution to the winds, all my good intentions, all my observations; I was happy and silly, I recited poetry... by God I did... you don't believe me? Well, by God I did recite, and in a trembling voice at that.... At dinner I sat next to her....

Yes... everything's going perfectly... My affairs are in good order, and if I did want to get married... But that's the problem. There's no deceiving her. I've heard it said that women cross swords with the best of them these days. And there's no knocking the sword out of her hand. Well, we'll see later.... In any case I had a marvelous evening.... But you seem lost in thought, Ivan Pavlych.

MUKHIN. Do I? I'm thinking that if you're not in love with Vera Nikolayevna, you're either a great fool or an intolerable egoist.

GORSKY. Who knows, who knows; but who.... Shh! they're coming.... *Aux armes!* I rely on your discretion.

MUKHIN. Oh, that goes without saying.

GORSKY *(looking through the drawing room door)*. Ah, Mlle. Bienaimé.... Always first... like it or not... Tea awaits her. *(Enter Mlle. Bienaimé. Mukhin rises and bows. Gorsky goes over to her.)* Mlle., *j'ai l'honneur de vous saluer.*

MLLE. BIENAIMÉ *(making her way into the drawing room and gazing mistrust - fully at Gorsky)*. *Bien le bonjour, monsieur.*

GORSKY. *Toujours fraîche comme une rose.*

MLLE. BIENAIMÉ *(with a pout)*. *Et vous toujours galant. Venez, j'ai quelque chose à vous dire. (She and Gorsky go into the dining room.)*

MUKHIN *(alone)*. What an odd fellow that Gorsky is! Who asked him to select me as confidant? *(Paces back and forth.)* Well, I've come here on business.... If only one could....

The glass door to the garden is suddenly thrown open. Enter Vera in a white dress. She is holding a fresh rose. Mukhin glances round and bows in some confusion; Vera stops in bewilderment.

MUKHIN. You... you don't recognize me... I....

VERA. Oh! Monsieur... Monsieur... Mukhin; I wasn't expecting you at all... when did you arrive?

MUKHIN. In the middle of the night.... Just imagine, my coachman....

VERA *(interrupting him)*. Mama will be so pleased. I do hope you will be our guest.... *(Looks around.)*

MUKHIN. You may be looking for Gorsky.... He just left.

VERA. What makes you think I'm looking for Mr. Gorsky?

MUKHIN *(not without embarrassment)*. I... I thought...

VERA. You're acquainted with him?

MUKHIN. From a long time back; we were in service together.

VERA *(going over to the window)*. What lovely weather we have today!

GORSKY. You've already been for a stroll in the garden?

VERA. Yes... I got up early.... *(Glancing at the hem of her dress and at her shoes.)* The dew is so....

MUKHIN *(with a smile)*. And your rose, look at it, it's dripping with dew....

VERA *(looking at it)*. Yes....

MUKHIN. May I ask... for whom you have picked it?

VERA. What do you mean, for whom? For myself.

MUKHIN *(meaningfully)*. Oh!

GORSKY *(emerging from the dining room)*. Would you like some tea, Mukhin? *(Catches sight of Vera.)* Good day, Vera Nikolayevna.

VERA. Good day.

MUKHIN *(hurriedly and with feigned indifference to Gorsky)*. Is tea really ready? Well, I'll be off then. *(Exits to the dining room.)*

GORSKY. Vera Nikolayevna, give me your hand.... *(She offers him her hand in silence.)* What's the matter?

VERA. Tell me, Yevgeny Andreyich, your new friend, Monsieur Mukhin—is he a fool?

GORSKY *(puzzled)*. I don't know... he's not supposed to be. What a question....

VERA. Are you good friends?

GORSKY. I know him well... but what can... could he have said something to you?

VERA *(hastily)*. No... nothing... I'm just.... what a glorious morning!

GORSKY *(pointing to the rose)*. I see you've already been for a stroll today.

VERA. Yes.... Monsieur... Mukhin just asked me who I picked this rose for.

GORSKY. And what was your reply?

VERA. My reply was, for myself.

GORSKY. And did you really pick it for yourself?

VERA. No, for you. You see, I am frank.

GORSKY. Then give it to me.

VERA. I can't now: I'll have to tuck it in my belt or give it to Mlle. Bienaimé. Such fun! And serve you right. Why didn't you come down first?

GORSKY. But I was down before anyone.

VERA. Then why didn't I run into you first?

GORSKY. That dreadful Mukhin....

VERA *(looking at him askance)*. Gorsky! You're playing games with me.

GORSKY. In what way....

VERA. Well, I'll prove it to you later.... But now let's go and have some tea.

GORSKY *(holding her back)*. Listen, Vera Nikolayevna! You know me. I am mistrustful, eccentric; I appear to be joking and casual when in reality I'm just shy.

VERA. You?

GORSKY. Yes, me. And then everything that's happening to me is so new.... You say I'm playing games.... Show a little kindness... put yourself in my position. *(Vera raises her eyes silently and looks at him intently.)* I assure you, it has never come my way to talk... to talk with anyone as I'm talking to you now... that's why it's so hard for me.... Yes, I admit I'm used to pretending.... But don't look at me like that... God knows, I deserve some encouragement.

VERA. Gorsky, I'm easily deceived.... I grew up in the country and haven't seen much of the world... I'm easily deceived; but what's the point? It won't bring you much glory.... and to make a game of me.... No, I refuse to believe it.... it's something I don't deserve, and I'm sure that it's not anything you want either.

GORSKY. To make a game of you.... just take a look at yourself.... Those eyes see through everything. *(Vera turns away silently.)* Do you know that when I am with you, I can't... well, I simply can't help saying everything that comes into my head.... In your quiet smile, in your calm gaze, even in your silence, there is a kind of authority....

VERA *(interrupting him)*. But don't you want to speak out plainly? You're still wanting to play hide-and-seek?

GORSKY. No, I'm not.... But listen, to be frank, which of us is ready to say everything that's on his mind? Take you, for instance....

VERA *(again interrupting him and with a mocking look)*. Exactly: Who speaks his mind entirely?

GORSKY. No, I'm talking about you now. For example, tell me frankly, are you expecting someone today?

VERA *(calmly)*. Yes. Stanitsyn will probably come and see us today.

GORSKY. You are a dreadful creature. You have the gift of not admitting anything and not concealing anything at the same time.... *La franchise est la meilleure des diplomaties*; probably because the one doesn't get in the way of the other.

VERA. So you knew he was coming.

GORSKY *(faintly embarrassed)*. I knew.

VERA *(smelling the rose)*. And your Monsieur... Mukhin also... knows?

GORSKY. Why do you keep asking me about Mukhin? Why do you....

VERA *(interrupting him)*. I think that's enough—don't be cross.... If you like, we'll go for a stroll in the garden after tea. We'll have a little chat. I'll ask you....

GORSKY *(hastily)*. What?

VERA. You are inquisitive.... We'll have a little talk, you and I... about an important matter. *(From the dining room comes the voice of Mlle. Bienaimé. "C'est vous, Véra?")*

VERA *(in an undertone)*. As if she couldn't hear my voice. *(Louder.)* Oui, c'est moi, bonjour, je viens. *(As she goes out she throws the rose on the table and says to Gorsky from the doorway.)* Meet me later, then. *(Exits into the dining room.)*

GORSKY *(slowly picks up the rose and remains motionless for a while)*. Yevgeny Andreyich, my friend, I have to tell you frankly that as far as I can see you've met your match in this little devil. You flounder about, and she doesn't lift a finger, but still you can't keep from blabbing. But what does it matter? Either I'll gain the victory—so much the better—or I'll lose the battle; and there's no disgrace in marrying such a woman. My blood runs cold, mark you... but, on the other hand, why cling to freedom? It's time you and I stopped behaving like children. But wait a moment, Yevgeny Andreyich, aren't you surrendering rather quickly? *(Gazes at the rose.)* What do you signify, my poor little flower? *(Turns round quickly.)* Ah, Mama and her lady friend.... *(Carefully puts the rose in his pocket. Mrs. Libanova and Varvara Ivanovna emerge from the drawing room. Gorsky goes to meet them.)* Bonjour, mesdames! I trust you are rested.

MRS. LIBANOVA *(extending the tips of her fingers)*. Bonjour, Eugène.... I have a slight headache today.

VARVARA IVANOVNA. You're late in getting to bed, Anna Vasilyevna.

MRS. LIBANOVA. You may be right.... And where is Vera? Have you seen her?

GORSKY. She's in the dining room at tea with Mlle. Bienaimé and Mukhin.

MRS. LIBANOVA. Oh yes, I gather Monsieur Mukhin arrived last night. Do you know him? *(Sits down.)*

GORSKY. I've known him a long time. You're not going to have any tea?

MRS. LIBANOVA. No, tea is bad for my nerves.... Guttmann doesn't allow it. But I won't keep you.... Off with you, off with you, Varvara Ivanovna! *(Exit Varvara Ivanovna.)* And you will stay with me, Gorsky?

GORSKY. I've already had some tea.

MRS. LIBANOVA. What a beautiful day! Le capitaine—have you seen him?

GORSKY. No, I haven't; he must be looking for mushrooms in the garden... as usual.

MRS. LIBANOVA. Just imagine the game he managed to win yesterday.... But do sit down... What are you standing up for? *(Gorsky takes a seat.)* I have the seven of diamonds and the king, along with the ace of hearts—hearts, mark you. I say: I'm playing, Varvara Ivanovna passes as usual; that rascal also says: I'm play- ing; I put down a seven; and he puts down a seven; mine of diamonds; his of hearts. I make a bid; but Varvara Ivanovna, as invariably, hasn't got a thing. And what do you think she does? She goes and plays a low spade... And there's me with a pair of kings. Well, naturally he won.... Oh, by the way, I have to send to town.... *(Rings the bell.)*

GORSKY. What for?

BUTLER *(emerging from the dining room).* What can I do for you?

MRS. LIBANOVA. Send Gavril to town for some chalk... you know the kind I like.

BUTLER. As you wish, ma'am.

MRS. LIBANOVA. And tell them to get plenty.... And how's the haymaking?

BUTLER. As you wish, ma'am. Haymaking is proceeding.

MRS. LIBANOVA. Good. And where is Ilya Ilyich?

BUTLER. He is walking in the garden, ma'am.

MRS. LIBANOVA. In the garden.... Call him, then.

BUTLER. Very good, ma'am.

MRS LIBANOVA. Be off with you then.

BUTLER. Very good, ma'am. *(Exits through the glass door.)*

MRS. LIBANOVA *(gazing at her hands).* And what are we going to do today, Eugène. You know I depend on you utterly. Think up something amusing. Now is that Monsieur Mukhin a nice young man?

GORSKY. He's a splendid fellow.

MRS. LIBANOVA. *Il n'est pas gênant?*

GORSKY. Oh, not in the least.

MRS. LIBANOVA. And he plays preference?

GORSKY. Naturally....

MRS. LIBANOVA. Ah! *mais c'est très bien....* Eugène, give me a stool to rest my feet on. *(Gorsky fetches a stool.)* Merci.... and here comes the captain.

CHUKHANOV *(entering from the garden; there are mushrooms in his cap).* Good morning, dear lady! Your hand, I beg.

MRS. LIBANOVA *(languidly extending a hand).* Good day to you, you rascal!

CHUKHANOV *(plants two successive kisses on her hand and laughs).* Rascal, rascal.... But I'm always losing. My humble respects to Yevgeny Andreyich.... *(Gorsky bows; Chukhanov stares at him and shakes his head.)* What a dashing young fellow! Ever thought of a military uniform, eh? And you, dear lady, how are you feeling? Here are some mushrooms I've picked for you.

MRS. LIBANOVA. Why don't you take a basket, captain? How could you put mushrooms in your cap?

CHUKHANOV. I obey, dear lady, I obey. It doesn't matter much to an old soldier like me. But for you, dear lady.... Look, I'll just empty them into a dish. And it seems our little bird Vera Nikolayevna has seen fit to wake up, has she?

MRS. LIBANOVA (not answering Chukhanov, to Gorsky). Dites-moi, is this Monsieur Mukhin well-off?,

GORSKY. He owns two hundred souls.

MRS. LIBANOVA (indifferently). Oh. Why are they taking so long to drink their tea?

CHUKHANOV. Do you order us to take them by storm, good lady? Give the order! We'll overcome them in a moment.... If only we had colonels like Yevgeny Andreyich....

GORSKY. What sort of colonel am I, Ilya Ilyich? For heaven's sake!

CHUKHANOV. Well not so much by rank as by physique.... It's physique I'm talking about....

MRS. LIBANOVA. Yes, Captain... do so... and see if they've done with sipping tea.

CHUKHANOV. As you wish, dear lady.... (Walking off.) Ah, but here they come. (Enter Vera, Mukhin, Mlle. Bienaimé and Varvara Ivanovna.) My respects to the entire company.

VERA (in passing). Good morning.... (She runs over to Anna Vasilyevna.) Bonjour maman.

MRS. LIBANOVA (kissing her on the forehead). Bonjour, petite.... (Mukhin bows.) You are welcome, Monsieur Mukhin.... I'm very glad you didn't forget us....

MUKHIN. I assure you... I... such an honor....

MRS. LIBANOVA (to Vera). And I see you've already been running about the garden, you naughty girl.... (To Mukhin.) Have you seen our garden yet? Il est grand. Lots of flowers. I'm terribly fond of flowers. Anyway, with us everyone is free to do as he pleases: liberté entière...

MUKHIN (smiling). C'est charmant.

MRS. LIBANOVA. That's my rule. I can't stand selfishness. It makes life hard for others and not too easy for yourself either. There you are, ask them.... (She gestures toward the entire company; Varvara Ivanovna smiles sweetly.)

MUKHIN (also smiling). My friend Gorsky has already told me about it. (After a short silence.) What a beautiful house you have!

MRS. LIBANOVA. C'est Rastrelli, vous savez, qui en a donné le plan to my grandfather, Count Lyubin.

MUKHIN (approvingly and with respect). Ah! (Throughout the conversation, Vera has deliberately turned away from Gorsky and walked over to Mlle. Bienaimé, then to Morozova. Gorsky immediately notices this, and glances stealthily at Mukhin.)

MRS. LIBANOVA (turning to the entire company). Why don't you go for a stroll?

GORSKY. Yes, let's go to the garden.

VERA (still not looking at him). It's hot outside now.... It will soon be twelve o'clock.... Now is the hottest time of day.

MRS. LIBANOVA. As you wish.... (to Mukhin.) We do have billiards, you know.... But liberté entière.... And you know what, Captain, we'll sit down to a game of cards.... It's a bit early.... But Vera says it isn't a good time for a stroll now.

CHUKHANOV *(who hasn't the slightest desire to play cards)*. Very well, dear lady, very well.... It's never too early. And you have to have your revenge.

MRS. LIBANOVA. Of course... of course.... *(Hesitantly, to Mukhin.)* Monsieur Mukhin... they say you have a liking for preference.... would you care to have a game? Mlle. Bienaimé doesn't know how to play, and it's ages since I played with four hands.

MUKHIN *(completely taken aback by this suggestion)*. I... yes, with pleasure....

MRS. LIBANOVA. *Vous êtes fort aimable....* But please don't stand on ceremony.

MUKHIN. Not at all... I'm very pleased....

MRS. LIBANOVA. Very well then... we'll go to the drawing room.... The table is already set up.... Monsieur Mukhin, *donnez-moi votre bras....* *(She gets up.)* And you, Gorsky, think up something for us to do later... do you hear? Vera will help you.... *(Exits to the drawing room.)*

CHUKHANOV *(going over to Varvara Ivanovna.)* Allow me to offer you my services....

VARVARA IVANOVNA *(thrusting her arm at him with vexation)*. You're a fine one....

Both pairs go quietly to the drawing room. In the doorway, Anna Vasilyevna turns and says to Mlle. Bienaimé: "Ne fermez pas la porte...." Mlle. Bienaimé comes back with a smile, takes a seat in the foreground to the left and with a preoccupied air takes up her canvas. Vera, who for a short time has stood undecided whether to stay or follow her mother, suddenly goes over to the piano, sits down and begins to play. Gorsky goes quietly to her side.

GORSKY *(after a brief silence)*. What is it you're playing, Vera Nikolayevna?

VERA *(without looking at him)*. A Clementi sonata.

GORSKY. Heavens! What an antiquity!

VERA. Yes, it is a most ancient and dismal thing.

GORSKY. Why did you choose it? And what's this whim of suddenly sitting down at the keyboard! Surely you haven't forgotten that you promised to have a stroll in the garden with me?

VERA. That's exactly why I sat down at the piano—so as not to go for a stroll with you.

GORSKY. Why this sudden disfavor! What kind of caprice is this?

MLLE. BIENAIMÉ. *Ce n'est pas joli ce que vous jouez là, Véra.*

VERA *(loudly)*. *Je crois bien....* *(To Gorsky, continuing to play.)* Listen, Gorsky, I don't like playing the coquette, and it isn't my style. I'm too proud for that. You know very well that I'm not playing the coquette now.... But I am cross with you.

GORSKY. What for?

VERA. I've been insulted by you.

GORSKY. I've insulted you?

VERA *(continuing to take apart the sonata)*. You really could have picked a better confidant. I'd hardly gone into the dining room when this monsieur... monsieur... what's his name?.. Monsieur Mukhin observed to me that my rose had probably reached its destination.... Then, seeing that I didn't respond to his courtesies, he suddenly began to sing your praises, but so awkwardly.... Why is it that friends always praise us so awkwardly? And in general he always makes such a mystery of himself, is so modestly discreet, gives me such looks of respect and sympathy.... I can't stand him.

GORSKY. And what do you conclude from all this?

VERA. I conclude that Monsieur Mukhin... *a l'honneur de recevoir vos confi - dences.* (*She pounds the keys.*)

GORSKY. What makes you think that?... And what could I have said to him?...

VERA. I don't know what you could have said to him.... That you're running after me, that you're playing a game with me, that you intend to turn my head, that you find me very amusing. (*Mlle. Bienaimé coughs dryly.*) *Qu'est ce que vous avez, bonne amie? Pourquoi toussez vous?*

MLLE BIENAIMÉ. *Rien, rien... je ne sais pas... cette sonate doit être bien diffi - cile.*

VERA (*in an undertone*). How she gets on my nerves.... (*To Gorsky.*) Why don't you say anything?

GORSKY. I? Why don't I say anything? This is what I ask myself: am I at fault before you? Yes, I am at fault, and I repent. My tongue is my worst enemy. But listen, Vera Nikolayevna..... Do you remember I was reading you Lermontov yesterday, do you remember where he talks of a heart where love is locked in a bitter struggle with enmity.... (*Vera quietly raises her eyes.*) No, no, I can't go on when you look at me like that....

VERA (*shrugging her shoulders*). Enough of that....

GORSKY. Listen.... I will make a frank confession: I am fighting against, I am terrified of yielding to that involuntary enchantment which I cannot for the life of me deny.... I try my hardest to escape with words, with mockery, with sto-ries.... I chatter away like an old maid, like a child....

VERA. But why is this? Why can't we stay good friends? Is it impossible for relations between us to be simple and natural?

GORSKY. Simple and natural.... That's easy to say.... (*With decision.*) Very well then, I am at fault before you and I beg your forgiveness: I've been playing a sly game—and I'm still playing it... but I can assure you, Vera Nikolayevna, that whatever my assumptions and intentions in your absence, at your first words they all vanish like smoke, and I feel—this will make you laugh—I feel that I am in your power....

VERA (*stops playing little by little*). You told me the same thing last night....

GORSKY. Because I felt the same way last night. I absolutely refuse to play the fox with you.

VERA (*with a smile*). Ah, there you are!

GORSKY. Let's talk about you: you must be aware that I am not deceiving you when I tell you....

VERA (*interrupting him*). That I find favor in your eyes... I should think so!

GORSKY (*with vexation*). You're as unapproachable and mistrustful today as a seventy-year-old money-lender! (*He turns away; both are silent for a while.*)

VERA *(now scarcely playing at all)*. I'll play your favorite mazurka, if you like.

GORSKY. Vera Nikolayevna! Don't torment me.... I swear....

VERA *(gaily)*. Enough is enough, give me your hand. You are forgiven. *(Gorsky quickly presses her hand.)* Nous faisons la paix, bonne amie.

MLLE. BIENAIMÉ. *(with feigned surprise)*. Ah! Est-ce que vous vous étiez querel - lés?

VERA *(in an undertone)*. Oh what innocence! *(More loudly.)* Oui, un peu. *(To Gorsky.)* Well, would you like me to play your mazurka?

GORSKY. I don't think so; that mazurka is too sad.... It's full of a kind of bitter yearning for far-off things; and I assure you I feel quite happy here. Play me something gay, radiant, lively, something that would dally and sparkle in the sunlight, like a little fish in a brook... *(Vera becomes thoughtful for a moment and begins to play a sparkling waltz.)* Heavens! How sweet you are! Just like that little fish.

VERA *(continuing to play)*. I can see Monsieur Mukhin from here. He must be having a good time! I'm convinced he invariably underplays his hand.

GORSKY. It's all the same to him.

VERA *(after a short silence, not ceasing to play)*. Tell me, why does Stanitsyn never express his thoughts in their entirety?

GORSKY. He obviously has a great many thoughts to express.

VERA. You're being malicious. He's no fool; he's a man of great kindness. I'm very fond of him.

GORSKY. He's a splendid fellow, thoroughly reliable.

VERA. Yes.... But why do his clothes have such a stiff and starchy look? As if they'd just come from the tailor's. *(Gorsky makes no reply and gazes at her in silence.)* What's on your mind?

GORSKY. I was thinking.... I was picturing to myself a little room, only not buried in our snows, but somewhere in the south, in some remote beautiful land....

VERA. But you were just saying that you have no yearning for far-off lands.

GORSKY. I wouldn't want to go alone.... Not a familiar face to be seen, sounds of a foreign tongue fall on your ear in the streets, the freshness of the nearby sea wafts from the open window... the white curtains bulge quietly, like a sail, the door gives onto a garden, and on the threshold, in the delicate shade of the ivy....

VERA *(embarrassed)*. Oh, you are a poet....

GORSKY. God forbid. I am only remembering.

VERA. Remembering?

GORSKY. The setting—yes; the rest—all that you didn't let me finish saying—is a dream.

VERA. Dreams don't come true... in real life.

GORSkY. Who told you that? Mlle. Bienaimé? For heaven's sake, leave such gems of feminine wisdom to old maids of forty-five and lymphatic youths. Real life... but how can the most ardent, the most inventive imagination hope to keep pace with real life, with nature? For pity's sake... take any shellfish you like it's a hundred thousand times more fantastic than all the tales of Hoffmann; and what inspired poetic masterpiece could compare... well say even with that oak tree growing on the hillside?

VERA. I'm willing to believe you, Gorsky!

GORSKY. I beg you to believe that the most extravagant, the most rapturous happiness envisioned by the fancy of an idle man cannot compare with the bliss that lies within his reach... if only he can stay healthy, if fate is not unkind, if his estate isn't auctioned off, and if only, when all is said and done, he can make up his mind what he wants.

VERA. If only!

GORSKY. But aren't we... but aren't I young and in good health, my estate isn't mortgaged....

VERA. But you haven't made up your mind what you really want....

GORSKY (decisively). I have made up my mind.

VERA (fixing her eyes on him). Well, tell me then.

GORSKY. Very well. I want you to....

SERVANT (enters from the dining room and announces). Vladimir Petrovich Stanitsyn.

VERA (getting up quickly). I can't see him now.... Gorsky! I think I understand what you're trying to say.... You receive him instead of me... instead of me, please... puisque tout est arrangé.... (Exits to the drawing room.)

MLLE. BIENAIMÉ. Eh bien? Elle s'en va?

GORSKY (a little embarrassed). Oui.... Elle est allée voir....

MLLE. BIENAIMÉ. Quelle petite folle! (She gets up and also exits to the drawing room.)

GORSKY (after a short silence). So what have I done? Have I got married?... "I think I understand what you're trying to say." See what she's getting at... "puisque tout est arrangé." At this moment I can't stand the thought of her! Reckless, reckless—that's what I am! I tried to put on a brave show in front of Mukhin, and now.... the poetic flights I indulged in! The only thing missing was the traditional: "You'll have to ask Mama...." Ugh what a ridiculous situation! But the business has to be tied up one way or another. Stanitsyn's arrival is convenient! O fate, o fate! prithee tell me, are you having a little joke at my expense or are you coming to my assistance? Well, we'll see.... But my good friend Mukhin is a fine one....

Enter Stanitsyn. He is dressed like a dandy. In his right hand is a hat, in his left a basket wrapped in paper. His face expresses agitation. At the sight of Gorsky he comes to a sudden stop, reddens. Gorsky goes to meet him with extended arms and the most affectionate expression.

GORSKY. Welcome, Vladimir Petrovich! I'm so happy to see you....

STANITSYN. I too... am very.... But have... you been here long?

GORSKY. Since yesterday, Vladimir Petrovich.

STANITSYN. Is everyone in good health?

GORSKY. Everyone, absolutely everyone, from Anna Vasilyevna down to the pet dog you gave Vera Nikolayevna.... And how are you?

STANITSYN. I... I, thank goodness.... But where are they?

GORSKY. In the drawing room!... They're playing cards.

STANITSYN. At so early an hour... and what about you?

GORSKY. This is where *I* am, as you can see. What's that you've brought? Some candy perhaps?

STANITSYN. Yes, Vera Nikolayevna was saying the other day... so I had some candy sent from Moscow....

GORSKY. From Moscow?

STANITSYN. Yes, they have the best stuff there. But where is Vera Nikolayevna? *(Places hat and candy on the table.)*

GORSKY. I imagine she's in the drawing room... watching them play preference.

STANITSYN *(peering timidly into the drawing room)*. Who is that new face?

GORSKY. You don't recognize him? Mukhin, Ivan Pavlych.

STANITSYN. Oh yes.... *(Shifting from one foot to the other.)*

GORSKY. Would you care to go to the drawing room?... Something seems to be disturbing you, Vladimir Petrovich.

STANITSYN. Oh no, it's nothing... the journey, you know, the dust.... And my head is also....

An *outburst of laughter from the drawing room. Everyone shouts: "He's four short, four short!" Vera says: "I congratulate you, monsieur Mukhin!"*

STANITSYN *(laughs and again peeps into the drawing room)*. What's going on... has someone overbid?

GORSKY. But why on earth don't you go in?...

STANITSYN. To tell you the truth, Gorsky... I would like to have a little talk with Vera Nikolayevna.

GORSKY. In private?

STANITSYN *(uncertainly)*. Yes, just a few words. I would like... now... or some time later today.... You know yourself....

GORSKY. What about it, then? Go in and tell her.... and don't forget your candy....

STANITSYN. You have a point. *(He gets as far as the door and still can't make up his mind to go in, when suddenly Anna Vasilyevna's voice rings out: "C'est vous, Woldemar? Bonjour... Entrez donc...." He goes in.)*

GORSKY *(alone)*. I'm not pleased with myself.... I'm starting to get bored and irritable. Heavens above! What is this that's going on inside me? Why does the bile rise to my throat? Why this sudden ill-omened cheerfulness? Why this readiness to play schoolboy pranks on the whole world, even on myself? Even if I'm not in love, then why this desire to pull everyone's leg, including my own? Get married? No, I'm not going to get married, whatever you say, especially like this, at the point of a knife. But if it comes to that, surely I'm capable of sacrificing my own vanity? Well, she will triumph, devil take her. *(Goes over to the Chinese bil - liard table and begins pushing the balls about.)* Perhaps it will be better for me if she marries.... But no, that's nonsense.... I won't be able to see her then, any more than I can see my own ears... *(Continues to push the balls about.)* I'll make a wager.... If I should hit the mark.... Dear God, what childishness! *(Throws down his cue, goes over to the desk and picks up a book.)* What's this? A Russian novel? Well, well, well. Let's see what the Russian novel has to say. *(Opens the book at random and reads.)* "And what then? Not five years passed after the wedding and the captivating, vivacious Maria was transformed into the buxom, loud-mouthed Maria Bogdanovna.... What had become of all her yearnings and dreams...." Oh my dear, respected authors, what children you are! So this is what you bewail! Is it surprising that people get older, put on weight, grow dull witted? But this is the dreadful thing: the dreams and yearnings stay the same, the eyes are still undimmed, the down is still on the cheeks, and our beleaguered spouse doesn't know where to turn.... Yes, that's how it is, a respectable man shakes with a fever before he plights his troth.... Now I think they're coming this way.... I must escape somehow.... Oh Lord, it's just like Gogol's *Marriage*.... But at least I don't jump out of the window, but go quietly through this door into the garden.... It's all yours, Mr. Stanitsyn!

As he hastily retreats, Vera and Stanitsyn enter from the drawing room.

VERA *(to Stanitsyn)*. Was that Gorsky running off to the garden?
STANITSYN. Yes... I... must confess... I told him I wanted... to have a few words with you in private... just a few words...
VERA. I see, you told him.... And what did he....
STANITSYN. He... didn't....
VERA. All these preparations!... You alarm me.... and I didn't completely understand that note of yours yesterday....
STANITSYN. What I want to say, Vera Nikolayevna.... For heaven's sake, forgive my boldness, I beg of you.... I know I'm unworthy.... *(Vera moves slowly toward the window; he follows her.)* What I want to say.... I... I have resolved to ask for your hand in marriage.... *(Vera says nothing and lowers her head.)* God in heaven! I know only too well that I'm not worthy of you... that on my part this is... but you have known me a long time... if blind devotion... the fulfillment of your slightest wish, if all this.... I beg you to forgive my boldness.... I feel.... *(He comes to a standstill. Vera quietly reaches out her hand to him.)* Surely, surely, I cannot have reason to hope?
VERA *(softly)*. You haven't understood me, Vladimir Petrovich.
STANITSYN. In that case... naturally... forgive me. But allow me to beg one thing of you, Vera Nikolayevna... don't deprive me of the happiness of seeing you, even just occasionally.... I assure you... I won't be any bother.... Even if there's someone else.... You... and the man of your choice.... I assure you... I will always be happy if you are happy.... I know I'm not worth much... how could I possibly.... Of course you are right....
VERA. Give me time to think, Vladimir Petrovich.
STANITSYN. What?
VERA. Yes, leave me now... for a little while... we shall meet... I'll talk with you later....
STANITSYN. I will submit to whatever you decide without a murmur. *(He bows, exits to the drawing room and shuts the door behind him.)*
VERA *(follows him with her eyes, goes over to the garden door and calls out.)* Gorsky! Gorsky, come here! *(She advances to the forestage. Gorsky enters in a few moments.)*

GORSKY. You called me?

VERA. Did you know that Stanitsyn wanted to talk with me in private?

GORSKY. Yes, he told me.

VERA. Did you know why?

GORSKY. No, not really.

VERA. He is asking for my hand in marriage.

GORSKY. And what was your answer?

VERA. I didn't give him one.

GORSKY. You didn't refuse him?

VERA. I asked him to wait.

GORSKY. Why?

VERA. What do you mean "why," Gorsky? What's come over you? Why do you look at me so coldly, speak with such indifference? What does that smile on your lips mean? You see that I've come to you for advice, I am reaching out my hand—and you....

GORSKY. Forgive me, Vera Nikolayevna:... I'm a bit slow sometimes.... I've been walking in the sun without a hat.... You mustn't laugh.... That's probably what it is.... And so Stanitsyn is asking for your hand, and you are asking for my advice... now I have a question for you: what's your opinion of family life in general? You might compare it with milk... but milk soon goes sour.

VERA. Gorsky! I don't understand you. A quarter of an hour ago, on that very spot *(gestures toward the piano)*, remember, was this the way you talked to me? Is this how I left you? What's the matter with you? Are you making fun of me? Gorsky, do I deserve this treatment?

GORSKY *(bitterly)*. I assure you that "making fun" is the last thing in my mind.

VERA. How do you explain this sudden change? Why can't I understand you? Why is it, on the contrary, that I.... Tell me, tell me, haven't I always been frank with you, like a sister?

GORSKY *(not without embarrassment)*. Vera Nikolayevna! I....

VERA. Or perhaps... look what you are forcing me to say... perhaps Stanitsyn aroused in you... how can I put this?.. something like jealousy?

GORSKY. And why shouldn't he?

VERA. Oh don't pretend.... You know only too well.... But what am I saying? How should I know what you think of me, what you feel for me....

GORSKY. Vera Nikolayevna! Let me tell you something: really it might be better for us to break off our acquaintance for a while....

VERA. Gorsky... what are you saying?

GORSKY. Joking aside.... Relations between us are so strange.... We are condemned to misunderstand and torment each other....

VERA. I don't object to being tormented; but I'm not inclined to let anyone make fun of me.... to misunderstand each other—why should that be? Don't I look you straight in the eye? Do I have a fondness for misunderstandings? Don't I always say what I think? Am I lacking in trust? Gorsky, if we have to part, let us at least part good friends!

GORSKY. If we do part, you won't give me a thought.

VERA. It's as if you wanted me to.... You seem to want some kind of declara-

tion from me. But I am not in the habit of lying or exaggerating. Yes, I like you—
I feel an attraction toward you in spite of your eccentric ways—and... and that's
all. These friendly feelings could develop, and they could come to an end. That
depends on you.... That's what's going on inside me.... But you, you must tell me
what it is you want, what you are thinking. Surely you understand that I'm not
asking out of empty curiosity, that I really do have to know.... *(She falls silent and
turns away.)*

GORSKY. Vera Nikolayevna! Hear me out. God created you happy. You have
lived and breathed in freedom since you were a child.... Truth is to you as light is
to the eyes, as air is to the lungs.... You look about you bravely and go forward
bravely, even though you have no knowledge of life, because life doesn't—and
won't—present any obstacles for you. But for heaven's sake don't expect the same
courage from a man as somber and confused as myself, a man who has much to
blame himself for, who has sinned and is still sinning.... Don't tear from me that
last, decisive word, which I do not say aloud in your presence, perhaps because I
have said it to myself in solitude a thousand times.... I say to you again... be
patient with me or rid yourself of me for good... wait a little....

VERA. Gorsky, can I trust you? Tell me—I will take your word—can I really
trust you?

GORSKY *(with an involuntary movement)*. God alone knows!

VERA *(after a short silence)*. Take some thought and give me a different
answer.

GORSKY. I always answer better when I don't take thought.

VERA. You are as capricious as a little girl.

GORSKY. And you are terribly shrewd.... But you must forgive me.... I think
I just said: "Wait a little." This inexcusably silly expression just slipped from my
lips.

VERA *(reddening at once)*. Did it indeed. Thank you for your candor.

*Gorsky is about to respond when the door of the drawing room is suddenly opened
and the entire company enters, with the exception of Mlle. Bienaimé. Anna Vasilyevna
is in an easy and cheerful mood; she is on Mukhin's arm. Stanitsyn throws a rapid
glance at Vera and Gorsky.*

MRS. LIBANOVA. Just imagine, Eugène, we completely cleaned out Mr.
Mukhin.... We did indeed. But what an enthusiastic cardplayer he is!

GORSKY. Really? And I had no idea!

MRS. LIBANOVA. C'est incroyable! He underplays at every step.... *(Sits
down.)* And now we can go for a stroll.

MUKHIN *(going over to the window, with restrained irritation)*. Hardly, it's
beginning to drizzle.

VARVARA IVANOVNA. The barometer has gone right down today....
(Takes a seat a little behind Mrs. Libanova.)

MRS. LIBANOVA. Really? Comme c'est contrariant! Eh bien, we'll have to
think of something else.... Eugène, and you, Woldemar that's your business.

CHUKHANOV. Would anyone care to do battle with me at billiards? *(No
one answers.)* In that case, how about having a little snack and emptying a glass of

vodka? *(Another silence.)* All right then. I'll go by myself and drink the health of all this respected company.... *(Goes into the dining room. Meanwhile Stanitsyn has gone up to Vera, but cannot pluck up the courage to enter into conversation with her. Gorsky stands to one side. Mukhin is examining some drawings on the table.)*

MRS. LIBANOVA. Well then, gentlemen? Gorsky, you think of something.

GORSKY. If you like, I'll read you the introduction to Buffon's natural history.

MRS LIBANOVA. Oh stop it.

GORSKY. Or how about playing *petits jeux innocents.*

MRS. LIBANOVA. Whatever you like... but I'm not speaking for myself.... My steward must be waiting for me in the office already.... Has he arrived, Varvara Ivanovna?

VARVARA IVANOVNA. I should think he probably has.

MRS. LIBANOVA. Do make sure, my dear. *(Varvara Ivanovna gets up and goes out.)* Vera, come here.... Why are you looking so pale today? Are you all right?

VERA. I'm all right.

MRS. LIBANOVA. That's all I wanted to know. Oh yes. Woldemar, don't forget to remind me.... I've got a little errand for you in town. *(To Vera.) Il est si complaisant.*

VERA. *Il est plus que cela, maman, il est bon. (Stanitsyn smiles blissfully.)*

MRS. LIBANOVA. What are you examining so attentively, Monsieur Mukhin?

MUKHIN. Views of Italy.

MRS. LIBANOVA. Oh yes... I brought them back with me... *un souvenir....* I love Italy... I was happy there.... *(Sighs.)*

VARVARA IVANOVNA *(entering).* Fyodor has arrived, Anna Vasilyevna.

MRS. LIBANOVA *(getting up).* So he's arrived! *(To Mukhin.)* You'll find... there's a view of Lago Maggiore.... An absolute delight!... *(To Varvara Ivanovna.)* Has the bailiff come too?

VARVARA IVANOVNA. The bailiff is there too.

MRS. LIBANOVA. Well then, good-bye, *mes enfants....* Eugène. I leave them in your charge.... *Amusez-vous....* Mlle. Bienaimé is coming to your aid. *(Mlle. Bienaimé enters from the drawing room.)* Let's be off, Varvara Ivanovna! *(Exits to the dining room with Morozova. A short silence falls.)*

MLLE BIENAIMÉ *(in a dry voice).* Eh bien, que ferons nous?

MUKHIN. Yes, what shall we do?

STANITSYN. That is the question.

GORSKY. Hamlet said that before you, Vladimir Petrovich! *(Suddenly ani - mated.)* But come to think of it, let's get down to it, let's.... See what a downpour we've had.... What's the point of sitting with our arms folded?

STANITSYN. I'm prepared.... What about you, Vera Nikolayevna?

VERA *(who has remained motionless all this time).* I too... am prepared.

STANITSYN. Well, that's just fine!

MUKHIN. Have you thought something up, Yevgeny Andreyich?

GORSKY. Yes I have, Ivan Pavlych! Here's what we'll do. We'll take seats around the table....

MLLE. BIENAIMÉ. *Oh, ce sera charmant!*

GORSKY. *N'est ce pas?* Write down all our names on scraps of paper, and the first to be drawn will have to tell some absurd and fantastic story, about himself, about someone else, whatever he likes.... *Liberté entière*, to use Anna Vasilyevna's expression.

STANITSYN. Good, good.

MLLE. BIENAIMÉ *(together with Stanitsyn's "Good, good.")*. Ah! *très bien, très bien!*

MUKHIN. But what kind of story do you have in mind?

GORSKY. Whatever comes into your head.... Well, let's sit down.... would you like to, Vera Nikolayevna?

VERA. Why not? *(Takes a seat, Gorsky sits down on her right, Mukhin on her left, Stanitsyn next to Mukhin, Mlle. Bienaimé next to Gorsky.)*

GORSKY. Here's a sheet of paper *(tears it up)*, and here are our names. *(He writes down names and rolls up the scraps of paper.)*

MUKHIN *(to Vera)*. You seem rather thoughtful today, Vera Nikolayevna.

VERA. And how do you know that I'm not always like this? You're seeing me for the first time.

MUKHIN *(with a smirk)*. Oh no, how could you possibly always be like this....

VERA *(with faint vexation)*. Do you think so? *(To Stanitsyn.)* Those candies of yours are delicious, Woldemar!

STANITSYN. I'm very glad... to have been of service....

GORSKY. Oh, a ladies' man! *(He mixes the scraps together.)* Here you are. And who will pick one out?... Mlle. Bienaimé, *voulez-vous?*

MLLE. BIENAIMÉ. *Mais très volontiers. (with a pout, picks out a scrap and reads.)* Meester Stanitsyn.

GORSKY *(to Stanitsyn)*. Well, tell us something then, Vladimir Petrovich!

STANITSYN. But what do you want me to tell you?... I'm really at a loss....

GORSKY. Tell us something or other. You're free to say anything that comes into your head.

STANITSYN. But nothing comes into my head.

GORSKY. Well, that's a bit awkward, of course.

VERA. I agree with Stanitsyn.... How can one, just on the spur of the moment....

MUKHIN *(hastily)*. I am of the same opinion.

STANITSYN. So set us an example, Yevgeny Andreyich; you begin.

VERA. Yes, you begin.

MUKHIN. Begin, begin.

MLLE. BIENAIMÉ. *Oui, commencez, monsieur Gorsky.*

GORSKY. You're quite sure you want.... Very well.... I'll be the first.... Hmm.... *(Coughs.)*

MLLE. BIENAIMÉ. *Hi, hi, nous allons rire.*

GORSKY. *Ne riez pas d'avance.* Very well, give me your attention. A certain baron had....

MUKHIN. Had a certain fantasy?

GORSKY. No, had a daughter.

MUKHIN. Well, that's almost the same thing.

GORSKY. Goodness how sharp you are today!... Anyway, a certain baron had a daughter. She was very beautiful, her father loved her dearly, she loved her father dearly, everything was as it should be—when suddenly, one fine day the young baroness took it into her head that life was a disgusting business, the world became a very dull place; so she burst into tears and took to her bed.... A lady in waiting at once ran to fetch her father, her father came, saw what was to be seen, shook his head, said in German: m-m-m-m-m, departed with measured step and summoning his secretary, dictated to him three letters of invitation to three young noblemen of ancient lineage and of pleasing demeanor. The very next day, dressed in all their finery, they clicked their heels in turn before the baron, while the young baroness smiled as she had in times past, if not more radiantly, and scrupulously examined her suitors, for the baron was a diplomat and the young men were suitors.

MUKHIN. You do spin it out!

GORSKY. My dear friend, accept my humble apologies!

MLLE. BIENAIMÉ. *Mais oui, laissez-le faire.*

VERA *(giving Gorsky an attentive look)*. Do go on.

GORSKY. And so the baroness had three suitors. Which to choose? The heart answers this question best of all.... But when the heart.... But when the heart is unsure?... The young baroness was a maiden of intelligence and fore-sight.... She decided to subject the suitors to a test.... One day, finding herself alone with one of them, the fair-headed one, she suddenly turned to him with a question: tell me, what are you prepared to do to prove your love for me? The fair-headed suitor, by nature a man of the greatest self-possession, but therefore all the more inclined to exaggeration, responded with ardor: at your command I am prepared to leap from the highest bell tower in the world. The baroness smiled cordially, and the very next day asked the same question of the next suitor, the auburn one, informing him beforehand of the fair-headed suitor's response. The auburn one answered in the very same words, possibly with even greater ardor. Finally the baroness turned to the third suitor, a chestnut head. Chestnut head was quiet for a moment for the sake of propriety and replied that he was willing to agree to anything else, but that he would not throw himself from a tower, and for a very simple reason: it would be difficult to offer anyone his hand and heart once he had smashed his head to smithereens. The baroness was angry at chestnut-head; but... perhaps... because she was a little more partial to him than the other two, she began to badger him: promise me, she says, at least.... I won't ask you to keep your promise.... But chestnut head, being a man of principle, was unwilling to promise anything....

VERA. You are in bad humor today, Monsieur Gorsky!

MLLE. BIENAIMÉ. *Non, il n'est pas en veine, c'est vrai.* Eet eez not good, not good.

STANITSYN. Another story, another one.

GORSKY *(not without vexation)*. I'm not in form today... every day you can't.... *(To Vera.)* Take you today, for example.... What a difference from yester-day!

VERA. What do you mean? *(She gets up; everyone gets up.)*

GORSKY (to Stanitsyn). You can't imagine what a wonderful evening we spent yesterday, Vladimir Petrovich! A pity you weren't with us, Vladimir Petrovich.... Mlle. Bienaimé here will bear witness. Vera Nikolayevna and I went boating on the pond together for more than an hour.... Vera Nikolayevna was so delighted with everything, she was in such a good mood.... She really seemed to take wing.... Tears welled up in her eyes.... I'll never forget that evening, Vladimir Petrovich!

STANITSYN (despondently). I can well believe it.

VERA (who has not taken her eyes off Gorsky all this time). Yes we really were rather ridiculous yesterday.... And I wasn't the only one to take wing, as you put it. Just imagine, gentleman, Gorsky read me poetry yesterday—such sweet, dreamy poetry, too!

STANITSYN. He read you poetry?

VERA. Indeed he did... and in such a strange voice... as if he wasn't well, with such heartfelt sighs....

GORSKY. You asked for all that yourself, Vera Nikolayevna!... You know that I rarely indulge in exalted feelings of my own inclination.

VERA. You astonished me all the more yesterday. I know that you find it much pleasanter to laugh than... than to sigh shall we say or... daydream.

GORSKY. Oh, I agree with that! And really, can you name something which is not deserving of laughter? Friendship, family happiness, love?... All these delightful things are good only for a moment's relaxation, then God grant me speed! A decent man shouldn't permit himself to wallow in these featherbeds (Mukhin, smiling, glances now at Vera, now at Stanitsyn; Vera notices this.)

VERA (slowly). It's clear you are now speaking from the heart!... But what are you getting excited about? No one doubts that this has always been your manner of thinking.

GORSKY (laughing constrainedly). Really? You were of a different opinion yesterday.

VERA. What makes you so sure? No, joking apart, Gorsky, allow me to offer a friendly word of advice.... Never allow yourself to sink into sentimentality.... It doesn't suit you at all.... You're so clever.... You can get along perfectly well without it.... Oh, I think it's stopped raining. Look how wonderfully sunny it is! Let's go into the garden.... Stanitsyn, give me your arm. (Turns quickly and takes Stanitsyn's arm.) Bonne amie, venez-vous?

MLLE. BIENAIMÉ. Oui, oui, allez toujours.... (Takes her hat from the piano and puts it on.)

VERA (to the others). And you, gentlemen, aren't you coming? On the double, Stanitsyn, on the double!

STANITSYN (running into the garden with Vera). As you wish, Vera Nikolayevna, as you wish.

MLLE. BIENAIMÉ. Monsieur Mukhin, voulez-vous me donner votre bras?

MUKHIN. Avec plaisir, mlle..... (To Gorsky.) Good-bye, chestnut head! (Exit with Mlle. Bienaimé.)

GORSKY (alone, goes over to the window). What a pace she's running at!.. and never a backward glance.... And Stanitsyn. Stanitsyn—he's falling over himself with joy! (Shrugs his shoulders.) Poor fellow! He doesn't understand the position he's in.... Enough said, but is he really to be pitied? I think I went a bit too far. But what is a man to do with his bile? All the time I was telling my story, that little devil never took her eyes off me.... I was wrong to mention our little stroll yesterday. If she had the idea that... it's all over, Yevgeny Andreyich, my good friend, you might as well be packing your bags. *(Pacing back and forth.)* Yes, it's time... I've landed myself in a fine mess. O chance, the fool's misfortune and the wise man's providence, come to my aid! *(Looks round.)* Who's there? Chukhanov. If only he could somehow....

CHUKHANOV *(entering warily from the dining room).* Ah, Yevgeny old fellow, how glad I am to find you alone.

GORSKY. What can I do for you?

CHUKHANOV *(in an undertone).* Well, it's like this, Yevgeny Andreyich... Anna Vasilyevna, God grant her health and long life, was kind enough some time ago to give me some timber for a little cottage, but she forgot to pass on an order to the office, and without an order there's no getting the timber....

GORSKY. Well, you should remind her then.

CHUKHANOV. I'm afraid to bother her, old fellow.... Be so kind, old fellow, and I'll pray to God for you for a hundred years... somehow to mention.... *(He winks.)* You really are a master at that... couldn't you, as you might say, just in passing? *(He winks even more meaningfully.)* And you might take into account that the house is already occupied... hee-hee!

GORSKY. Is that so? Very well then, I'll be delighted....

CHUKHANOV. I'll be in your debt to the grave, old fellow.... *(Loudly, in his former manner.)* And if you're in need of something, just give me a wink. *(Throwing back his head.)* Ehh, what a fine fellow!

GORSKY. Very well... I'll take care of everything; don't worry.

CHUKHANOV. I obey, your excellency! But old man Chukhanov doesn't bother anyone. He has made his report, put in his request, had recourse, and now it's up to the boss. Much gratitude and satisfaction. To the left about turn, march! *(Exits to dining room.)*

GORSKY. Well I don't think anything can be squeezed out of this "occasion".... *(Hurried footsteps are heard on the steps outside the garden door.)* Who's that running? Good Lord! Stanitsyn!

STANITSYN *(rushing in).* Where's Anna Vasilyevna?

GORSKY. Who is it you need?

STANITSYN *(comes to a sudden halt).* Gorsky.... Oh, if you only knew....

GORSKY. You are beside yourself with joy.... What's the matter?

STANITSYN *(taking him by the hand).* Gorsky... I really didn't ought to... but I can't help it—I'm suffocating with happiness.... I know you always took my part.... Just imagine.... Who would have thought it....

GORSKY. Well, what is all this?

STANITSYN. I asked Vera Nikolayevna for her hand, and she....

GORSKY. And she what?

STANITSYN. Just imagine, Gorsky, she gave her consent... just now, in the garden... gave me permission to approach Anna Vasilyevna.... Gorsky! I'm as happy as a child.... What a wonderful girl!.

GORSKY *(barely concealing his emotion).* And you are going to Anna Vasilyevna now?

STANITSYN. Yes. I know she won't refuse me.... Gorsky, I am happy, immeasurably happy... I could embrace the entire world.... Let me embrace you at least. *(Embraces Gorsky.)* Oh, how happy I am! *(Runs off.)*

GORSKY *(after a lengthy silence). Bravissimo! (He bows in Stanitsyn's direction.)* I have the honor to congratulate you... *(Paces angrily about the room.)* I admit I didn't expect this. The sly minx! But I must be off right away... On second thought, I'll stay.... Fie, how painfully my heart is beating.... disgusting. *(Having pondered a moment.)* Well, I'm defeated then.... But how shamefully defeated... neither in the manner or in the place I would have chosen.... *(Going over to the window, peers into the garden.)* They're coming.... At least we'll die with honor.... *(Puts on his hat as if preparing to go into the garden but in the doorway bumps into Mukhin, Vera and Mlle. Bienaimé. Vera is holding Mlle. Bienaimé by the arm.)* Oh, you're coming back so soon. I was just about to join you.... *(Vera does not lift her eyes.)*

MLLE. BIENAIMÉ. *Il fait encore trop mouillé.*

MUKHIN. Why didn't you come with us earlier?

GORSKY. Chukhanov held me up.... And you've been doing a lot of running about by the look of you, Vera Nikolayevna?

VERA. Yes... I feel hot.

Mlle. Bienaimé and Mukhin move a little to one side, then begin to play on the Chinese billiard table, which stands slightly to the rear.

GORSKY *(in an undertone).* I know everything, Vera Nikolayevna. I didn't expect this.

VERA. You know.... But I'm not surprised. He's not the kind to keep secrets.

GORSKY *(reproachfully).* You'll regret this.

VERA. No, I won't.

GORSKY. You acted under the influence of anger.

VERA. Perhaps, but I acted wisely and I won't regret it.... You applied Lermontov's lines to me, you told me that I will go where chance leads me and never return.... Besides, Gorsky, you know yourself that I'd be unhappy with you.

GORSKY. You do me much honor.

VERA. I say what I think. He loves me, but you....

GORSKY. But I?

VERA. You aren't capable of loving anyone. Your heart is too cold and your imagination is too hot. I'm talking to you as to a friend of things that happened long ago....

GORSKY *(tonelessly).* I've offended you.

VERA. Yes... but you didn't love me enough to have the right to offend me.... Anyway, all this belongs to the past.... Let us part friends.... Give me your hand.

GORSKY. You amaze me, Vera Nikolayevna! You are as transparent as glass, as guileless as a two-year-old, and as resolute as Frederick the Great. I give you my hand... but don't you feel what a bitter hour this must be for me?...

VERA. Your vanity is wounded... never mind, it will heal.

GORSKY. Oh, you're a philosopher as well!

VERA. Listen.... This is probably the last time we'll be talking about this.... You're an intelligent man, but you've been sorely mistaken about me. Believe me, I didn't put you *au pied du mur*, as your friend Monsieur Mukhin would express it, I didn't subject you to any ordeals, but was searching for truth and simplicity, I didn't require you to jump from a bell tower, but rather than that....

MUKHIN. *J'ai gagné.*

MLLE. BIENAIMÉ. *Eh bien! la revanche.*

VERA. I didn't allow myself to be made a plaything, that's all.... I assure you I don't have any resentment.

GORSKY. I congratulate you.... magnanimity becomes a victor.

VERA. Give me your hand.... Here is mine.

GORSKY. I beg your pardon, your hand is no longer yours to give. *(Vera turns away and goes toward the billiard table.)* All the same, everything is for the best.

VERA. Exactly.... *Qui gagne?*

MUKHIN. I've been winning so far.

VERA. Oh, you're a great man!

GORSKY *(clapping him on the shoulder).* And the best of friends, aren't you, Ivan Pavlych? *(Puts his hand in his pocket.)* Oh by the way, Vera Nikolayevna, would you mind coming over here.... *(Goes to the forestage.)*

VERA *(following him.)* What do you have to say to me?

GORSKY *(takes a rose from his pocket and gives it to Vera).* Well, what do you say to that? *(Laughs, Vera blushes and lowers her eyes.)* Well? Funny, isn't it? You see, it hasn't had time to fade yet.... *(With a bow.)* Allow me to return it to its owner....

VERA. If you had the slightest respect for me, you wouldn't choose this moment to give it back.

GORSKY *(withdrawing his hand).* In that case, allow it to remain in my possession, this poor little flower.... But sentiment isn't my style, is it? Yes, indeed, long live gaiety, mockery and malice! I'm quite myself again.

VERA. Splendid!

GORSKY. Look at me. *(Vera fixes her eyes on him. Gorsky continues, not with - out emotion.)* Fare thee well.... Now would be a fitting moment to exclaim: *Welche Perle warf ich weg!* But what's the point? Everything is for the best.

MUKHIN *(exclaims).* *J'ai gagné encore une fois!*

VERA. Everything is for the best, Gorsky.

GORSKY. Perhaps... perhaps.... Ah, and now the door of the drawing room is flung open.... The family polonaise is about to proceed!

Anna Vasilyevna enters from the drawing room. She is led by Stanitsyn. Varvara Ivanovna advances behind them... Vera runs to meet her mother and embraces her.

MRS. LIBANOVA *(in a tearful whisper).* *Pour-vu que tu sois heureuse, mon enfant....*

Stanitsyn is in a daze. He is on the point of bursting into tears.

GORSKY (to himself). What a touching picture! And to think that I might have been in this dolt's place! No, I certainly wasn't born for family life. (Loudly.) Well, Anna Vasilyevna, have you finally concluded your sage disposition of household affairs—accounts and reckonings?

MRS. LIBANOVA. Yes I have, Eugène—why?

GORSKY. I suggest we harness the carriage and take a trip to the woods—the entire company.

MRS. LIBANOVA (feelingly). With pleasure. Varvara Ivanovna, my sweet, would you give the order.

VARVARA IVANOVNA. Very well, very well. (Goes to the anteroom.)

MLLE. BIENAIMÉ (rolling her eyes). Dieu! que cela sera charmant!

GORSKY. See how we're going to play the fool. I'm merry as a cricket today.... (To himself.) Today's happenings have made the blood rush to my head. I feel intoxicated.... God, how sweet she is!... (Loudly.) Get your hats then; let's be off, let's be off. (To himself.) Go to her then, you silly man!... (Stanitsyn goes up to Vera awkwardly.) That's settled then. Don't worry, my friend, I'll take care of your little business in the course of our outing. I'll arrange for you to appear in your full brilliance. How lighthearted I feel! And how bitter, dammit! Well never mind. (Loudly.) Mesdames, let's go on foot—the carriage will catch us up.

MRS. LIBANOVA. Let us go, let us go.

MUKHIN. What is this? It's as if a devil had taken possession of you.

GORSKY. A very devil.... Anna Vasilyevna! Do give me your hand.... I'm still master of ceremonies, aren't I?

MRS. LIBANOVA. Yes, yes, Eugène, of course you are.

GORSKY. Delighted to hear it... Vera Nikolayevna, be so kind as to give Stanitsyn your hand.... Mlle. Bienaimé, prenez mon ami monsieur Mukhin, and Captain... where's the captain?

CHUKHANOV (entering from the anteroom). At your service. Who's calling me?

GORSKY. Captain, give Varvara Ivanovna your arm.... She's just coming in now.... (Enter Varvara Ivanovna.) And God be with you! Quick march! The carriage will catch us up. Vera Nikolayevna, you will lead the procession, Anna Vasilyevna and I will bring up the rear.

MRS. LIBANOVA (softly, to Gorsky). Ah, mon cher, si vous saviez combien je suis heureuse aujourd'hui.

MUKHIN (taking his place with Mlle. Bienaimé, into Gorsky's ear). Well done, old fellow. Well done: you don't lose your nerve... but you have to admit one thing—the weakest link is where it breaks.

Exeunt.

CURTAIN

ALEXEI PISEMSKY

BAAL

Will ye steal, murder and commit adultery,
and swear falsely, and burn incense unto Baal.

Jeremiah VII, 9

CHARACTERS

Alexander Grigorievich Burgmeyer, a rich businessman.
Cleopatra Sergeyevna, his wife.
Vyacheslav Mikhailovich Mirovich, deputy of the elective district council.
Pyotr Fyodorovich Kunitsyn, a lawyer practicing on his own.
Ismail Konstantinovich Tolokonnikov, an architect and builder.
Avdei Igafraksovich Samakhan, a famous doctor.
Simkha Ruvimich Rufin, a Jew.
Evgenia Nikolayevna Trokhgolovova, a young widow.
Tatyana, a cook.
Servants.

ACT I

Scene 1

Large study, a man's room, luxuriously decorated. Malachite fireplace, large mirror hanging above it. Original paintings, Rubens and Van Dyck, on the walls.

Cleopatra Sergeyevna and Evgenia Nikolayevna, both beautiful young women, are on stage. Cleopatra Sergeyevna has her hat on, as if ready to go out, but something her friend has just said has excited her curiosity. She has stopped for the moment, as if looking into the mirror, but listens to Evgenia Nikolayevna who is sitting in the armchair.

EVGENIA NIKOLAYEVNA. As you like, of course. But I assure you you'll convince no one.

CLEOPATRA SERGEYEVNA *(turning to her)*. Who, may I ask, do I want to convince, and about what?

EVGENIA NIKOLAYEVNA. Really! It's as if you saw and understood nothing. I mean that Mirovich is madly in love with you!

CLEOPATRA SERGEYEVNA *(slightly embarrassed)*. I'm not saying that I don't understand. Of course I've seen and understood that very clearly. But so what?

EVGENIA NIKOLAYEVNA. Oh, for heaven's sake! Don't you even feel a little sorry for him? Or maybe I should say doesn't your conscience bother you?

CLEOPATRA SERGEYEVNA *(obviously astonished)*. Why should my conscience bother me? I haven't flirted with him or led him on.

EVGENIA NIKOLAYEVNA *(with a quick penetrating glance at her friend)*. Cleopatra you'd say anything! You haven't flirted with him? My dear, you can say almost anything, anything, but not that.

CLEOPATRA SERGEYEVNA *(confused at her friend's vehemence)*. You're quite wrong. I assure you I can say that, and boldly too.

EVGENIA NIKOLAYEVNA *(half closing her eyes and speaking in a mocking voice)*. And all those walks in the country together... the parlor games, all evening? What a passionate card player you became all of a sudden. What was the meaning of all that?

CLEOPATRA SERGEYEVNA *(becoming more confused)*. Oh, it's true in the beginning I was a bit incautious with him. But it was only that his company was so pleasant. After all he's the most intelligent human being around here. He's handsome in his own way too, besides being educated and, well, sophisticated. I assumed that we could become friends. But, naturally, as soon as I realized his feelings were more than those of friendship, I began to withdraw, and instead of warmth I gave him coldness and formality.

EVGENIA NIKOLAYEVNA *(with an ironical smile and a shrug of her shoulders)*. May I ask why you did all this? For whom and for what purpose?

CLEOPATRA SERGEYEVNA *(again visibly astonished)*. What do you mean, for whom and for what purpose? Do you really mean you don't understand why?

EVGENIA NIKOLAYEVNA *(with another shrug)*. No, I don't understand.

CLEOPATRA SERGEYEVNA. You don't understand that I'm married, that

I love my husband, that he loves me, and that for me it would be stupid, ridiculous, and, yes, dishonest, to let myself become infatuated with a man, oh a boy almost, with whom there could never be anything serious.

EVGENIA NIKOLAYEVNA (with a wicked smile). Out of all these fine words of yours I gather that you love your husband! Was that how you expressed yourself? You respect him? That's true at any rate, and he thoroughly merits your respect.

CLEOPATRA SERGEYEVNA. How, may I ask, do you know so much about my feelings towards my husband, whether it's love or respect?

EVGENIA NIKOLAYEVNA. My dear Cleopatra, by the very fact that you are twenty-five and your husband is forty-five. With such a difference in age it's hardly natural for a woman to feel a burning passion for the man. And particularly in your case. You are so different from each other. You'd like to indulge in sentimental nonsense occasionally, the usual lover's endearments, and with all respect for the esteemed Alexander Grigorievich, I am convinced he's totally devoid of such desires.

CLEOPATRA SERGEYEVNA. And what if he is? I love him regardless, simply because he loves me.

EVGENIA NIKOLAYEVNA (heavily emphasizing the "well"). Well! He loves you!

CLEOPATRA SERGEYEVNA. What do you mean by exclaiming in that tone of voice?

EVGENIA NIKOLAYEVNA. Exclaiming? Simply because a very clever, elderly gentleman who's been around for a long time, told me that he didn't know of one marriage where the husband had remained faithful to his wife for more than five years, and you, my dear Cleopatra, have been married for eight years.

CLEOPATRA SERGEYEVNA (indignantly). Then your elderly gentleman is mistaken. Alexander is faithful to me, and has been up to now.

EVGENIA NIKOLAYEVNA (with a shrug of her shoulders). Blessed are those who believe for they shall be complacent! Dear God, how blind we women are when it comes to husbands. I lived with mine for only three years, and you saw for yourself that he loved me to distraction, but for all that when he died I discovered to my horror that our housemaid had more than once been the object of his passions.

CLEOPATRA SERGEYEVNA. And so Evgenia, by all that you are trying to tell me that my husband doesn't love me, and that he cheats too?

EVGENIA NIKOLAYEVNA. No, indeed I am not. We are discussing matters in general.

CLEOPATRA SERGEYEVNA. Strange discussions! If you are as fond of me as you seem to be, and you know something about my husband, you shouldn't beat around the bush, but tell me frankly and honestly. That's how I'd treat you.

EVGENIA NIKOLAYEVNA. But my dear what can I say? I honestly don't know anything.

CLEOPATRA SERGEYEVNA. Then why all these discussions and hints? You've brought this up more than once, and nevertheless it bothers me.

EVGENIA NIKOLAYEVNA (rising impetuously from the chair and even with some heat). I bring them up because Mirovich asked me to.

CLEOPATRA SERGEYEVNA *(again astonished).* Why should Mirovich ask you? What kind of friendship has suddenly sprung up between you two?

EVGENIA NIKOLAYEVNA. Oh, not friendship as you understand the word, but, for heaven's sake, I used to see him nearly every day at your place, and long ago I used to make fun of him for it. But strangely enough I met him in the country a couple of days ago and got him to tell me everything.

CLEOPATRA SERGEYEVNA *(disconcerted and annoyed).* And what did he tell you?

EVGENIA NIKOLAYEVNA. He said that he'd told you he loves you. He did, didn't he?

CLEOPATRA SERGEYEVNA *(with emotion).* Unfortunately, he did.

EVGENIA NIKOLAYEVNA. And you completely turned him down?

CLEOPATRA SERGEYEVNA *(with a half smile).* That goes without saying, of course. Do you know, Evgenia, you have a most disgusting habit of worming secrets out of everyone.

EVGENIA NIKOLAYEVNA. What's disgusting about it? On the contrary, I find it very pleasant.

CLEOPATRA SERGEYEVNA. But it's hardly pleasant for the victims.

EVGENIA NIKOLAYEVNA. Oh, what about that!

CLEOPATRA SERGEYEVNA. Oh, merely that no one could be pleased that his secret, no matter how trivial it is, should be spread around. A secret is only a secret until others know about it.

EVGENIA NIKOLAYEVNA. Do you mean you think I'll go around gossiping about what Mirovich told me?

CLEOPATRA SERGEYEVNA. Indeed, it's likely you will. No woman could guarantee not to, even though in this case there isn't much to tell.

EVGENIA NIKOLAYEVNA. Even if there were something, rest assured it would be safe with me. I'm certainly no gossip. Have you ever heard me say anything reckless about anyone?

CLEOPATRA SERGEYEVNA. Oh, maybe you don't actually tell. But you honestly suspect everyone of reckless behavior, and are ready to suspect everyone and to believe anything about anyone. Why don't I show the slightest interest in someone else's affairs? Is anyone courting you, for instance? Are you in love with anyone?

EVGENIA NIKOLAYEVNA *(interrupting).* Oh if you like, do inquire and find out. I won't be angry, I promise you. But I'm a widow. Everything is permissible to a widow. I questioned Mirovich only out of pity for him because the last time I saw him he was absolutely lost—sunk in despair at the thought of your anger because he told you he loved you.

CLEOPATRA SERGEYEVNA. I wasn't really angry, but I'd be happier if he hadn't told me.

EVGENIA NIKOLAYEVNA. Well, can he still come and see you occasionally?

CLEOPATRA SERGEYEVNA *(smiling, but still a little embarrassed).* Of course, I'd like it better if he didn't visit us, though I don't feel I've any right to forbid him the house.

EVGENIA NIKOLAYEVNA. But you didn't tell your husband about it?

CLEOPATRA SERGEYEVNA. Why on earth should I bother my husband with all that nonsense? Look Evgenia, please warn Mirovich that I'm going to be both formal and completely cold if he comes.

EVGENIA NIKOLAYEVNA. For God's sake! He doesn't expect anything. He neither hopes nor waits. For him it'll be enough if he can sit and worship you, his cruel goddess, at a distance.

CLEOPATRA SERGEYEVNA (pretending indifference). If it's not too boring for him he may, as you say, "sit and worship his cruel goddess." (Putting on her gloves.) But so long. I've got to go and make my rounds of visits. You'll wait for Alexander Grigorievich?

EVGENIA NIKOLAYEVNA. Yes, I want his advice on a financial matter.

CLEOPATRA SERGEYEVNA (she advances towards the door, stops halfway and turns to Evgenia with a warning gesture). And about my husband—I ask you never again to try to put suspicions in my mind. I'm very touchy on that subject, and if I ever found that he cheated me, I'd become a completely different woman in my relations with him. I've too much self-respect for that.

EVGENIA NIKOLAYEVNA. Oh don't worry, I won't.

CLEOPATRA SERGEYEVNA. Well, I beg you, don't! (She leaves the room.)

Scene 2

EVGENIA NIKOLAYEVNA (alone). Cheats you? Well! I think I should know better than some others, my dear, how faithful he is to you! Not that I haven't noticed from a dozen trivialities that he took up with me only for a joke. He sees a young woman, beautiful, and well, willing! She almost told him herself that she was in love with him. So... why not take what was offered, and even give some cash in return? Ah, but here he made a mistake. I am not one of those meek silly fools, to be made love to for his amusement and then dropped whenever he chooses. As for that stupid wife of his—I'll pair her up with Mirovich. She's lying anyway. She's up to her ears in love with him—so much so that she's scared to meet him. But they'll be matched without fail. Burgmeyer of course will explode then. He'll shove her out, and I'll come along opportunely and take her place. And then dear Alexander Grigorievich will see what it means to take up with me for a pastime!

But how unjust fate is! I grew up with Cleo. We went to school together, and I was always smarter than she was. Cleverer, more astute, and far more practical. But all of a sudden she marries a rich man, a millionaire no less. And I had no choice but to marry a half-witted boy, who, God knows, hadn't told me anything about his financial affairs, so that when he died I found out I was still as poor as ever.

Well, if it's true that there's little happiness and less luck in the world, at least one should do something with one's brains. And even if most men imagine that they're so much smarter than women, with keener insight and all that, the truth is that as far as guile is concerned, we're a hundred times ahead of them.

What I'd like to know right away, however, is why Alexander Grigorievich has been so down in the mouth these last few days. (She goes to the window.)

Here he comes. What does he look like? As if he'd had his death sentence. I'm going to question him today, right now.

Scene 3

Alexander Grigorievich Burgmeyer enters. A man with graying hair, his countenance is somewhat stern, and his expression is one of puzzlement or confusion. He is wearing several rings on his thin hands, and his watch chain and key are also adorned with precious stones. His clothes look as if they have all come from an English tailor.

BURGMEYER *(holding out his hand to Evgenia)*. Good day, dear lady. I'm afraid Cleopatra isn't at home.

EVGENIA NIKOLAYEVNA. No, she went out calling, and asked me to wait for you here.

BURGMEYER *(having put aside his hat and cane)*. Apparently she isn't jealous.

EVGENIA NIKOLAYEVNA. Oh, not in the least. She doesn't suspect anything.

They sit down and Burgmeyer falls into deep thought.

EVGENIA NIKOLAYEVNA *(looking at him attentively, and speaking in a low, seductive voice)*. I actually came to see you and waited so that I could tell you how happy I was at the meeting of your shareholders. It's unbelievable how enthusiastic they all were about you.

BURGMEYER *(with a fleeting smile)*. Yes, there were plenty of shouts.

EVGENIA NIKOLAYEVNA *(still with the same ingratiating seductive voice)*. Oh, it was more than shouts. Look, in the theater they shout and rave about an actor or a singer sometimes, but at that meeting there were actually tears, tears of gratitude for you, prayers for you! There was an old man sitting next to me, apparently not rich and if he gets, as you promised, thirty percent on his little capital, then he'll be able to get along fairly comfortably with his two grandsons. He kept whispering, "Mr. Burgmeyer's giving me a pension. A pension!"

And besides you were very interesting—I mean the way you looked. When you finished reading your report and everybody applauded, and you got up like this, and leaned over with your hands on the table, you looked so pale and disturbed—it was just the way I used to imagine, when I was a young girl, that great men would look, in their moments of triumph. You know, when the people welcome a hero, or when an orator brings them to their feet with his eloquence, the great man should be a little pale and nervous.

Burgmeyer, having hardly listened to a word, and apparently deeply disturbed about something, gets up and walks to the proscenium. He turns away from Evgenia, who, in turn, at first looks at him in astonishment, and then gets up quickly and gracefully like a cat, and, approaching Burgmeyer, puts both hands on his chest.

EVGENIA NIKOLAYEVNA. Let's assume that yesterday you had a reason for being sad and disturbed, but why do you have to be disturbed today?

BURGMEYER (turns towards her and tries to smile in a friendly manner). Oh, it's nothing—just that nothing seems to please me anymore.

EVGENIA NIKOLAYEVNA. But my dear what can be the reason for that? It'll soon be months since you've been yourself. For what or for whom is all this sadness? You're a millionaire. You've a beautiful wife, who loves you, and whom you love. And as well as all that, Alexander, you have, as you can see for yourself, someone who makes no demands on you, but who asks only permission to love you, and that you'll be just a little frank and honest with her occasionally.

BURGMEYER (as if suddenly relieved). Yes, Jenny. I do want to be frank with you. I have thought of telling Cleo, but why worry her before I need to. Look out and see that there's no one in the next rooms to overhear us, and then shut the doors.

EVGENIA NIKOLAYEVNA (looks out the doors, shuts them and then returns). There isn't a soul in sight.

BURGMEYER (takes her hand, and throughout the whole of the following speech he taps her fingers lightly but nervously). My dear, you've just said "You're a millionaire! You're a benefactor to society. Everyone's praising your name. Old and young alike are praying for you." But Jenny, the truth is that I'm not a millionaire. I'm destitute, a beggar, and far from being a benefactor, I'm a destroyer of all those who were praising me.

EVGENIA NIKOLAYEVNA. Alexander! Is this possible after all that I saw with my own eyes yesterday? Are you sure you're not the victim of some kind of morbid imagination?

BURGMEYER (smiling, but with a certain sadness). Ha, Ha, Ha! Morbid imagination? Unfortunately what worries me doesn't take place only in my imagination. It exists in reality. However, there's something important to be done right now. (He goes to the desk and takes from it a thick packet of papers, which he hands to Evgenia.) Here's your little capital my dear, which you entrusted to me. I'm afraid I need to extricate it from my affairs so that you'll have the use of it. I added a little bit to it—something to help you to remember our friendship.

EVGENIA NIKOLAYEVNA (frightened). Alexander, do you mean you're sending me away from you?

BURGMEYER. No, Jenny, no. Please don't think that. But anything can happen. I might have to leave suddenly for abroad. I might die unexpectedly. No man's life is in his own hands, but God's.

EVGENIA NIKOLAYEVNA. Alexander, your words terrify me. No matter how little you love me, even if you don't value or respect me at all, still I love you. My dear, your peace of mind is dearer to me than my own. I implore you to be honest with me. (She weeps openly.)

BURGMEYER. All right, all right. I'll tell you everything. (He makes an obvious effort to compose himself to begin the story.) My last contract, which, as you know, is one of the biggest I've ever had, has taken all the assets of those shareholders you saw yesterday. And, moreover, a large part of my capital is all tied up in that contract. Its terms are going to be examined for acceptance within the next few days, but these terms, my dear, are far from being above board. I might even say they are downright dishonest.

EVGENIA NIKOLAYEVNA. I simply cannot believe what you are saying. Is this your way of behaving?

BURGMEYER. I didn't behave like that, Jenny, when I was rich. But now I'm poor.

EVGENIA NIKOLAYEVNA. But where has all your money gone?

BURGMEYER. All my capital, and almost all the money which was to be used in the job vanished in last year's stock market. And the fine building for which I have the contract is to be erected from puttied-up and painted scrap material, and even that is on credit.

EVGENIA NIKOLAYEVNA (astonished at his statements). Oh! Good God! Why did you play the stock market, Alexander?

BURGMEYER. Why? Because the new devil Greed is sent from Hell to seduce us. A man has thousands, but he wants hundreds of thousands. He has hundreds of thousands, but he wants millions, tens of millions. The money is there, it seems, just before his eyes and not out of his reach. All he needs to do is stretch out his hand and take it. And there's no lack of lepers like us in the world, possessed of that devil, and compelled to self-destruction, and to the destruction of our families and of countless others who entrusted us with all they had.

EVGENIA NIKOLAYEVNA. But is there no way out? Can't you do something to rectify your affairs?

BURGMEYER. Oh yes, it is perfectly possible. There's really not much to it. Given a year I could make myself twice as rich as I was before... in a day or two I could be awarded a concession on which I could immediately realize a million, not to speak of retrieving the losses on my fallen shares. If I could only keep those until then, they're bound to rise back to normal. And just like that, all my losses on the stock market would be wiped out—indeed they might even turn to profit too. But it all hinges on that concession—it will only be approved if my credit is sound. But my credit will remain sound only if my latest contract is accepted. And they're not going to accept it!

EVGENIA NIKOLAYEVNA. But Alexander, everybody knows the responsible officials can always be bribed. All one needs for that is money. So here, take this money of mine. For the rest, I'll ask my friends to lend money to you.

BURGMEYER. It isn't a question of money. There's enough money for bribes. But there's a man sitting on the commission who can't possibly be bribed.

EVGENIA NIKOLAYEVNA. Where is there a man like that?

BURGMEYER. Mirovich! A mere boy, but elected to the job by the zemstvo, the Elective District Council.

EVGENIA NIKOLAYEVNA (unable to believe her ears). Mirovich?

BURGMEYER. Yes.

EVGENIA NIKOLAYEVNA (laughing boisterously). But my darling, my angel, my dear Alexander, surely you are now talking childishly. Are you honestly afraid of Mirovich, of only one Mirovich?

BURGMEYER. No, I'm not afraid of him. But I'm afraid of his objections, and of the report he will give. Please try to understand what will happen. His report will be spread around, and the shares of our last contract will tumble from a ruble to fifty kopecks. That, of course, will be noticed in government circles, and as a result I won't get the concession, and my reputation will be undermined right away in all my business connections.

EVGENIA NIKOLAYEVNA. But I don't think Mirovich will register any protest.

BURGMEYER. Ah, but he has registered a protest already. It's already an accomplished fact.

EVGENIA NIKOLAYEVNA. He registered it because he thought it was necessary for him to use some kind of weapon. Alexander, haven't you noticed that Mirovich is madly in love with your wife?

BURGMEYER (turns from Evgenia with an angry frown). Of course I saw a little of that. But of what advantage is that here?

EVGENIA NIKOLAYEVNA. Only that Cleo can be a perfect solicitor in the case. He won't be able to refuse her anything.

BURGMEYER. But why won't he be able to refuse her anything? I hope there's nothing more between them than the fact that Mirovich is in love with her—for heaven's sake nothing more.

EVGENIA NIKOLAYEVNA. Now please, Alexander, don't betray me—I'm going to tell you this confidentially—but what exists between them is that Mirovich told your wife he's in love with her. She rejected him completely, but that's all to the good, because if she gives in to him now, even in the slightest degree—well, I simply don't know what he wouldn't be ready to do for her.

BURGMEYER (still frowning, and with evident irritation). So what? That's all very wonderful. But how's it all to be accomplished?

EVGENIA NIKOLAYEVNA (as if she doesn't understand him). But what's to be accomplished?

BURGMEYER (a cynical smile appearing). Yes, of course. Simply to indicate to Cleo—and ask her—right—that she behave, well, shall we say in a natural way? You won't take on the job of asking her, will you?

EVGENIA NIKOLAYEVNA. Dear Alexander! You know that I'd be ready to at any time. But at this moment I'm convinced that I wouldn't be able to do anything here as far as that affair is concerned. I think honestly it would be better if you discussed it with Cleo yourself. Because no matter how she puts me off, I can see quite plainly that she isn't totally indifferent to Mirovich. And if she's terribly prudent with him now, it's simply that she's afraid of you. She's afraid she might hurt you and make you furious with her. But if you give her the merest hint, delicately of course, she'll understand at once that it wouldn't be such a very crushing blow to you.

BURGMEYER (in a burst of laughter). Who wouldn't understand? Explained as agreeably as that, particularly as she knows how morally upright I am.

EVGENIA NIKOLAYEVNA. Well, I don't know. But judging by myself—even though I'm not your wife—and Mirovich were in love with me, without hesitation I'd put him into such a whirl he'd never come down to earth.

BURGMEYER (interrupting). Ah, but that's you! What about my wife?

EVGENIA NIKOLAYEVNA. Where's the difference? Do you really mean to say that anything's possible for me, but not for your wife?

BURGMEYER. Oh! For God's sake get on with it. *(Goes to the window.)* Cleo's coach! She's just pulled into the yard.

EVGENIA NIKOLAYEVNA *(also looking out of the window)*. Yes, it's Cleo. She'll head straight in here to you, of course. Should I stay, or is it better for me to go?

BURGMEYER. You'd better leave, I think.

EVGENIA NIKOLAYEVNA *(getting ready to leave, and talking to him rapidly)*. My dear, if you suddenly take it into your head to leave the country, Cleo probably won't go with you. But take me. I'll do anything, be anything, your servant if you like. I won't take this money. *(Puts the packet on the table.)* It should remain with you now, more than ever. *(Goes out through one of the doors.)*

Scene 4

BURGMEYER *(putting his hand on his brow)*. What devil made Evgenia suggest that idea? As if it hadn't been already in my own mind for the last few days! But of all the foul blows of fate—I, myself, am to go to that innocent angel, to my wife, and say to her: "Go on. Get busy. Bring out all your wiles and tricks, all your sweet smiles and big eyes to seduce a man who's practically a stranger to you, just so that he'll keep his hands out of my business." But good God, what is there left for me to do? To plunge straight to ruin with the feeble hope of starting to work all over again? But what work can I do? I'm only good for one job, contracting, and for that a man's got to have either credit or cash. I've got neither. I can see nothing ahead of me but utter misery, total poverty. But God, that misery is far more frightening today than it used to be. Before there was always, somehow, somewhere, a relative, or a faithful friend, or some benevolent good angel who could offer a corner somewhere... a crust or two and a decent cast-off coat to the ruined millionaire. But now—nobody would give you a place to warm yourself for an hour. What can Cleo and I do? Die on the streets from exposure? Ha! Well, it's for her and her only that I'll have to take this final chance....

Scene 5

Enter Cleopatra. Burgmeyer pulls himself together to greet her normally.

CLEOPATRA. You're alone? Is that why Jenny left?

BURGMEYER. Yes, that's why she left.

CLEOPATRA SERGEYEVNA. Why didn't you tell me about the ovation you got yesterday? Jenny told me they greeted you with applause and saw you off with applause. I'm terribly sorry you didn't take me with you. I'd have loved to have seen your triumph.

BURGMEYER. Don't think too much about my triumph, Cleo. You may see my disgrace also.

CLEOPATRA SERGEYEVNA. Your disgrace? But when and where?

BURGMEYER. Any day now I may have to declare myself bankrupt.

CLEOPATRA SERGEYEVNA *(worriedly)*. But... but... how could you become bankrupt?

BURGMEYER. By my last job, which they're not going to accept. And if they don't accept it, then they won't accept the other deal either, and I expected to make a big enough killing from it to pay all my debts....

CLEOPATRA SERGEYEVNA (becoming more disturbed). Well, but who is it? The commission doesn't approve of this work, is that it?

BURGMEYER. Not all of the commission. On the contrary, just about all the members accept it—with one exception... Mirovich!

CLEOPATRA SERGEYEVNA (shocked on hearing the name). But why doesn't he accept it?

BURGMEYER. He says the contract hasn't been fulfilled according to specification.

CLEOPATRA SERGEYEVNA. But in what particular? He's hardly a judge, in my opinion.

BURGMEYER. He found many things wrong.

CLEOPATRA SERGEYEVNA (smiles as if reassured). It's strange. (She pauses and after a moment of thought turns to her husband.) Listen—of course I didn't want to tell you about all this—I thought it all too silly. But now I think I should tell you. Mirovich isn't indifferent to me—in fact he even hinted.... Of course I stopped him in mid-flight. I gave him quite a lecture in fact. But is it possible that his refusal to accept the terms of the contract is his way of taking revenge? I've always considered him to be of the utmost integrity.

BURGMEYER. I'm afraid it's not revenge. The contract actually was carried out in the shoddiest, most disgraceful way. You see, I lost all the money I had alloted to it in the run on the stock market last year.

CLEOPATRA SERGEYEVNA. But that's terrible! I honestly never expected that to happen. I feel as though the sky has fallen!

BURGMEYER. The most terrible thing about it is that if the building were accepted, and provided my new deal went through, I'd use all the profit to jack up and put in decent condition the present construction, even if it were accepted as it is. You know how reliable I've always been in my deals.

CLEOPATRA SERGEYEVNA. Of course! But explain all that to Mirovich! Still, I'm convinced he's a good-hearted and clever man.

BURGMEYER. What would be the good of explaining it to him? Do you think he'd believe me? He'd simply answer that every contractor is ready to swear on a stack of Bibles that he'll make everything right after the contract has been accepted, but of course, sneak out of the promise later. He apparently thinks all contractors are no better than small-time swindling storekeepers.

CLEOPATRA SERGEYEVNA. How stupid of him to think that....

BURGMEYER. Shrewd or stupid, that's how he thinks. (He smiles at her.) Cleo, what if you went to him and softened him up a bit? Who could refuse anything to a young woman at the height of her beauty?

CLEOPATRA SERGEYEVNA (noticeably surprised at the suggestion). I should go to him, you say?

BURGMEYER (again smiling). Yes, my dear.

CLEOPATRA SERGEYEVNA (frowning and taking a moment to reply). No, Alexander, I can't do it. I threw Mirovich out—and now to go to him, to eat humble pie, to beg him... No, it would be too much for my self-respect. I abso-

lutely can't do it. Besides, I don't think it would be of any use anyway. He probably still feels furious at me.

BURGMEYER *(with a slight yelp of laughter)*. Then be obliging to him, lead
him on a trifle.

CLEOPATRA SERGEYEVNA *(again astonished)*. You mean I should actually flirt with him?

BURGMEYER *(as if still amused)*. Oh, you know, the way women usually
flirt.

CLEOPATRA SERGEYEVNA *(with outraged face)*. What you want is not
that I should simply ask Mirovich, but that I should flirt with him?

Burgmeyer makes no reply. He avoids his wife's gaze.

CLEOPATRA SERGEYEVNA *(getting more and more worked up)*. Listen,
Alexander! What if in playing your little game, I should find myself getting involved with Mirovich?

BURGMEYER *(with a grimace of distaste)*. Well...

CLEOPATRA SERGEYEVNA. And if I... Well, I'll tell you honestly. I'm
not as indifferent to Mirovich as I appear. But I suppressed the feeling—refused
to feed it. Don't you see, Alexander, it would be like setting fire to powder?

BURGMEYER *(his face convulsed)*. I see very well. But what's to be done? If
this is the last resort?

CLEOPATRA SERGEYEVNA *(stubbornly)*. It seems then that it's of little
consequence to you if something happens between me and Mirovich?

BURGMEYER *(again as if smiling)*. But what could happen that would be so
very important?

CLEOPATRA SERGEYEVNA *(taking a few steps away from him)*. Yes! In
your mind it isn't that important. *(She clutches her head in her hands.)* Dear God!
(To her husband.) Wait! Let me come to my senses and understand clearly all that
you have said. *(She falls into a chair. Her eyes become somber.)* You not only wish,
you'll be very happy if I, your wife, in order to persuade Mirovich, would even
become his mistress. That's what you've been saying to me it seems. That's what
you've been leading up to with all your talk. *(With laughter but through tears.)*
And here I've been believing—idiot that I am— that you loved me so much that
you'd hardly be able to live through it if I cheated you....

BURGMEYER *(astonished and frightened by his wife's words)*. But why neces-
sarily his mistress? How did you get that meaning from my words?

CLEOPATRA SERGEYEVNA *(getting up from the chair)*. What do you use
for brains? Is it possible that you can imagine every man will do anything in the
world for me because I've beautiful eyes and a pretty little nose? And after all,
why should I hold back from enjoying the other man's company so that you can
amuse yourself with your mistresses at my faithfulness. Rumors were right apparently, that said you had them. No! I've finished with self-control. You may as
well realize that I love Mirovich—and now, give me your orders as to what I am
to do? Do I go to Mirovich? No? Now, immediately? Do I make him sign the
paper?

BURGMEYER *(totally taken aback)*. Cleo, calm down! I only meant it as a
joke. I didn't expect you to take my words literally like that.

CLEOPATRA SERGEYEVNA. How did you expect me to take them? Alexander, day and night I've prayed to God to help me overcome this passion; but you, yourself, are throwing me into this, to ruin. You alone are to blame. I'll be pleased—oh, delighted—to go to Mirovich, but only to stay there. I'll never come back to you.

BURGMEYER (with supplication in his voice). Cleo, forgive me. Don't do anything. Don't go anywhere. Let me be ruined. Only forgive me for my moment of human weakness.

CLEOPATRA SERGEYEVNA. It's too late now. You've told me once, that's enough. I've found out what's been hidden in your soul concerning me; now I'm no longer your wife, but a slave, a servant who's staying in your house for the time being, so that she can get her orders as to what she's to do—to pay for the bread you gave her, and the stuffs you dressed her in. I'll await your orders. (She leaves the room.)

BURGMEYER (following her). Cleo, I beg you! Forget what I said. It was the devil who moved my lips. I never thought of anything like this. Losing you would be the greatest loss of my life.

CLEOPATRA SERGEYEVNA (turning to him, her eyes flashing with anger). It's not true. I don't believe you! I can see right through you. You really are what Mirovich took you for, a petty storekeeper. Everything's a commodity for you—even I am. (Shuts the door after her and locks it.)

BURGMEYER (in total despair). God, this is beyond me.

Curtain

ACT II

Small sitting-room in Mirovich's suite, supplied with desk and multitude of papers and books.

Scene 1

Mirovich, a young man with a thick mane of hair, short fashionable beard, intelligent face, sensitive, poetic expression. He is dressed in a grayish lounging jacket with red edging, and wide checkered trousers.

Kunitsyn, his friend, also young, a very tall, handsome man. Appears he might be an inveterate dandy, although not dressed in completely good style. His jacket seems somehow too short, his trousers too narrow, and his boots have excessively thick soles. His beard is trimmed, and his moustache is dyed and turned slightly upwards.

MIROVICH *(with apparent heat)*. Look, I'm telling you that such swindling takes place that it's hard to imagine. Swindling all carried out in the quietest way possible. I've known Mr. Burgmeyer and his family for four months. I went to see him almost every day and practically every time he was telling me with the greatest ease that soon I'd be getting his contract to approve, and that probably there would be a few omissions. But he said that he'd rectify everything immediately, so of course, I didn't worry. Not for a minute did I dream that I'd find such a sinkhole of meanness and trouble.

KUNITSYN *(quickly)*. Why trouble? Fine, all you need to do is strip some more money off Burgmeyer.

MIROVICH. Let the ground swallow him and his money. As if I needed his money! But the damnedest thing on their part, it seems, is that they counted on bribing me on the stupidest pretext. On the very day of the inspection, all of a sudden, Burgmeyer calls to pick me up in his carriage, and along with him is his technician, a silly weathercock of a fellow, but possessed of indescribable cheek. We all went along together, but of course it turned out that only half the building could be seen—the other half for some reason or other was locked. In another place the windows were covered on some pretext. It came time for breakfast, and right after it started pouring cats and dogs, so that it became too uncomfortable to inspect exterior walls. And then, at every stop there was champagne, cognac! In short we flew through the inspection like a shot from a cannon, and suddenly the gentlemen turned to me: "How have I found it?" I said, "Nohow! Because I saw nothing." "For heaven's sake, what's that? We thought....in fact we already have the certificate of the inspection survey ready. Your friends have signed it." And they actually showed me the certificate signed by all these gentry!

KUNITSIN. I see... I see... They've all been taking bribes from a long time back, and they've talked about you, too. Your approval was to be achieved by way of the dame in the case. You're in love with Madame Burgmeyer, they say. Charming creature she is!

MIROVICH *(noticeably confused by these words)*. Even if I were in love with her, it wouldn't serve any purpose.

KUNITSYN. It would serve the purpose that she wouldn't be reluctant. *Attendez!*... she wouldn't keep saying....

MIROVICH. Keep on lying! You see everything from only one point of view. Madame Burgmeyer is such a saintly, honest, moral being that no matter what relations might exist between us I know she'd never influence me to take a wrong step.

KUNITSYN. Yes, of course. "Honest saintly being!" Ah, my friend, when just once hundreds of thousands of rubles begin to be threatened, then each one of those saintly beings starts to spin like a carp on a hot frying pan and takes any course available.

MIROVICH. Oh, for God's sake, control your cynicism just a bit.

KUNITSYN. What do you mean, cynicism? Old friend, I'm speaking the truth. Tell me, though, how did you act afterwards?

MIROVICH. I did exactly this—the very next day I went with my technician and examined everything thoroughly. Here's the result of that inspection. *(He hands Kunitsyn a sheet of paper covered with writing.)*

KUNITSYN *(looking over the sheet)*. Oh, oh! The dear, dear little souls. Forty-seven articles in the contract not fulfilled!

MIROVICH. Exactly forty-seven.

KUNITSYN. That means that not even Madame Burgmeyer will be able to do anything.

MIROVICH. Indeed she won't!

KUNITSYN. Get after them, my boy. Get after them. Fix them properly. Let me tell you something about myself. I hate all millionaires. That is, I simply can't stand even meeting one in the street. I'd like to grab a knife and pierce his belly. Why do we feel envious and annoyed? We run, damn it, year in and year out, with our tongues hanging out, and get absolutely nothing. But the million-aire only has to stretch out his little hand, to sign some little contract—and then watch the millions come flocking into his pocket.

MIROVICH. What are you complaining about? You make enough in your trade. The law is profitable.

KUNITSYN. Bah! That's peanuts! Peanuts, if you compare the lawyer's prof-its with the railway business. There's where the stuff is, old chap. If I were al-lowed, just for a moment to stick my finger in that pie, what plums I could pull out. And what's in law after all? I'm not even sure it's the kind of business I'm suited for. They're all yelpers, old fellow, aren't they? "Honorable judges, honor-able jurors, let the voice of your conscience be heard!" And at the same time he's uttering his private prayer, "God, show me how to get a few more rubles out of this client, legally, of course." As for the clients—they're all rogues too. As soon as you win a case for a man he's off like an arrow—as for the loser, you couldn't track him down with a bloodhound. It's a lousy profession! Listen! I've just re-membered another low deal. You see this suit I'm wearing? Nice, isn't it?

MIROVICH. Not bad.

KUNITSYN. For fifteen hundred I've got myself all kinds of stuff like this, and every day I'm out dancing at a masquerade or a private affair. I'm deter-mined to marry the daughter of a nice rich businessman, and if nothing comes of that I'll oblige some overweight husband-hunting female.

MIROVICH. What kind of a complex have you got, Kunitsyn, to convict yourself of these foul ideas. I'm certain you'd never be able to carry out one of them.

KUNITSYN. Why not? Oh, I'll do it for sure. Life today's for those who help themselves, my friend, out of everybody else's pockets, but keep tight hold of what they've got themselves. You see a swindler here, a knave there, and a dirty dog in the third place, and living among roses, one involuntarily breathes in their fragrance. If I don't get married after all my dancing, I'll squeeze into a bank somewhere as treasurer, grab a million and light out for America. Look for me there!

MIROVICH. Tell me, what kind of miraculous happiness do you see in money? You can't buy everything with rubles.

KUNITSYN (with both hands on his hips and standing disdainfully in front of his friend). What can't be bought with money? What? In this age of steam, railroads, electricity? The devil knows what!

MIROVICH. The love of a real honest woman! One can't buy that. Nor the ability to be an artist! Nor honest fame. None of those can be bought with money.

KUNITSYN. Love? You say love can't be bought. Ha, ha, ha! My dear Mirovich, you should just see the beauty I'll buy. What's charm? She'll be red-hot with passion for me. She'll worship me. As for fame—friend, fame nowadays has been transferred from heroes to business men.... Not more than a few days ago at a shareholders' meeting Burgmeyer got more applause than any honest king. And as far as talent is concerned... unless you can strum away on a baby grand, or write doggerel like our mutual friend, that idiot Muromtsev, there is no talent. Well, that I certainly don't need! That's for free!

Scene 2

Servant enters and hands three visiting cards to Mirovich.

MIROVICH (looking them over). What's this? Simkha Ruvimich Rufin. Moscow merchant of the First Guild.

KUNITSYN (carrying on). Rufin pufin, the Jew boy!

MIROVICH (continuing). Ismail Konstantinovich Tolokonnikov, architect-builder!

KUNITSYN (again continuing). I know him. He even got his ugly mug beaten up because of his swindling, but keeps on just the same.

MIROVICH (throwing the cards on the table). And finally, Monsieur Burgmeyer.

KUNITSYN (almost with delight). So he came! Well, hello! Speak of the devil....

MIROVICH (annoyed). He's been to my place five times already; and now this time—he comes in company with these men? What do they want from me? I'd like to know?

KUNITSYN. They need you apparently. (Taking his hat.) I'm going to leave now. But let them come in. And give them hell, every one of the dirty dogs. Give them a tongue lashing they won't forget. But look, get that little Jew, Simkha Ruvimich. He's a no-good so-and-so. As for Monsieur Burgmeyer—well, if he offers you fifty or sixty thou', the hell with it, forgive him!

MIROVICH *(annoyed)*. Get out with your thousands.

KUNITSYN. No sir! There's nothing as excellent as a few thousand. *(He leaves singing a couplet he made up.)* "Were I a prince in Arcady, I'd grab what I could, pray thee."

SERVANT *(impatiently expecting Mirovich's orders)*. May the gentlemen enter?

MIROVICH. And what's your worry?

SERVANT *(with disgruntled voice)*. No worry! They came to you, not to me....
(Turns around ready to leave.)

MIROVICH *(yells after him)*. Show them in.

Servant leaves.

Scene 3

MIROVICH *(alone)*. I'm convinced Burgmeyer has bribed my servant, because almost every time the idiot grabs me by the neck to let Burgmeyer in at once. Even here these gentry can't walk in without bribing! Kunitsyn is perfectly right! I should bawl them out, and soundly, so that they'll understand at last that they can't abuse me forever. *(He gets behind one of his armchairs, and leans on it proudly with his hand on its back.)*

Scene 4

Burgmeyer enters, followed slowly and cautiously by Simkha Ruvimich Rufin, a young and very handsome Jew. Both of them bow to Mirovich without speaking, and then stand to one side.... Tolokonnikov, on the other hand, comes directly to Mirovich, a book in his hand, and greets him in somewhat military fashion, that is, slightly raising his shoulders and even clicking his heels as if he still felt spurs fastened to them.

TOLOKONNIKOV *(in a bold voice)*. You found it proper yesterday to send us your sentiments concerning the fulfillment of the contract.

MIROVICH *(in turn likewise harshly)*. Yes, I sent them, and I want those same remarks included in the report, where they will constitute my independent opinion.

TOLOKONNIKOV *(bows slightly to Mirovich, but nevertheless is openly sneer-ing)*. I certainly can't obstruct that wish in any way. But I can allow myself to observe that quite a few mistakes have crept into those remarks.

MIROVICH *(proudly)*. Indeed! What mistakes?

TOLOKONNIKOV *(still sneering, but completely in possession of the situation)*. You allowed yourself to set down that the walls are fastened together with wooden nails instead of with steel ones... Wonderful! But you should have stated where, and how often, because perhaps some idiot, a drunken worker, too lazy to go for a steel peg, nailed in a wooden one. But that doesn't mean anything. *(He shrugged his shoulders.)*

MIROVICH. Of course, it's not the question of one wooden peg, but of hundreds, and they are painted black, to look like steel a short distance away.

TOLOKONNIKOV *(lifting his shoulders even higher)*. Nevertheless, they should be counted, from the first nail to the last.

MIROVICH. Are you suggesting I should climb on your roofs to accomplish that?

TOLOKONNIKOV *(speaking strongly)*. Absolutely! Absolutely! You'll agree that from your report an action will probably be brought against the contractor and since that means money, we'll have to get the facts straight. What's more you state that the layer of road metal is only one and three-quarter inches thick, when it actually should be seven inches. Well, I've the honor to show you the legal position on that. *(He opens the book he's carrying, and hands it boastfully to Mirovich.)* Article 1207, second paragraph! *(Mirovich begins to read the article, and Tolokonnikov regards him with a sneer. As if interpreting the article, he keeps on speaking.)* It clearly states in that article that when the distance is given officially to the contractor, it is not necessary to pay any attention to the thickness of layers of road metal, because road metal isn't flour. You can't make dough out of it to spread in even layers. And in actual practice it usually happens that in one place a layer could be one inch and in another it could even be fourteen.

MIROVICH *(returning the book to Tolokonnikov)*. That article doesn't concern our case in the slightest. It refers to subsequent submissions: as far as preliminary submissions are concerned, every bid is considered as having fulfilled the contract. The contract states that the layer of road metal must be a uniform seven inches thick. And that's what it must be.

TOLOKONNIKOV *(in exclamatory voice)*. But it's physically impossible to fulfill that condition. It would be easier to jump up to the moon.

MIROVICH *(quite coolly)*. If it is physically impossible to fulfill the contract then you shouldn't have taken it on.

TOLOKONNIKOV *(again lifting his shoulders)*. What can't be fulfilled! Excuse me, but that would put a cramp on every enterprise. Everybody, not only lawyers, will tell you that the law's more binding than any contract. And why today when everything's on the forward move would anyone set up such obstructions? I must admit it's mighty strange to me to hear such ideas from a man of your education.

MIROVICH. It's likely you'll find a lot more things in my ideas that are even stranger to you, just as I will in yours.

TOLOKONNIKOV *(sneering and advancing with shuffling steps towards Mirovich)*. Of course, of course, my ideas are low and vulgar. But let's get back to business. In your report you go on to state that frame buildings are built only of posts, panelled on the outside, and inside are only boards. You're right there, but the contractors are not responsible—they didn't have to do that part.

MIROVICH *(retreating a step)*. What do you mean, didn't have to be responsible for that?

TOLOKONNIKOV *(with noticeable self-confidence, and with some self-satisfac -
tion)*. They're simply not responsible. The contract only states that so many
buildings have to be erected, of such and such specifications, but in what manner is not stipulated.

MIROVICH *(at last losing his temper and raising his voice)*. But it's barracks
you built, not buildings!

TOLOKONNIKOV *(still self-possessed)*. Barracks, well, maybe. But surely
every contractor wants to take advantage of every loophole he can in a contract—
that's understandable.

MIROVICH *(with terrible anger)*. Look here, Mr. Tolokonnikov, take time to
realize what you're saying. At one point a contract means everything, and at the
next moment it means nothing. What are you trying to do? Intimidate me with
your words? Well, realize here and now that I'm no coward. And although I'm
young, I'm learning early to understand swindling and double-dealing.

TOLOKONNIKOV *(in his turn losing his composure)*. Excuse me, but there's
no swindling or dirty tricks here.

MIROVICH *(grabs the paper he had been showing to Kunitsyn and shakes it vio -
lently in front of Tolokonnikov's nose)*. You say there's no swindling and muck in
this? None?

TOLOKONNIKOV *(pushing the paper aside)*. Just a minute, just a minute.
Don't shove your papers in of my face and yell at me. I'm not your clerk, and I
repeat that there's no swindling here, and if you do find any *(with an ironic smile)*
you, no doubt, have ulterior reasons....

MIROVICH *(advancing to him)*. What ulterior reasons do I have? What? I
demand that you explain yourself immediately, or I'll find a way to make you be
sorry for what you've said, and teach you to be more careful of your tongue.

BURGMEYER *(afraid of the belligerent attitude of the two men)*. Mr. Mirovich,
calm down. Mr. Tolokonnikov, shut up!

TOLOKONNIKOV *(with the same mocking, though not quite so self-confident
smile, addresses Mirovich)*. I think you'd better learn how to use your words. I
said what I did because you said a lot more to me.

MIROVICH *(furious)*. I have a perfect right to speak as I did, and you
haven't. Do you understand?

TOLOKONNIKOV *(still appearing composed outwardly and smiling)*. No, I
don't understand. Someone perhaps could say that you have that right, and others that I.... In any case I can see that further explanations would be useless. I
have the honor to leave you. *(He bows, clicking his heels.)* It's a pity that after only
the second meeting in our lives, we should part in such an unfriendly manner.

MIROVICH. I'm only sorry that we ever met!

TOLOKONNIKOV *(blazing up)*. The feeling is mutual.

He leaves, no longer bowing to Mirovich.

Scene 5

Mirovich, Burgmeyer and Rufin

MIROVICH *(greatly displeased)*. How patient does a man have to be? I'm going to order my door to be shut, and no one admitted.

BURGMEYER *(confused, and warily addressing Mirovich)*. Mr. Tolokonnikov, my dear sir, really wanted only to explain things to you as a technician, and justify himself in a technical sense.

MIROVICH *(still annoyed)*. Why did he have to justify himself to me? I'm absolutely convinced that in a technical, intellectual, and moral respect the fellow is an ignorant, impudent scoundrel. *(He looks at Rufin.)* And what does that gentleman want from me?

BURGMEYER *(shifty-eyed and embarrassed)*. That's a new contractor, who'd like to take on the job of rectifying the discrepancies in my contract.

MIROVICH *(to Rufin)*. You're a Jew?

RUFIN. A Jew, sir.

MIROVICH. How long have you been a member of the Moscow Guild?

RUFIN. Since the 12th of April.

MIROVICH. That is you've been a member since yesterday?

RUFIN. Yes.

MIROVICH *(laughs)*. It's almost ridiculous! You mean you are ready to take on Mr. Burgmeyer's contract?

RUFIN. I'm ready sir. I don't need a penny ahead of time for it, not even half a penny. You found forty-seven defects. I'll undertake the job in this way... I'll correct the first item—you'll pay me for it from Mr. Burgmeyer's securities. I'll rectify the second item—you'll pay me for the second item from Mr. Burgmeyer's money. I'll correct the third—you'll pay me for the third.

MIROVICH. That's all very well, but, unfortunately, it's hardly up to me.

RUFIN. What do you mean, my dear sir, it's not up to you? It's in the interests of your superiors.

MIROVICH. Yes, but my superiors didn't empower me to do that. I was told to pass the construction if, in my opinion, I found it fulfilled all the articles stipulated in the contract. But I didn't. So I'm not accepting it. That is my role in this matter.

RUFIN. But my dear sir, what am I to do? Where should I go now?

MIROVICH. You should wait until the contract's taken away from Burgmeyer. The repairs will be subsidized from securities—probably decided at an auction. Then you should go to the auction and make a bid.

RUFIN *(with apparent anger)*. But I won't be able to make an offer then. As time passes employment will pick up... tradesmen and materials will be twice as dear, and I'd have to charge four or five times more. My prices are now advantageous to you. Here they are! *(He thrusts a paper almost forcibly at Mirovich.)*

MIROVICH *(throwing the paper on the table)*. I assure you I believe you. Nevertheless, I can't do anything.

RUFIN *(again with a show of anger)*. I've just told you what my price is. If later on the work is to be paid for from Mr. Burgmeyer's securities at a higher cost than mine, then Mr. Burgmeyer will start demanding the difference from you.

MIROVICH. What's to be done then? I'll pay him if the judgment goes against me. You've figured everything out very cleverly, but you've forgotten to consider that I saw you at Burgmeyer's, and that I know quite well that you're one of his men.

RUFIN (without confusion). I was Mr. Burgmeyer's steward. But I left him and now make my own contracts. I am a member of the Moscow Guild.

MIROVICH. Yes, as of yesterday. But you're not a member of the Guild, you're only a bribed figurehead. That's who you are. (Addresses Burgmeyer.) Mr. Burgmeyer, aren't you bored with taking part in all this comedy? Apparently it isn't enough that you've talked at me God knows how many times, but you even sic your noble gang on to me, who try to trick me as if I were a complete idiot.

BURGMEYER (his head bent). Vyacheslav Mikhailovich, I'm in such a state that I don't know what I'm doing nor what's happening to me. They've only wanted to help me if they could. I'm going to ask only one favor from you—that you'll let me talk to you no longer as a contractor trying to swindle you, but as a man almost down and out by what's happened.

MIROVICH. I don't know what there is to say. But talk if you feel you must. (Again he stands beside an armchair with his hand on the back.)

RUFIN (turning humbly to Burgmeyer). You don't need me any more sir?

BURGMEYER (completely confused by the question). No!

Having put his coat under his arm, Rufin leaves quietly, with the step of a Jew, as if he were saying with every movement, "No, not everything was tried. We could have tried even harder!"

MIROVICH (laughing at Rufin's demeanor, looks at the audience and then at Burgmeyer). I'm listening.

BURGMEYER (with a catch in his voice). I admit, Vyacheslav Mikhailovich, that the terms of the contract haven't been fulfilled, and not only should repairs be made, but the whole thing should be begun again from scratch.

MIROVICH (almost arrogantly). Why did you carry it out this way?

BURGMEYER. Not for profit I swear, as God's my witness, not for profit. But because last summer I lost a million on the American stock market.

MIROVICH. For that, of course, you have my complete sympathy. But what can be done?

BURGMEYER. Something could be done, and very simply. With my turnover that million is a drop in the bucket. Any day now I stand to get a concession on a deal which should net me a million. With that money, I'd not only put the present construction into first-class condition, I'd make it a model of architectural and engineering skill.

MIROVICH (sneering). When the construction actually becomes an example of architectural and engineering skill, I'll acclaim it as such, but right now I describe it as it is.

BURGMEYER. But look, please understand this, I can still be given a concession. And here I'm not pleading for myself, but for my unfortunate shareholders—not rich, but poor little men whose last cent is tied up in those shares.

MIROVICH. All that, as I've said already, is pretty hard and it's hard on me. But regardless, I will not start lying publicly and recklessly for anyone or anything in the world.

BURGMEYER. But please listen. Here's another development. I got this telegram yesterday. *(Takes a telegram from his wallet and gives it with shaking hands to Mirovich.)* Look, they say in it that I might get a concession before the submission of the report on the last construction. Now, take your statement back. Pretend you're ill.... While they're deciding on a substitute for you time will pass. I am asking only for a delay. I've got five thousand workmen all ready to go. As soon as I get an O.K. for the new enterprise, I'll start them on the present construction. Then even if you enter into the commission again, even if you send no matter how many other commissions to check up on me, I won't be scared, because I swear to you by everything a man holds sacred that it'll be done ten times better than what I was pledged to do. My reputation is more important to me than anything else.

MIROVICH. I don't doubt that at all, Mr. Burgmeyer, but I can't do that for you either. I began to investigate this thing and I must get on with it. Just now your technician hinted that very likely I have ulterior motives for finding everything wrong. And now all of a sudden I find everything satisfactory, or I prudently remove myself. Then, of course, they'll say openly that my change of heart came about in some dubious way.

BURGMEYER. That technician's an idiot and a blockhead. I'll get rid of him, send him out of the country, if you like, and won't let him come back for twenty years.

MIROVICH. But your technician's not the only one who will talk. The same thing will be in the minds of everyone. I'm only beginning my career, Alexander Grigorievich, and it would be strange indeed for me to undertake one of the biggest, low-down acts imaginable at the very outset.

BURGMEYER. The public will know nothing. How could anyone find out if the construction was put up badly or well? Why were you prevented from accepting or refusing it? Even if the public did find out, they'd value you all the more and be grateful, because you'll save not only me and the savings of a thousand people, who trusted their little capital to me, but you'll save the enterprise itself. You're still young, and you don't know yet how things are done. But as it is, you'll prejudice my interests so that they'll take the whole thing out of my hands and give the reconstruction job to someone else. He, looking after his own interests, of course, will tinker about, mend matters here and there, strengthen the building and paint it up. Let's say you won't accept the job from him either. A third person will do exactly the same thing. Finally, you'll have to accept it some time or other, but it will still be in the shape it's got no right to be in. I'm the only one, the one who did wrong in the first place, who's ready to bring real sacrifice into the job, to make up somehow by correcting everything. Because of all that I'm even ready to go down on my knees and beg you to be merciful.... *(Wants to kneel.)*

MIROVICH *(preventing him).* Please stop this. So help me God, these scenes won't get us anywhere! *(He looks out of the window.)* Good God, Cleopatra Sergeyevna's just arrived!

BURGMEYER. My wife? That finishes it! *(Rushes out, completely lost.)*

MIROVICH *(to himself and equally disturbed).* Is it actually possible that even she is going to attack me about this.

Scene 6

Cleopatra enters, and speaks in a distraught voice.

CLEOPATRA SERGEYEVNA. I didn't stop to announce my arrival, but just came in. Don't turn me out of the house. Let me stay. Give me a chair. I'm exhausted.

Mirovich gives her a chair. She sits down.

CLEOPATRA SERGEYEVNA. Is my husband here? Has he left?

MIROVICH. He left all of a sudden. I don't know what happened.

CLEOPATRA SERGEYEVNA. It's a good thing he left. Mirovich, sit down beside me.

He moves a chair and sits down next to her. Cleopatra puts her hand on his.

CLEOPATRA SERGEYEVNA. Tell me, were you speaking the truth when you said you loved me?

MIROVICH. My adored one, how can you think that I would lie to you. *(He bends over Cleopatra's hand and kisses it.)*

CLEOPATRA SERGEYEVNA. I believe you, Mirovich. And I'm going to confess that I love you. But first, I want to tell you something about myself. I've got a lot of pride Mirovich; I'm proud and think a great deal of myself. Maybe that's why God punishes me. You should know that Burgmeyer has been the benefactor of our family from years back. He helped my father out of a financial hole, supported my poor invalid mother, and even paid for my education. It was drummed into me incessantly that he was our savior and that I must marry him. I didn't like him at all, but couldn't bear to be under perpetual obligation to him for favors to our family, so I decided to pay him back everything with myself. Afterwards I began to get used to him. It seemed to me that he loved me excessively. Every little wish of mine was law to him. I was often capricious, but he put up with it all. When I pretended I was sick, he was completely lost. I used to think that if I ever did fall in love with anyone, it would be a greater blow to Burgmeyer than the loss of his honor, his money, his position, even life itself. Last year I met you, Vyacheslav, and I fell in love with you almost from the first moment. You began to talk to me—about what I don't know, but it was completely different from the talk I was used to hearing. All my life I had heard only about what goods were more profitable to buy, how much the season tickets for the Italian opera cost. I was taken to the dressmakers and dressed up. So that you seemed to me like a man from another planet. At first my feeling was one of ecstasy, but then I got scared. I felt sorry for Burgmeyer, and frightened for myself. It appeared to me that your love was only the fleeting kind, so I refused to hear you. But how long I would have had the strength to keep you away from me I do not know. Of course, sooner or later I would have had to tell you the truth, but now things have speeded everything up. *(She smiles sadly.)* After all the love I credited my husband with having for me, he came to me a couple of days ago, and said: "My business affairs are in a sad muddle, and much depends on Mirovich. Go to him, flirt with him, seduce him, but squeeze out of him his consent not to obstruct my dealings." Vyacheslav, have you ever heard of a husband saying such a thing, even to the worst, the most immoral wife? At that instant I tore out of my heart every shred of feeling for Burgmeyer and came to you. Do it his way. Do as he asks. Give him that as payment for me. And take me for yourself.

MIROVICH *(having listened to her with growing emotion, stands up at her last words)*. Cleopatra Sergeyevna, for your frankness I will repay you with equal frankness. To have you would be the greatest blessing possible, you know that. But have you really thought about it? As things stand at present, we could be united, as you wish it, only by... I won't say "crime," but something worse than that, something more horrible. In this case we'd be united by my despicable and dishonest actions.

CLEOPATRA SERGEYEVNA. Vyacheslav, there'd be no dishonest action on your part. My husband told me himself—and there was no need for him to lie to me—that later he would complete the contract honorably.

MIROVICH. And of what use would the completion be to me? All the same I'd be involved in this swindling deal, and finally, I wouldn't say a word, if it concerned only me. Let them disgrace me and brand me. No one would believe, of course, that I'm burning with a love for you that I can't control. No one believes in that nowadays! They'd simply call me a Don Juan ready to commit any crime for the sake of a good-looking woman. I could bear all that but, my darling, you'd be implicated as well. They'd swear you were your husband's accomplice.

CLEOPATRA SERGEYEVNA. No, Vyacheslav, I am not his accomplice! I love you more than anything in the world, and I ask you to be my husband, because I want once and for all to call it quits and leave him.

MIROVICH. I know, Cleo. I can see everything. If you only knew the infernal, agonizing struggle I'm going through right now. Here—the very paradise of love, and there—a farce! If I commit this action I'd have to be false to the banner I thought I'd live under for the rest of my life. My generation, that is, me and my contemporaries, when we'd still hardly left the classroom, began to boast, reproaching and cursing our parents, and grandparents for taking bribes, giving false judgments, being embezzlers, for their complete lack of honor or sense of civic duty. All we read with feeling was what told us about how they disgraced themselves and how they were ridiculed. Now we have graduated into public service, and I, as one of these public servants, rushes straight into the same kind of behavior our fathers used to practice, with the very same partiality and lying, except that perhaps I have a few more romantic reasons. But I'm not going to give the right to these old dotards to point at me maliciously and say "Here, look at our strict critics, see how nobly they act!" But Cleo, you, as a woman perhaps aren't able to understand my feelings about all this.

CLEOPATRA SERGEYEVNA. On the contrary, my darling, I understand you perfectly, and I'm beginning to love and respect you even more because of it. God be with you. Go your own way. I won't bother you. *(She rises from the arm - chair.)* Good-bye.

MIROVICH *(with sad perplexity)*. But where are you going?

CLEOPATRA SERGEYEVNA. Where? Home!

MIROVICH *(breathlessly)*. Wait, Cleo. Wait just a minute.

CLEOPATRA *(submissively)*. All right.

MIROVICH *(clutches his head in despair)*. What an insignificant and cowardly dolt I am. Why do I tremble? What am I afraid of? She gives her whole self to me, her whole life. And I'm grinding myself to dust because of a phantom created by my imagination and because of what a few cretins will say about me. *(He sits at a table and his head sinks into his hands.)*

CLEOPATRA SERGEYEVNA *(quietly approaching and lightly touching his shoulder)*. Listen, Vyacheslav, if both this way and that are too difficult for you, then, if you want me to, I'll stay with you anyway. Don't do anything for my husband. Let what has to happen to him, happen. I know that you are more precious to me than he is.

MIROVICH *(taking his hands from his face and turning towards her, speaks with a sad ironic voice)*. Just like that! Without doing one thing, just take you away from him! But won't it be just a bit too cruel on my part to take away from him his most precious jewel and give him nothing in return. No! Let him at least keep his millions. I'll save them for him.

CLEOPATRA SERGEYEVNA *(somewhat gloomily)*. But what if you repent later?

MIROVICH. How can I repent? You offered to stay with me without any sacrifice on my part and now what I am doing is of my free will! *(He sits at the table and begins to write with extreme haste. Having written this hurriedly and as if uncon - scious of what he's doing, he rings. The servant hurries in.)* Here, you know where the commission meets? Take this paper there. Tell them that I'm ill, that I can no longer take part in business, and am resigning for good. Ask them to send my previous report back with you.

SERVANT. Yes, sir. *(Leaves.)*

MIROVICH *(addressing Cleopatra Sergeyevna in a tone of feigned happiness)*. Cleopatra Sergeyevna, I've done everything your husband wished.

Curtain

ACT III

Scene 1

An even more luxurious study than in the first act. A huge safe can be seen behind the heavily ornamented desk.

BURGMEYER *(he has grown very old and is almost completely gray. He is sitting on a sofa beside a small inlaid table, and leans his head on his hand).* Such a rush of blood goes through my head, I feel as if I'm going mad, and that for me would be worse than death.... If you lie in the grave at least you feel nothing, but who would take care of me here? I can't rely much on Evgenia Nikolayevna. I'm beginning to see through her all right. It seems she worries about nothing except her own amusement.

Scene 2

Enter Rufin.

RUFIN *(speaks in a quiet, almost timid voice).* The doctor is coming.
BURGMEYER *(without even looking at him).* When?
RUFIN. Soon, sir. At first he asked me if it was for Mr. Burgmeyer, the local capitalist. I said yes, so then he said "Tell him I'll come, but I'll have to make the journey from the country to the town, so that I'll have to get a thousand rubles in silver for the visit." I wanted to say to him "But, doctor, that's too much. You won't be coming only for my employer. And, besides, how far is your country cottage from town?" But I got scared. He's so angry, so fierce! He chased away two servants right in front of me. Then he said "I don't intend to heal the gentry, your masters, merely for the sake of Jesus Christ."
BURGMEYER *(smiles at the story, then takes a key from his pocket and hands it to Rufin).* In the safe, on the second shelf a thousand is already counted out. Take it out and give it to me.

Rufin adroitly and skillfully unlocks the safe with the same key, takes out the designated thousand, then having locked the safe, he hands the key and the money together to Burgmeyer with a certain servility. Burgmeyer sticks both carelessly in the side pocket of his coat.

RUFIN *(apparently still busy with the thought of the doctor).* If that doctor went to ten houses like this, that would be ten thousand a day. In no other business, Mr. Burgmeyer, can that much profit be realized.
BURGMEYER *(who has hardly listened to him).* And about those other two.... did you make the inquiries around the countryside as I asked you to?
RUFIN. About Mr. Mirovich and our Cleopatra Sergeyevna?
BURGMEYER. Yes.

RUFIN. Yes, I did inquire. They live very poorly, in a tiny house.

BURGMEYER. But isn't it possible to send them money, a bit more skill-fully?

RUFIN. Well, how? I don't know how many times I've offered them money, Mr. Burgmeyer. They've refused every time. They're crazy... and young!

BURGMEYER. Can't we at least try to find him work?

RUFIN. What kind of work, Mr. Burgmeyer? Somehow he can't find a job in the civil service at all. As for finding him something in the commercial world—well, he won't conform. He won't join us! He's too proud! He won't sub-mit to you! If you recommended him to others, later you'd be blamed for it. I'm afraid he has a reputation for being a frivolous, shallow sort of man.

BURGMEYER. But why not put it like that to one of our business friends, that he is a shallow sort of fellow and shouldn't be trusted with anything impor-tant, and I'd secretly pay his wages, as if it came from the employer.

RUFIN. But my dear sir, who would agree to that? They'd ask why we should pay the wages of someone in their employ, and why they should keep a worth-less person?

BURGMEYER. Maybe they could be persuaded to agree. Arrange it, Simkha, somehow, please.

RUFIN. I'm ready to serve you. *(Then, avoiding the other's eyes.)* Here's some more bills. I dropped into a couple of stores and they handed me these. *(Gives Burgmeyer two bills.)*

BURGMEYER *(glancing at them)*. What's this? Evgenia Nikolayevna has suc-ceeded in spending another eight thousand?

RUFIN *(with a secretive smile)*. Well, the lady is young. She wants to dress up to enjoy life.

BURGMEYER. What's all this dressing up? Some months she's gone through forty thousand. Besides, I don't see any special clothes on her. What's she doing with them? Go today round the stores and tell them that she is not to be given anything on credit without my note. Otherwise I won't pay the bills.

RUFIN. But Mr. Burgmeyer, won't she be disturbed by this.... Should you talk to her first?

BURGMEYER. I've talked to her twenty times, and explained that though I'm rich I'm not in the least accustomed to have my money thrown to the winds or into the fire. As far as she is concerned the words merely boomerang and she keeps on her own course. Look, right now, go to the stores and warn them.

RUFIN. There's a lawyer waiting downstairs to see you.

BURGMEYER. What lawyer?

RUFIN. I don't know sir. I've never seen him before. He's a conspicuous sort of man, big....

BURGMEYER. Invite him in.

Rufin leaves.

Scene 3

BURGMEYER *(alone)*. A strange quirk of fate! I practically adopted that little Jew-boy, Simkha, when he was a youngster, brought him up, taught him a little, and now he turns out to be the most useful fellow imaginable, and practically the only man in the world who's sincerely attached to me....

Scene 4

Enter Kunitsyn. He seems a little uncertain, and bows to Burgmeyer with undue familiarity.

KUNITSYN. May I introduce myself, Kunitsyn, a member of the legal profession.

Without rising from his place, Burgmeyer bows silently.

KUNITSIN. Excuse me for intruding upon you, but I've come to you on business which, I believe, should interest you.
BURGMEYER *(dryly)*. Please, sit down.
KUNITSYN *(sits and gains composure)*. I should tell you that I'm not a shy individual, but, damn it, there are times when you don't know for sure that a thing should be done or not.
BURGMEYER. If you don't know, then I imagine it's better not to do it.
KUNITSYN. But perhaps not to do it, in the present case, will be—what shall I say?—not quite just may be the word. And as for your part, it will surely be very bad. This isn't an everyday matter. In fact it's like something out of a novel.
BURGMEYER. A novel, you say?
KUNITSYN. Very much like a novel. And it has a preface which I must explain to you. Two years ago, because of my financial circumstances, which, between ourselves, are almost always in bad shape, I used to attend masquerades in the hope of improving my situation. I dance excellently, and in short, I made quite a name for myself. At one of these masquerades a masked figure approached me, disguised as a goddess. "Mortal," said she, "is your heart free for love?" "Completely free," said I. "And can a creature loving you have confidence in you?" she asked. "As much as it pleases you," said I, "wherever and whenever it pleases you," said I. At this she takes me by the arm, and we walk away. I look at her hand. It's absolutely beautiful, as if chiseled from ivory, a tender matte skin, covered with delicate bloom, and beautifully warm. The figure of the goddess was sylph-like. We danced a can-can. Her legs were divine! Her dress moved as she danced in the most exquisite way. Well, I thought, her face might be an ugly mug! Disappointments like that have happened to me before. "Beautiful stranger," said I, "wouldn't you like me to get a loge, where you could take off your mask and breathe freely?" "No, Pierre." (Notice, she calls me Pierre right from the start.) "There are too many people here. It's better somewhere

else." "*Et bien, madame,*" and off we go, just like that, for some marvelous, but secluded spot, on Peter's Boulevard. Here she took her mask off. Well, it turned out that she was not an ingenue, but nevertheless it was unbelievable! The oval of that face, the smooth matte skin, the great black eyes, straight little nose and the mouth, the very outline of delight. Well, I'll tell you, I fell for her like some utter fool.

BURGMEYER *(listening with growing attention).* And when, may I ask, did that meeting with the lady take place?

KUNITSYN. Last year. It was still autumn. But the strangest thing about this little love affair, as you will see for yourself, is that the lady never did reveal who she was: "Varvara Nikolayevna, Varvara Nikolayevna" and nothing more. Incidentally that didn't worry me too much. As long as two people are doing what comes naturally, thanks be to God, who needs labels and rank. What's in a name? So we carry on just like that for about a year. But once, smack on St. Varvara's Day, I met her at the same inn. This time she filled *me* up with wine, right up to the gullet. You understand that she treated me as if it were her name day. And she drank too much as well. Those marvelous eyes of hers blazed, and her cheeks flared up too, you know, as the poet said "As if she were a bride, but without the wreath." "Pierre," she said, "you must know that I'm a married woman, my husband is a millionaire. I hate him! But he's still in love with me, so I can't be completely faithful to you. Get me out of this humiliating situation. Somewhere get us two forged passports, foreign ones, and we'll slip off abroad with them. As for funds for the trip, I'll get six hundred thousand from my husband's safe." Well, rascal that I am, the thought at first appealed to me very much indeed. On one hand, suspicion stirred within me, but later... to skip off with a pretty woman, to settle somewhere in the Pyrenees, breathing clear air, and at the same time feel six hundred thousand in your pocket—everybody would agree that that would be very pleasant. So within a week I fixed up the little deal. Through various dishonest sources I got hold of two phony passports and brought them to her. She immediately thrust them into her handbag, and in a somber voice said, "My husband is going away next week. I'll grab the six hundred thousand and go off with you." I felt as if someone had hit me on the head with a hammer and I woke up as if from a dream. I said nothing to her at the time, but I came home and thought. This woman is going to take six hundred thousand from her husband, or to state it truthfully she's simply going to steal it from him. And I'm to be her closest accomplice. I became terrified, simply terrified. Did it ever occur to you to think that within a few days you'd become a thief?

BURGMEYER *(with a slight smile).* No, thank God, that never happened.

KUNITSYN. Take my word for it, it's an ugly thought, loathsome! So all that night I twisted and turned, and the next day I was strong enough to hurry to our rendezvous and say, "My Angel, let's forget it. Let's spit on it. It's not worth it." She stared at me, furious, even her face was distorted with anger. "So," she said, "that's how much you love me!" "But darling!" I cried, "it's not only a low-down dirty trick, it isn't even safe. Because we're thieves they'll find us in a foreign country, and have us brought back here." "Nonsense," she said. "You're a coward, afraid of everything." Well, there was no other alternative. I went to get my law books to show her how the law viewed these things. But even though I showed her, she doesn't try to understand anything. And finally she said maliciously, "If you don't want to run away with me, I'll find someone else." And since that moment she's disappeared out of my sight and I haven't heard a word.

BURGMEYER (again, as if smiling). All this is very curious of course. But why do you think it should interest me personally?

KUNITSYN. Very simply. Because the lady we've been discussing, must interest you personally, a fact which I discovered by chance. Once I walked past your house. My friend, Mirovich, whom you know, told me that the house belonged to you, and that a charming young woman lived with you. Well, I saw a buggy drive up to your house, and a lady hopped from the carriage and went straight in by the front door. I glanced under her hat, and good God, it was my Varvara Nikolayevna!

BURGMEYER (surprised and startled). What! Your Varvara Nikolayevna? She came into my house?

KUNITSYN. Exactly. And to tell you the truth, at first I thought maybe she came to visit that Mademoiselle.... They visit one another once in a while. I approached and asked the coachman, "Who's that lady you just brought to Mr. Burgmeyer's house?" "That's his housekeeper." My doubts began to be dispelled, and the curtain fell from my eyes. But I must tell you I was thrown! Most important, I didn't know how to take it. On one hand, I thought, she's a pretty young woman. I loved her. How could I give her up? I felt sorry! On the other, I knew that with her character she'd soon pick up some other swindler and they'd steal you blind, which could mean that some day she might lose her head for it. I thought and thought and then went to my friend Mirovich—the most decent fellow, clever! I told him the story and asked him what I should do. At first he was confused, too. "I think," he said, "you should go to Mr. Burgmeyer and get him first of all to promise that he wouldn't prosecute the woman, and then tell him everything. There's no question, one shouldn't let a man be fleeced. And besides, there would be no harm in giving a good lesson to—not Varvara Nikolayevna, as she pretended to be, but Evgenia Nikolayevna, who's proved herself to be no good." So now I've done what Mirovich suggested.

BURGMEYER (much embarrassed). I appreciate your confidence very much. But after all I've seen you now for the first time. How can you prove that you've been telling the truth?

KUNITSYN. Honest to God I don't know. Maybe if you looked among her papers for the passports—one made out to the French citizen Emily Jourdan and a Belgian, Kleimel.

BURGMEYER (knitting his brows). Do you know if she has kept them safe?

KUNITSIN. I think, I even suppose, that if she hasn't found someone else to take my place, then she's searching for him. As soon as you can lay hands on those passports, give them back to me right away. I'll dispose of them immediately, for if I don't, dammit, I could be in a fine mess. And something else—don't prosecute Evgenia Nikolayevna! That's important to me.

BURGMEYER. You made that one of the terms of giving away the secret, and I'll abide by the agreement.

KUNITSYN. Please do. Well, I'll say good-bye to you.

BURGMEYER (extending his hand). Good-bye. If what you've told me turns out to be the truth, then I'll certainly feel obliged to reimburse you with some cash.

KUNITSYN (at first delighted). Good. That's not a bad idea. (Thinks about it.) But don't you think it will look as if I've sold her down the river?

BURGMEYER. How could you sell her? As you yourself put it well, you told me out of a sense of justice.

KUNITSYN (happy at that explanation). Of course, of course. And to tell the truth, on my way here I had a dim thought that maybe Mr. Burgmeyer should pay me, because, no matter how one puts it, I am saving him six hundred thousand. Every man, I tell you, is rotten to the core. Buona sera, Signor! (He bows and leaves.)

Scene 5

BURGMEYER. My premonition that this lady is a completely lost soul has come true. (He rings the bell. A servant enters.) As usual Evgenia Nikolayevna isn't at home?

SERVANT. No, she isn't. They went out.

BURGMEYER. Call Simkha.

SERVANT. He went out, too. He's not here.

BURGMEYER. Well, you're here! Get a carpenter and take him to Evgenia Nikolayevna's room and break open all the drawers in the tables and chests of drawers and bring the drawers here. (Servant stands puzzled.) What are you standing there for? Don't you understand my words? Get going! Break the locks on all drawers or boxes which have papers in them, and bring the stuff to me. (Servant leaves in puzzlement.) If I don't find those passports Evgenia will certainly never mention them. Not more than three days ago she was complaining about my being cold, and trying to reassure me that she loved me, while maybe at the very same time she was getting poison ready to do away with me, and grab my money. It serves me right—an old lecher getting carried away by the ease of his success and by beauty, having forgotten that snakes can be lurking under beautiful flowers. (Going to the door he shouts impatiently.) What're you doing there? God knows why it's taking them this long!

SERVANT'S VOICE. We're bringing the things at once.

BURGMEYER. At once! They've strange ideas about "at once!" (Servant and carpenter bring two boxes each.)

BURGMEYER (ransacking the first box in a great hurry). They're not here! (Looks into the next box.) Nothing here either. (To the carpenter.) Give me the boxes.... why are you standing there like a lout? (Carpenter hands him the boxes, and he rummages through them both at the same time. Suddenly, turning pale, he yells.) It's them, I think. Indeed, it is! (He pulls two passports from the box and waves them in the air.) Here they are, my treasures! (Puts the papers in his pocket.) Well, well, she'll dodge me no longer, play no more tricks. (Turns to servant and carpenter, who are looking at him in wonder.) Take all that back and throw it on the floor!

SERVANT. Without putting the drawers back in the tables?
BURGMEYER. You were told what to do. Dump it on the floor!
SERVANT (to carpenter). Let's go.

They carry the boxes out.

Scene 6

BURGMEYER. She won't escape from me now. Indeed she won't! That's her coming in now! She's bumped smack into the servant. Ha! What a row she's making! (From rooms further along Evgenia Nikolayevna's shouts can be heard: "What's the meaning of this? How dare you? You thieves! Oh, you gangsters, look what you've done.") What a tigress! What a hyena hidden under the gentleness she'd have you believe was hers. Now she'll be coming to me for explanation, and to complain! Please do come in!

Scene 7

Enter Evgenia Nikolayevna, scarlet in the face, with her hair ruffled on her forehead. She has gained weight since we saw her last and become much less attractive.

EVGENIA NIKOLAYEVNA (her voice is distorted with anger). Alexander Grigorievich, all the drawers in my room have been broken into, and they tell me that it was done at your orders.
BURGMEYER (outwardly calm). Yes! I ordered it done.
EVGENIA NIKOLAYEVNA. But for what purpose? I'd be interested to know. Were you looking for love letters from someone to me?
BURGMEYER. It's likely that I'd find those also, but I wasn't looking for love letters, but for something else. And I found what I was looking for.
EVGENIA NIKOLAYEVNA. What did you find?
BURGMEYER. I found two phony passports, and now I have them here, in my pocket. You got them so that you could skip off abroad after you'd fleeced me.
EVGENIA NIKOLAYEVNA (turning even redder, and at the same time behav-ing as if she were much surprised at what she has just heard). Fleece you? Run abroad? With false passports? Have you finally lost your mind? It's true that a couple of foreign passports were lying somewhere among my things—I picked them up accidentally on the street, and have been asking among my friends what I should do with them.
BURGMEYER. You picked them up on the street? Listen Evgenia. It's possi-ble to be a depraved woman. It's possible to prefer a young lover to an old one—a handsome one! It's possible to want to leave the old lover, fleecing him first. All this I can understand, but to believe that you can still lie to that old idiot, still convince him of anything you please, well, that's stupidity on your part.

EVGENIA NIKOLAYEVNA. One can hardly keep quiet in the face of such slander. By what you're saying you make me appear like a villainess, a heroine of a French novel. Who could, on what grounds, and for what purpose, make up such charges about me to tell you? I can't understand it! *(She turns around and tries not to look at Burgmeyer.)*

BURGMEYER. Your former lover, Kunitsyn, told me the whole story—the one who got you two false passports in order that you might run off together abroad.

EVGENIA NIKOLAYEVNA *(retaining more an air of being insulted than con - fused).* So! Some man called Kunitsyn became my lover? That's all I needed!

BURGMEYER. Nevertheless you *do* know some man called Kunitsyn?

EVGENIA NIKOLAYEVNA. Yes, I used to meet someone by that name in public.

BURGMEYER. In public was it? Not in some secluded place, like some tavern for example?

EVGENIA NIKOLAYEVNA *(with a shout of forced laughter).* Ha, ha, ha! Ha, ha, ha! The more absurd the better! All right, suppose Kunitsyn is my lover, and suppose that we met somewhere and that he got the two passports. Why on earth would Kunitsyn tell you about this himself?

BURGMEYER. Apparently because he still isn't quite as low as you. He felt ashamed of the whole thing. More than that, an honest friend advised him.

EVGENIA NIKOLAYEVNA *(interrupting).* And that friend is Mirovich of course?

BURGMEYER. Mirovich—yes?

EVGENIA NIKOLAYEVNA *(with another malicious shout of laughter).* Ha, ha, ha! The truth is it's not Mirovich, but your wife! It's strange to me that you, Alexander Grigorievich, consider yourself an intelligent man, and yet you can't see through such simple lies. Your wife will, of course, be pleased to see us quarrel and separate...

BURGMEYER *(interrupting her with irritation in his voice).* Don't dare use your spiteful tongue on my wife.

EVGENIA NIKOLAYEVNA *(also falling into rage).* Oh, that you can never forbid! Never! Not only will I say it to you, but I'll go and tell her lover! Let him also find out how much she loves him. The fact that she cheated you doesn't mean that you must accuse everyone else of dirty dealings.

BURGMEYER *(with the same voice).* Who could dirty you? Who? When you've rolled yourself in the mud all over the place? Your very heart and soul are pitch black!

EVGENIA NIKOLAYEVNA. Wonderful words! What nobility! And for whom, after all, did I soil myself? You were the first for whom I fell in the mud, and now, you shameless brute, you have the courage to throw it back in my face. *(She begins to cry.)* Of course, it's only my poverty that gives you the courage to hurl such insults at me. But no matter how little I have, I'd rather condemn myself to starvation and misery than put up with this kind of humiliation any longer.

BURGMEYER. You don't alarm me with your hunger and misery. Besides your own capital—I trebled that for you in my business—and all the cash I paid out at the stores, which incidentally didn't go for clothes, but was transferred to your pocket—oh, I know all about that. I noticed! But I'll even give you a chance to fleece me blind! *(Coming to the safe and pointing at it.)* You thought there were six hundred thousand in here—well, there's even more. But you could have used only ten thousand, because the rest is in my name. *(Quickly and with shaking hands, he opens the safe and pulls out a huge bundle of banknotes.)* Here is the money! Take it! *(He throws the money at her, almost in her face. She catches it, as if accidentally. He continues to speak in a maddened, hysterical voice).* Only get out of my house. Right now! Don't stay another minute! If you do, I'll have the servants throw you out... *(He pulls the bell cord and shouts.)* Hey, come here!

EVGENIA NIKOLAYEVNA *(now somewhat scared).* I can see you really have gone insane. Imagine yelling for the servants to come! But I too am hot-tempered. I could scratch your eyes out, and spit in your face, you idiot, you scoundrel! Oh, you pig, you old goat! *(She goes toward the door.)*

Servant hurries in.

BURGMEYER *(pointing at Evgenia Nikolayevna, who is leaving).* This lady is leaving. Her things are to follow her wherever she's going. Nothing belonging to this powder fuse is to stay here. And you're not to let her into the house, not so much as to the kitchen or the kennel, not even as far as the watchdog!

SERVANT *(smiling faintly).* Yes sir! We won't let her in.... The doctor has just arrived.

BURGMEYER *(hasn't heard the servant. Addresses the audience).* It's as easy for that slut to lie as to drink water, and without a trace of shame at that.... I led her into trifling sins? Huh! Have I exposed her to attempted theft? Even if it weren't true, she as a woman should be appalled at the mere horror of the accusation. But to feel nothing!! Lord, what are we coming to?

SERVANT. The doctor is coming, sir.

BURGMEYER *(having finally heard him).* Who?

SERVANT. The doctor has arrived and is coming up to see you.

BURGMEYER. Let him come! God, you'd think he was announcing the emperor! *(He sits down and begins to tap nervously with his foot.)*

Scene 8

Enter Doctor Samakhan. He is pockmarked, has a sloping posture, and bristling black hair. Altogether he has the features and figure of a ruthless man. The servant stands respectfully to one side and then leaves.

SAMAKHAN *(looks at Burgmeyer impudently and arrogantly).* You are the landlord and patient?

BURGMEYER *(scowling).* Yes, I am.

SAMAKHAN. You want me to give you a check-up?

BURGMEYER. If you think it necessary.

SAMAKHAN. Of course, it is. You're not a horse to be given a drench to no purpose.... *(He takes a chair opposite Burgmeyer. He looks at him intently for some time and then roughly puts back one of Burgmeyer's eyelids with his thumb, and be-gins to speak as if discussing the case with himself.)* There's anemia, and a some-what intensified separation of the gall is noticeable. *(Then settling himself back in his chair, he begins to question Burgmeyer.)* How old are you?

BURGMEYER. Forty-eight.

SAMAKHAN. Have you any definite or pronounced pain?

BURGMEYER. I often have headaches. That's why I sent for you. I suffer from *Tic-Douleureux*....

SAMAKHAN *(sneeringly)*. Let me decide whether it's *tic douleureux* you have or something else. Have you any particular bad habits? I mean, do you drink hard, are you a big eater, and how about women? Are you excessive?

BURGMEYER. I have no such inclinations.

SAMAKHAN *(with great self-importance)*. Aha! Stand up please. *(Burgmeyer stands up. Samakhan puts his ear to Burgmeyer's chest, then immediately looks at him in open-mouthed surprise, and moves away a step.)* What's the meaning of all these terrible heart palpitations? It's me you're scared of, isn't it?

BURGMEYER. No. I had to get terribly angry at my servants!

SAMAKHAN *(smiling scornfully)*. You had to, indeed! Well, except for that I see nothing untoward in your chest. Lie on the couch. *(Burgmeyer lies down. Samakhan stands before him.)* Bend your legs a little. *(Burgmeyer bends them. Samakhan begins to tap Burgmeyer's stomach with a little hammer he takes from his pocket. Burgmeyer cries out at that. Samakhan smiles.)* You're too tender, too sensi-tive. There's nothing wrong with your stomach either. Turn over. *(Burgmeyer again turns with reluctance. Samakhan runs his thumb down Burgmeyer's spinal col-umn, and Burgmeyer yells out this time.)* Where did you feel the pain? In some par-ticular vertebrae, or in the whole spinal column?

BURGMEYER *(getting up to show his lack of desire for any further check-up)*. Everywhere! You nearly broke my spine.

SAMAKHAN. It can hardly break all of a sudden, just like that. It's still quite strong. You felt the pain because I applied strong pressure with my thumb. Now sit down.

Burgmeyer sits down, but avoids looking at the doctor.

SAMAKHAN *(also sits down)*. And please listen to what I'm about to say. In the morning you have a thirst and crave something sour....

BURGMEYER. That, and something more....

SAMAKHAN *(interrupting)*. And you feel the urge to be out in the fresh air as soon as possible....

BURGMEYER. Maybe! But as I told you, in addition to that I...

SAMAKHAN *(shouting)*. Don't interrupt me, please. You've talked enough already. Allow me now... I know without any of your "in additions" what's wrong with you. Your illness is anemia, attended by nervous disorder. Your cure should consist of eating more meat, and being out in the air all day. And also, get less irritated at your servants.

BURGMEYER. More than anything else I'd like you to get rid of my *tic douleureux*.

SAMAKHAN *(mimicking him). Tic douleureux! Tic douleureux,* he's learned it
by rote. All your *tic douleureux* is the result of anemia, and the form it takes is
nothing but disguised fever. I'll prescribe arsenic for you... *(Gets up from the
chair.)*

BURGMEYER. What do you mean? Arsenic?

SAMAKHAN. Just that! *(Sits at the desk and begins to write.)* You think I want
to poison you? Every poison depends on the degree of concentration—coffee is
poison, nevertheless you drink it every day... *(Getting up from the table and show -
ing the words on the prescription.)* To be taken as it says here... *(Reaches for his
hat.)*

Burgmeyer rises also and hands him the designated fee. He puts it in his pocket.

SAMAKHAN. Thank you!

BURGMEYER. Doctor, I'll thank you to take your prescription back as well.
I'm not going to follow it.

SAMAKHAN *(beginning to laugh).* What's the matter? Are you scared of arsenic?

BURGMEYER *(in an irritated voice).* No, I'm not scared of the arsenic. I got
scared when you stated ahead of time that you wanted to charge me a thousand
rubles. A doctor with an attitude like that towards his patients is not one I can
trust.

SAMAKHAN *(glancing at Burgmeyer with a sneer on his face).* And what, in
your opinion, should my attitude be? Thousands of people need me every day.
How should I decide whom to treat? Of course, I go to him who pays the most.

BURGMEYER *(growing more irritated).* You should, of course, choose to go
to the most dangerously and seriously ill. You should go there, and in a hurry.

SAMAKHAN *(with noticeable anger).* Here's a new moralist! That you, of all
people, Mr. Burgmeyer, should be a preacher! If I make a lot of money, and I
don't hide the fact that I do, and in what might be called a crude and forceful
way, you can be quite sure that I get it for my professional skill, my know-how.
When you... I don't know what... were doing business in your parents' store or
playing knucklebones with the village boys at the serfs' farmhouses, I was study-
ing and working. But you should ask you conscience how you accumulated your
millions, with what effort and knowledge, and then you'd better keep quiet. And
follow my prescription as I advise. The arsenic will probably help you. *(He nods
very slightly to Burgmeyer, and then leaves, having put his hat on while still in the
room.)*

Scene 9

BURGMEYER *(remaining alone. He seems totally embittered).* Will help, he
thinks! But what a pleasant situation. I can't even ask help from a doctor with
any confidence, because it's a whole lot more agreeable to all those charlatans to
stretch out an illness than to cure it. And to top it all, to have to listen to their
rudeness. Here, come on all of you, thirsty for money, grubbing for millions,

come and feast your eyes on me. Have a good look and see how much pleasure I get out of those millions. To some people I've even stopped being a man, but am simply a sack full of money, from which everybody in one way or other expects to get a share. No matter what I set my heart on, no matter what I want, regardless of what it is, everywhere in my way stands that money, like an implacable enemy, money, money, my money! And at the end of it, when I die, to whom can I leave it, except to that fool Simkha! If I will it to my wife, will she take it? In any case, she left me, and shamed me before the world. But didn't I push her into that? No! God knows I didn't want that. I told her at the time, thinking that for the sake of our mutual well-being she might seduce Mirovich, but with cunning, with artful design, so that he'd do what she wanted... How could I be expected to know that she was in love with him to such an extent that my appeal would at one and the same time insult her and make her happy. When she came to Mirovich when I was at his place, I was of course, foolish not to take her away from him forcibly if necessary, to drag her out.... But would she have obeyed me? Her character isn't the most submissive. And God knows a great scandal would have come out of it. My main fault is that I worried too much about gathering the kind of treasure which the moths will destroy and the worms corrupt, and I gave little consideration to other things. That's why the doctor is right: I can hardly blame anyone.... My wife can do as she pleases later but I'll do my part.... Simkha! Tell him to come here!

Scene 10

Simkha runs in at his call.

BURGMEYER. Where do you go to all the time? Don't you know you're the only one I have?

RUFIN. I went to inquire about Mr. Mirovich, sir. The firm Belli is going to take him, but only if he will go to America. "We know him," they said. "He's an honest man, and we need an honest man there!"

BURGMEYER. What a wonderful imagination you have? Then Mirovich will take my wife away from me completely. No one will even know where she might be.

RUFIN *(slyly)*. Oh, but sir, he won't take her. There'll be no means to take her with him. Anyway Cleopatra Sergeyevna won't go with him... *(Mysteriously.)* They quarrel all the time nowadays, they say.

BURGMEYER *(almost with satisfaction)*. What could they quarrel about?

RUFIN. Poverty. Sir, it seems that when people are poor one or the other is always doing something wrong.

BURGMEYER. Simkha, is it possible that even after my death Cleopatra Sergeyevna won't accept anything from me?

RUFIN. That I don't know sir, I don't know!

BURGMEYER. However, it doesn't matter! Fetch me a clever notary! I want to write a codicil. In it I'll provide for you... provide handsomely....

RUFIN *(kissing Burgmeyer's shoulder)*. I'm grateful, sir... *(Stands for a moment, shifting from one foot to the other.)* I'm going to ask you for another favor, sir. It suited you to get angry with Evgenia Nikolayevna. It suited you to have her sent away from you. What do you want of her now, sir? Won't you permit me to marry her?

BURGMEYER *(much startled)*. You? Marry Evgenia Nikolayevna?

RUFIN *(a little embarrassed)*. Yes sir, I met her just now, and she said, "Mr. Rufin, if you so desire I will marry you."

BURGMEYER *(with a flash of anger)*. What grounds could she have for saying that to you? Obviously you've been talking to her in this vein before.

RUFIN *(his face reddening)*. How could I, sir?

BURGMEYER. Then why did you become shifty-eyed just now, and your face turn red?

RUFIN. Oh sir, I'm very much afraid I've made you really angry.

BURGMEYER *(holding his hands around his head)*. Now, it seems, everything is becoming clearer to me. *(Turns to the audience, pointing at Rufin.)* That's why he...was taken into Evgenia Nikolayevna's favor instead of Kunitsyn and that's why he always pacified me over her debts. Altogether I was completely surrounded by a gang of thieves... *(Suddenly he turns to his desk and quickly takes out a revolver. He approaches Rufin, grabs him by the collar and shoves the revolver against Rufin's forehead.)* Go on, talk! You were Evgenia Nikolayevna's lover?

RUFIN *(shaking)*. Oh no, sir.

BURGMEYER *(in furious tones)*. Talk! Talk or I'll shoot you like a dog if you keep quiet even for a minute....

RUFIN *(trying vainly to kneel down)*. I am guilty sir. I was in love with her but I only made eyes at her.

BURGMEYER *(holding him fast by the collar and preventing him from kneel - ing)*. What about fleecing me? You planned it with her, and then meant to escape from the country? Admit it, or I'll pull the trigger.

RUFIN *(completely lost)*. It was she, sir, who used to say to me: "Let's go. Let's take the money from the safe!" "But you have your own money," I would say.

BURGMEYER *(shaking him)*. Why didn't you tell me all this and forewarn me? I saved you from death by starvation. I brought you up, educated you.... I wanted to make you heir to my possessions, but you came to terms with thieves to steal from me! I won't kill you. I don't want to go to Siberia because of you. *(Throws down the revolver, and shouts to his servants. They rush in. Burgmeyer al - most hurls Rufin into their hands.)* Put him in the cellar, in the cellar! And call the police here at once.... The police!

RUFIN *(regaining his senses with difficulty)*. Good fellows, the master's knocked my teeth out. He's made me bleed. *(Spits on his palm and shows the blood to the servants.)* Look, this is my blood.

BURGMEYER *(frantically)*. Get him out of here this minute! *(The servants hustle Rufin out, as he continues to bellow, "The master made me bleed. I'll lodge a complaint against him.")*

Scene 11

BURGMEYER *(alone)*. So that one cheated me too! Every last one of my employees has at least one person who would neither cheat nor steal from him, but around me there are only enemies. They're all cheats and traitors. I'm absolutely terrified to go on living. A man can't sleep quietly on a bed of daggers. God gave me the one and only faithful custodian, my wife, but I couldn't keep her either. But I will bring her back to me, even if it's the last thing I do. *(Shouts)* Who's there? Bring Simkha back here!

Scene 12

Two servants bring Rufin back by the arms. He's trembling like an aspen.

BURGMEYER. Listen swindler! I thought of spending a hundred thousand to get you sentenced to hard labor. But I'll forgive you everything, everything, do you understand? I'll let you marry Evgenia Nikolayevna, and I'll even give you a dowry with her—but only separate Mirovich from my wife and reconcile her with me.

RUFIN *(immediately gaining composure, as if he'd never been attacked)*. Sir, but how can I do that? I don't know....

BURGMEYER. You're lying, you're lying! You Jews steer the world through money, and you tell me that with money you can't reconcile me with one woman?

RUFIN *(apparently beginning to grasp the idea)*. Well, sir, maybe Mr. Mirovich will go to America. He, himself, will leave Cleopatra Sergeyevna to you.

BURGMEYER. He won't go. Get that straight. He hasn't a mean little soul like yours. He wouldn't sell his love for money.

RUFIN *(excitedly)*. Then I'll buy off that note he signed when he borrowed the two thousand. I'll buy it and send him to jail with it....

BURGMEYER *(looks steadily at Rufin)*. The note? Jail? *(Turning away from Rufin and waving his hand.)* Buy it! Put him in jail. He took more freedom away from me. He took the joy and happiness of my entire life. Get him locked up.

RUFIN *(completely out of the grasp of the servants, and raising his arms to the au - dience)*. I will.

Curtain

ACT IV

Interior of a small country cottage in Zikovo. On one side of the stage stands a small battered desk, unpainted wooden chairs, and on the other side a tattered sofa.

Scene 1

MIROVICH *(he has already become quite bald. His jacket is shabby and his boots are patched. He is walking thoughtfully around the room)*. No matter what I do, there's no money to pay for this cottage, nor to rent an apartment in the city, and still no work! I hurled myself at the Department of Justice, offering my services—they told me straight that I'd gone off with the wife of a rich contractor, and thus destroyed his peace. On what grounds could a man who'd do a thing like that get a job? But suddenly, out of the blue, appears this tender-minded outfit Belli and for God knows what reason, they make me an offer—I can work for them on condition that I go to America. "You're an honest man, and we need one over there!" *(He smiles sadly.)* I'm very thankful, of course, for their flattering opinion, but nevertheless I can't accept the job. If I were alone I'd take it like a shot, but as things are, how can I? I have a woman on my hands, and we can hardly make ends meet here. What would it be like to go off to some absolutely unknown country—maybe get in a row with the company, and find myself right down on my uppers? Yes. It only takes a man to make one false step, and he can never correct it—not with repentance, nor his willingness to work, nor with the utmost toil—with nothing! He dies, and rots, and that's it. But what's the matter with me? I've got to get on with correcting the proofs. *(Again he smiles sadly.)* A proofreader is what I've become, rather than die of starvation. *(He sits down at the desk and begins to work.)*

Scene 2

A servant enters—a fat, slatternly, dirty, old woman, obviously quite drunk. Having come into the middle of the room, she stands straddling her legs.

COOK. Sir! My fine sir!
MIROVICH *(without looking up)*. What do you want?
COOK. A fine gentleman with a young lady is asking for you, fine sir.
MIROVICH *(still not looking at her)*. For me?
COOK. Yes, you. He's sure no Russian! He's black, like a gypsy. The young lady with him, now she's Russian.
MIROVICH. What's all this Russian, no Russian? Is Cleopatra Sergeyevna not here?
COOK. No, she never come in yet. They're not asking for Cleopatra Sergeyevna, but for you!

Scene 3

Standing in the doorway are Evgenia Nikolayevna, beautifully and expensively dressed, and Rufin equally finely clad, with a gold chain, white gloves, and a fine new hat in his hands.

COOK *(pointing out Mirovich to them).* There he sits, all alone! *(She turns round to leave, but misses the opening and hits her head on the door jamb. At this she laughs.)* Missed it! *(She moves to the other side of the door, saying to herself)* Hold it, old cow! Don't fall to pieces. *(She gets out of the room.)*

Mirovich, having raised his head at her maneuvers, sees Evgenia Nikolayevna and Rufin before him. He is visibly astonished and stands up.

EVGENIA NIKOLAYEVNA *(very courteous and friendly).* Of course, you didn't expect to see me, Vyacheslav Mikhailovich, did you?
MIROVICH *(shrugs his shoulders).* I admit I certainly didn't.
EVGENIA NIKOLAYEVNA *(coming to the proscenium).* I knew Cleopatra Sergeyevna wasn't home. That's why I purposely came directly to you... *(Points to Rufin.)* May I present my husband, Rufin.
MIROVICH *(still more astonished).* Your husband?
EVGENIA NIKOLAYEVNA *(with a little confusion).* Yes. We got married just three days ago.
MIROVICH *(peering at Rufin).* I know you a little.... That's why you got baptized?
RUFIN. That's why I got baptized. Mr. Tolokonnikov was my godfather. *(With a slight smile.)* I'm now Semyon Izmailich, after my godpappy.
MIROVICH. And for that, of course, you'll get an award in cash?
RUFIN. I will. They say they're giving fifty rubles. I'll get it.
MIROVICH. Of course you will. Why lose a penny? And are you still Mr. Burgmeyer's steward?
RUFIN. No. I'm independent now.
MIROVICH. But how? Do you live as you did when you were dependent?
RUFIN. No. I'm no longer with him in any way.
EVGENIA NIKOLAYEVNA *(extremely irritated by Mirovich's questions, inter-rupts her husband).* We live in a completely separate house. My husband has no dealings with Burgmeyer, except of the most insignificant kind, and by the way, one of which is your concern.
MIROVICH. What is my concern?
EVGENIA NIKOLAYEVNA. I shall tell you. But will you allow us to sit down? You have not asked us to. *(To her husband.)* Sit down.

Rufin at once sits on a chair but can't manage to dispose of his hat, and in addition is hampered by his too-tight gloves. Evgenia Nikolayevna, with signs of disgust, brushes the dust from the sofa and sits down. She takes out a very beautiful cigarette case, extracts a cigarette and matches, and begins to smoke. Instead of exhibiting the manners and appearance of a graceful woman, as formerly, she has become too free and bold, so that having sat down, she sticks out her foot in a beautiful shoe, and begins to wiggle it. Mirovich sits back in his chair.

EVGENIA NIKOLAYEVNA *(puffing away carelessly at her cigarette).* It used to seem to me, Vyacheslav Mikhailovich, that you believed in my friendship. But I'm afraid now you're a little disappointed in me.

MIROVICH. A bit.

EVGENIA NIKOLAYEVNA I'm sorry about that. But the purpose of my visit will, I hope, convince you that I'm still your friend. You know of course, that I've been living in Mr. Burgmeyer's house, and that recently I quarreled with him.

MIROVICH. Yes, I heard about that.

EVGENIA NIKOLAYEVNA. And you heard also that your friend Kunitsyn, God knows what a liar he turned out to be, told a screed of rubbish to Burgmeyer about me. Burgmeyer at first believed everything, but now he's beginning to doubt... *(She smiles ironically.)* So much so that not only did he present me with a small dowry, he married me off to his former steward, as the old rich nobles used to do.

At that Mirovich smiles disdainfully.

EVGENIA NIKOLAYEVNA *(noticing that).* That Kunitsyn, with his incurable frivolity, is able to do anything in the world he likes, doesn't surprise me. But I did hear something, which if it is true, really surprised me, and that is that he came to Burgmeyer on your advice. Is that true, or isn't it?

MIROVICH. Perfectly true!

EVGENIA NIKOLAYEVNA *(somewhat taken aback by his ready answer).* Well, I don't blame you too much in this instance. Most likely you, yourself, were deceived, because I strongly suspect that the whole thing was fabricated by none other than your own Cleopatra Sergeyevna, and that she forced Kunitsyn to tell it to Burgmeyer.

MIROVICH *(his voice now stern).* Cleopatra Sergeyevna? What do you mean?

EVGENIA NIKOLAYEVNA. I'm almost convinced of it—and moreover that she did it because she wants to go back to her husband. Of course, I don't expect you to believe my story.

MIROVICH *(still with the same voice).* You make no mistake there. I don't believe anything you are saying!

EVGENIA NIKOLAYEVNA It's entirely up to you. I just want to say again that I only suspect Cleopatra Sergeyevna, but I have positive and indisputable proof that Burgmeyer wishes to have her back.

MIROVICH. He can wish all he likes—there's no law against that.

EVGENIA NIKOLAYEVNA. But apparently along with his wishing he has high hopes of bringing it to reality.... His first intention was to move you off somewhere, far from here. To manage that he got Belli's to make you an offer of a job in America. I know you got such a proposition.

Mirovich remains silent.

But, as I heard, you were clever and astute enough not to fall into that trap and you turned down the marvelous offer. Mr. Burgmeyer then decided to use more exact means... my husband here can confirm what I am telling you.... Burgmeyer told him to buy up some note you signed for that money you borrowed. Then if you don't pay Burgmeyer, he has instructed my husband to get you thrown in jail—and then of course, it will be very convenient for Cleopatra Sergeyevna to go back to her husband.

MIROVICH *(with blazing face)*. I've never doubted that Burgmeyer is ready to treat me in the worst possible way.

EVGENIA NIKOLAYEVNA. Well... maybe Mr. Burgmeyer isn't the only one at fault here.... I really came here to say to you again and again "Beware... Beware!" *(Addresses her husband.)* Well, will they soon proceed against Mr. Mirovich?

RUFIN. Soon! Mr. Burgmeyer instructed me to hurry. A warrant has been issued by the court. They'll begin proceedings today or tomorrow.

EVGENIA NIKOLAYEVNA. So soon! Well, by today or tomorrow you'll finally be completely convinced....

Scene 4

Cook enters.

COOK. My fine sir, the young lady's come back and is asking who you have as guests?

MIROVCH. Tell her that Evgenia Nikolayevna—oh, you'll muddle it all up.

COOK. I'll muddle it, your lordship!

MIROVICH. Wait, I'll write it out for you, and you give it to the lady. *(He writes on a scrap of paper and hands it to the cook, who leaves as before, with not very firm but noticeably careful steps, and this time she gets through the door directly.)*

EVGENIA NIKOLAYEVNA *(getting up)*. I'm afraid we've stayed too long. Anyway Cleopatra Sergeyevna probably wouldn't get much satisfaction out of seeing me.... *(To her husband.)* Let's go.

He gets to his feet at once.

Good-bye, Vyacheslav Mikhailovich. At least shake hands on parting.

MIROVICH *(refusing to hold out his hand)*. No. I'm sorry, but I don't offer my hand to slanderers, male or female.

EVGENIA NIKOLAYEVNA *(smiling)*. And you still take us for slanderers? Well, you'll find out for yourself.... *(Leaves with her husband.)*

Scene 5

MIROVICH *(Alone, begins to talk to himself)*. So, still more new joy! It gets harder with every hour!

Just then Cleopatra Sergeyevna comes in from another door, from an inside room. She is dressed in black silk, but her gown is very shabby.

CLEOPATRA SERGEYEVNA. Your guests left?
MIROVICH.They left!
CLEOPATRA SERGEYEVNA. But who on earth is this Evgenia Nikolayevna Rufin? Is it Jenny?
MIROVICH. Jenny!
CLEOPATRA SERGEYEVNA. But why is she called Rufin?
MIROVICH. Because she just married Burgmeyer's steward, Rufin.
CLEOPATRA SERGEYEVNA. That's news! *(She is noticeably tired, and walks to the sofa to sit down.)* But why did she come to see us? I certainly don't want to see her.
MIROVICH. She didn't come to see you, but to see me.
CLEOPATRA SERGEYEVNA. But why you?
MIROVICH. Oh, with various pieces of news... *(He observes her closely.)* But what's wrong with you, Cleo? Look at yourself. Your dress is dirty, your face is all splotched and your hair isn't combed.
CLEOPATRA SERGEYEVNA *(at first smiling somewhat ironically)*. I got very tired. I walked from town.... I couldn't afford to take a cab. And besides I got angry. *(She is silent for a moment and her tears well up.)* That woman wouldn't pay me a penny for the dress I took her.
MIROVICH. But why?
CLEOPATRA SERGEYEVNA *(now completely in tears)*. She said I had spoiled her dress, and that she'd have to give it to someone else for alteration. She'll have to buy additional material, and that's why I even owe her money, and not the other way round.... *(She covers her face with her handkerchief to hide her tears.)*
MIROVICH. But why all the tears? Because of such a trifle? Aren't you ashamed, Cleo! Here, have a drink of water. *(Fills a glass and gives it to her.)*
CLEOPATRA SERGEYEVNA *(Pushing the glass aside, says capriciously)*. I don't want it. Leave me alone!

Mirovich, noticeably insulted by her tone, moves away, puts the glass down and sits at his desk with his papers.

CLEOPATRA SERGEYEVNA. Such an idiot! She's stingy and greedy, and ready to cheat any poor woman.
MIROVICH *(without leaving his work, and somewhat venomously)*. But maybe you did sew it badly.
CLEOPATRA SERGEYEVNA. I did it quite well. She picked on me for absolutely nothing....

MIROVICH *(again somewhat maliciously)*. Well, I don't think you sewed it that well....

CLEOPATRA SERGEYEVNA. You think not!

MIROVICH. Not all Russian women, it would seem, can sew that well, especially you ladies.

CLEOPATRA SERGEYEVNA. You men are so much better?

MIROVICH. Men are more talented, and more sensible.

CLEOPATRA SERGEYEVNA *(angrily)*. Oh, terribly sensible! But what kind of passionate love do you have for me nowadays, Vyacheslav, that you have a dig at me in every conversation, and hint all the time that I'm stupid and can't do anything.

MIROVICH. When did I say that?

CLEOPATRA SERGEYEVNA. You're always saying it, and trying to prove it too. But I've already told you several times that I'm proud and have lots of self-respect. And if I saw that a man didn't respect me, and laughed at me, I just don't know what I'd be ready to do.

MIROVICH. For God's sake, let's not have a long drawn-out scene about that. We've got serious and grievous matters to discuss....

CLEOPATRA SERGEYEVNA. I don't know. For me this kind of thing is very serious. I don't know what else could be more serious.

MIROVICH. All this stuff that your one-time friend Evgenia Nikolayevna has just been telling me.

CLEOPATRA SERGEYEVNA. What could she possibly be telling you?

MIROVICH. She was trying to tell me that the whole story Kunitsyn produced about her is a complete lie, and insinuates that you made it up and persuaded Kunitsyn....

CLEOPATRA SERGEYEVNA Me? Oh, the wretched fool! What would I get out of making up stories about her? I'd even forgotten her existence.

MIROVICH. Then she warned me that your husband very much wants to make up with you again, and in order to separate us he's even given instructions to have one of my promissory notes bought up, and me thrown in jail.

CLEOPATRA SERGEYEVNA *(completely shocked)*. You... in jail?

MIROVICH. Yes!

CLEOPATRA SERGEYEVNA *(still hardly believing what she hears)*. Well, there can't be the slightest doubt that she made up all that story by herself.

MIROVICH. Why would she make it up? One can expect anything from your husband.

CLEOPATRA SERGEYEVNA. But could he have you locked up for long?

MIROVICH. Until I pay him.

CLEOPATRA SERGEYEVNA. But you can never pay him. You have no money.

MIROVICH *(sneeringly)*. No money!

CLEOPATRA SERGEYEVNA. Well, there is none. I'm sorry, but I won't allow my husband to do it.

MIROVICH. And how, may I ask, will you manage this "won't allow him"?

CLEOPATRA SERGEYEVNA. Just like that! I won't allow him. *(She stands up and begins to walk around the room.)* You borrowed that money and spent it on me. That's why my husband is obligated to pay it back. After all I am his wife.

MIROVICH *(waving his hands and grinning)*. True female logic, and female morality! A woman's lover borrows money and spends it on her, and that's the reason the husband has to take over the debt.

CLEOPATRA SERGEYEVNA *(with growing fervor)*. He must! He must! He oppressed my youth, all my early life, and that's not your concern, but mine... Call it my logic and morality if you like... *(Thinks a little.)* All these things are mere trifles. I won't let it happen. There's something much more important to me. *(Stops suddenly.)* Please give me some water, I feel that something awful is happening to me. *(She points to her throat. Mirovich gives her some water. She greed - ily drinks the whole glassful.)* But kiss me, tenderly, you know, as you used to do in the beginning of our love.

Mirovich hugs her. She kisses him passionately, and then makes a gesture of pushing him away.

CLEOPATRA SERGEYEVNA. That's enough. Go and sit down again. I'll sit down too. My legs are bending... *(She sinks onto the sofa. Mirovich sits down also. It is noticeable that he has some apprehension of the talk that is to follow. She speaks with certain trepidation.)* Listen, please. I've meant to ask you this for a long time, but somehow it always seemed too dreadful. The question is very important to me. Tell me—but I beg of you, speak openly, as you would before God and your conscience. Don't answer quickly, but only after having thought about it. Tell me, do you love me, at least a little? Or have you completely stopped loving me? From your treatment of me, it is easier to believe that you no longer love me, that you even almost hate me.

MIROVICH *(grim-faced)*. Cleo!

CLEOPATRA SERGEYEVNA *(persisting)*. No, tell me the whole truth, completely!

MIROVICH *(his eyes on the floor)*. How can I tell you the truth? How can I tell you definitely whether I've stopped loving you or not? I can't, because it's a mystery to me myself. I'm only conscious of one thing clearly—even under the most favorable conditions, when he has neither to worry nor to work, a man cannot hang around a woman doing nothing but perpetually making love to her. It's impossible. It's humiliating, disgraceful!

CLEOPATRA SERGEYEVNA *(in a toneless voice)*. That's true, absolutely true!

MIROVICH *(continues)*. And when, in addition to that, he's sunk in poverty, when he knows that it's necessary to earn each piece of bread for himself and the woman, and at the same time knows there is no work—well even the very interlude of lovemaking is a torture—it's a torture made up of the pangs of conscience, of boredom, of self-disgust, distaste, amounting, if you like, even to hatred.

CLEOPATRA SERGEYEVNA *(her face blazing)*. I've felt that all along and at the same time I understand completely, and I'm glad you have told me. I see a real man again, a man who wants to follow a decent road. But why, my dear, knowing all this, don't you decide to look for a job, resolutely and persistently? It doesn't have to be here, after all. It could be somewhere else in the provinces. People are getting jobs all the time!

MIROVICH (*scornfully*). Just now the Belli Company has offered me a job. But I'd have to go to America. Is that a very suitable offer?

CLEOPATRA SERGEYEVNA. Why on earth shouldn't you go to America?

MIROVICH (*sneering again*). It's too far! Your noble husband thought up that trip for me. They're making me the offer on his initiative, and that's why I can't believe it could ever be favorable or advantageous for me. Of course he undoubtedly counted on the fact that with my having to go so far off, and all the incidental expenses before leaving, I wouldn't have the money to take you with me.

CLEOPATRA SERGEYEVNA (*in the same toneless voice*). There's no need to take me with you.

MIROVICH. But how can I leave you here? To say nothing of our separation—we can't even conceive when we'd meet again—I'd be simply condemning you to poverty.

CLEOPATRA SERGEYEVNA (*as if realizing something*). Why poverty?

MIROVICH. Because I wouldn't be able to spare you anything. They're offering a very small salary. And if you tried to rely on your own work, you'd be mistaken. You can't even work because of your health, so what would be left to you? (*He grins sarcastically.*) To go back to your husband?

CLEOPATRA SERGEYEVNA (*breathing hard*). And what if I did?

MIROVICH (*greatly shocked*). You know quite well that that would be worse for me than anything! I'd lose all respect for you then.

CLEOPATRA SERGEYEVNA (*sorrowfully but firmly*). But why? Be so good as to tell me why you would lose all respect for me? Vyacheslav, I can see that you are a cruel and merciless egotist as far as I am concerned. You don't love me any more. I'm a burden to you, both morally and financially. But you demand that I should behave as if I were a block of wood, understanding nothing, but continuing to be a burden. As for my going back to my husband, what's that to you? I won't take a new lover.

MIROVICH. The latter would be less humiliating as far as I am concerned. It would only mean that you'd met a better man than I and the world is full of them. But to take up with your husband again would mean that you've evaluated the situation and deliberately decided to love a rotten little bounder, a man all made up of greed and vice, but humble in front of his superiors, and atrocious to those under him; a man incessantly complaining of being swindled, but himself cheating and lying all over the place. In short, the very quintessence of a successful, crooked businessman.

CLEOPATRA SERGEYEVNA (*shaking her head in denial*). No, he is not like that. Can't a businessman be decent and honest?

MIROVICH. No, he can't. Do you know what a businessman is in human society? He's a parasite, an oppressor of the working man, a consumer of labor and money.

CLEOPATRA SERGEYEVNA. But society can hardly exist without the businessmen. They also serve a useful purpose.

MIROVICH. None! Right now all the efforts of the best and most honest brains are directed to doing away with businessmen, at taking away all power from capital. The hour is coming soon for the gentry. Accounts will be settled with them, and more drastically than they were settled once with feudal noblemen.

CLEOPATRA SERGEYEVNA. According to you, then, all businessmen, without exception, are evildoers?

MIROVICH (shrugging his shoulders). Oh, maybe among those who've been tradesmen for generations, a few honest men might be found, since it's possible that need or circumstances put them in the place where they find themselves. But your husband picked a profession to his taste. And you can say that with his whole soul he has striven to cheat and lie. And now if you prefer him to me, what must I appear in your eyes? A piece of trash for which a name can hardly be found. Not only will you stop loving me, you'll probably despise me.

CLEOPATRA SERGEYEVNA. Whether I've stopped loving you or not, Vyacheslav, I don't know. And if you don't see that, God must be your judge! I know that with my love I've caused you a great deal of trouble, and it's high time to come to my senses. I'm no longer a stupid dreamer. But enough of that. I'm very tired. I've lived through a great deal today. Come, let me kiss you again.

(Mirovich approaches her, hugs her and she kisses him passionately.) Now I must go and lie down. For some reason I feel a lot worse.

She leaves.

Scene 6

MIROVICH (alone). What unfortunate beings the two of us are. What's to be done here? What? It's all very well for the wise men who astonish the world with their wisdom, their willpower and the force of character to solve the big problems... and as for people who are individuals, nonconformists—bah! They're moved like checkers! But let everyone fly, topsy-turvy, whereever he pleases? No! Let those wise ones untie this little Gordian knot!

Loud voices and laughter are heard. He listens.

It can't be Kunitsyn?

Scene 7

Kunitsyn enters, waving his hands in astonishment.

KUNITSYN. What an incident, what an incident, as they say in vaudeville!
MIROVICH. What is it?
KUNITSYN (repeating). What an incident, what an incident! But wait, first I must discharge a debt. Tanya, eh, Tanny, my darling little cook!

Goes through the doorway from which the cook had entered.

MIROVICH. A most inopportune time for a guest!

KUNITSYN *(returning)*. No one there. The bed's empty. Only a girl sitting about.

MIROVICH. But where is Tanya?

KUNITSYN. The girl says the lady sent her to Moscow with a letter.

MIROVICH *(puzzled)*. What do you mean? To Moscow with a letter? Why?

KUNITSYN. I don't know. She's probably lying. The charming Tanny, I think, has simply run to the tavern. But I'll begin my story. Having entered the park, I felt like taking a stroll. My head was splitting—I got too drunk yesterday—and right near the church who did I bump into, face to face, but Evgenia Nikolayevna. It's the first time we met since our fatal parting. There was an air about her like a Parisian... The most excellent carriage being driven alongside her. It turned out that even her husband was with her, that little Jew of Burgmeyer's. As soon as Evgenia Nikolayevna saw me, she jumped at me and gave me a dressing down, I'll tell you, in the most foul language. I used the same on her, and then her husband butted in. I threatened him with a stick.... And then, not having come to any kind of agreement, we parted. Suddenly at the gate of your cottage I saw—do you remember Khvorostov, who quit when he was still in the first year because he couldn't understand what was going on at the School of Jurisprudence? And whom, by the coincidence of his resemblance in physiognomy to *musculus gluteus*, we usually called "Mr. Gluteus." He's a bailiff here. How do you like that? "Hello, Mr. Gluteus," I said. "And where do you think you are going?" "Why are you abusing me as you always did?" said he, with those swollen cheeks and stupid, lisping mug. "I am going on business." "But will they send you anywhere on business, Gluety? Why are you lying to me?" He got angrier. "What do you mean by saying I'm lying? I'm going to Mirovich to demand payment of money from him, two thousand rubles." "What lying yelp is this," I say. "Show me right now what this money is about?" He gave me the paper, and it was indeed a warrant demanding payment of the money. I figured that the poor fellow hasn't a penny and since there's no goodness in the world—they'll throw him in jail. I plucked out my wallet. It was a good thing, damn it, that at this moment I happened to have money. I shoved two thousand into the hand of that dolt, led him to a nearby shop and took the note from him. Then, having brought him back to the sidewalk, as if in a joke I turned him around and give him such a smack on the neck that I nearly had him in the dirt. He cursed and spat. "That's all right," I said, "bark, scoundrel...." In the future you won't go to an old friend to demand money!" And here's the note. *(He puts the note solemnly on the table.)*

MIROVICH *(at first burned with shame while listening to his friend's recital, now takes him by the hand)*. I am grateful, my good friend. But I am ashamed. Why, for what reason, did you do it? And where did you get the money? How could you have two thousand to spare?

KUNITSYN *(naively)*. That money, my friend, is from Herr Burgmeyer. Remember, he promised to thank me if my words proved true. This morning, suddenly I got a package promising nothing special by its appearance, but I opened it, and see—money! I counted it. Two thousand rubles and a short note that it's from Mr. Burgmeyer, brief, delicate and noble!

MIROVICH *(retreating almost with horror)*. And you paid my debt with

Burgmeyer's money? See here, Kunitsyn, it's obvious there isn't any distinction in your mind between honesty and dishonesty. Weren't you ashamed to accept the money from Burgmeyer? In taking it you openly admit that you sold a woman who loved you. What's more, with his money you pay off a debt of his wife's lover. Can't you see all sorts of revolting, despicable implications in this transaction? And finally, you put me in a completely hopeless position. Now I'll have to go around bowing and scraping to everyone in order to collect two thousand so that I can hurl it back at Burgmeyer. But who on earth would trust me with such a sum? It was cruel, inhuman, of you, Kunitsyn. And if you didn't understand this you should have asked me about it beforehand. You shouldn't dispose of somebody else's dignity in that fashion.

KUNITSYN *(taken aback, and scratching his head).* By God, you're right. I can see now that it was damned clumsy on my part. But at first sight I thought I was doing you a favor. "Now at least they won't lock that man up," I said.

MIROVICH. What's all this talk of jail? They wouldn't be putting me in jail because I'd committed a crime, but even in jail my pride would suffer much less than it does now.

KUNITSYN *(almost through tears).* I understand at last. Forgive me, old friend. So help me God, I never expected to upset you like this. But wait—the thing can be corrected. In a few days I'm going to have some more money, this time through a totally private deal. I kicked in that last little bit of real estate of mine—I don't want to be a landed proprietor. You'll surely accept the money from me to pay off your debt to a devil, for if you don't, I'll be through with you forever. Ergo: as soon as I get the money, without a moment's delay I'll send Burgmeyer his two thousand, and write: "*Merci,* I don't deal with the flesh and blood of an old woman." And then, of course, you will owe me.

MIROVICH *(touched).* Thank you. Naturally I've never doubted your friendship—it's only when you try to show your friendship on a financial basis you're unscrupulous.

KUNITSYN. What else is there to do? I've smelt far too many Russian roses. Here and there among them one smells a swindler, and before long one joins the gang. Is somebody knocking? *(Listens.)* Somebody is. *(He sings out.)* "Open, open!" as Mme. Reckht sang for us. *(To Mirovich.)* Should I open it?

MIROVICH. Yes.

KUNITSIN *(opens door and speaks in surprise).* Mr. Burgmeyer!

MIROVICH *(also exclaiming).* Burgmeyer!

Scene 8

Burgmeyer enters, his eyes on the ground, not addressing anyone in particular.

BURGMEYER. Can I see Cleopatra Sergeyevna?

MIROVICH *(haughtily shaking his head, with his hair falling in locks before his face).* No, you cannot.

BURGMEYER. She herself sent the woman to ask me to come and see her.

MIROVICH *(reddening with anger).* Cleopatra Sergeyevna sent for you?

BURGMEYER. Yes, here's her note. Some misunderstanding has occurred here. I instructed my steward to buy up one of your promissory notes, with a view to destroying it. But he misunderstood me, and got a warrant for the recovery of the debt.

MIROVICH *(laughing in his face)*. And if your steward is really as thickheaded as that, why do you keep him?

BURGMEYER *(still looking at the ground)*. I've already given him notice. And now I've come to actually destroy the warrant.

MIROVICH. In that case you've had your trouble for nothing. The note has already been paid.

BURGMEYER *(still more confused)*. I'm very sorry I wasn't in time to correct the mistake... but nevertheless I would like to ask your permission to see Cleopatra Sergeyevna. I want to discuss something else with her.

MIROVICH. Cleopatra Sergeyevna is ill, and it is unlikely that she will see you.

BURGMEYER. But she herself wrote me a note.

MIROVICH. When she wrote the note she felt well—now she feels ill.

BURGMEYER. But a husband, I suppose, can see his wife, even if she is lying ill in bed.

MIROVICH. A husband? Yes! But it seems you have somewhere lost that right. You've forgotten that I saved your millions for you, because of that woman, and, in addition, I paid with more than my blood. I paid with my honor. And that's why I do not consider you to be Cleopatra Sergeyevna's husband.

BURGMEYER. You can consider me as her husband or not as you please, the law still does not deprive me of that right.

MIROVICH. Oh, I see. You want the support of the law? In that case go back to where you came from, and come back with the police. Otherwise I won't permit you even to approach the gate.

BURGMEYER *(lifting his eyes at last)*. Vyacheslav Mikhailovich. God knows I didn't come here to argue with you, but to try at least in a small way to help my poor wife. I hear on all sides that she has lost her health, and because of her circumstances she hasn't the wherewithal to call a doctor. She doesn't have a dry comfortable corner or even proper nourishment. Surely in the face of this, no one in the world can forbid me to help.

MIROVICH. No one, except Cleopatra Sergeyevna herself.

BURGMEYER. But even she will not forbid me, I hope.

MIROVICH. If she does not, it's her business. But I, personally, don't want to be the messenger carrying your blessings, nor, more especially, do I want to deprive her of them.

BURGMEYER. As far as you and your position are concerned, I know I have no right to either worry or think about you.

MIROVICH. Aha, but unfortunately you worry and think about me altogether too much. You were so thoughtful that you even found me a job with the Belli Company, so that I'd be sent off to America. Your steward, by mistake, of course, bustled about trying to put me in jail, and arrange free lodging for me there. To all that, I'm going to tell you, my dear sir, that honorable men do not choose mean, backhanded ways to get their wives back, and if they do want them back, then they choose a bullet or a sword.

BURGMEYER. I am too old for that. And it's obvious to me that I would lose if I resorted to such means.

MIROVICH *(with a snort of laughter)*. You were too old long ago for any noble action—long ago... Since childhood!

BURGMEYER *(bursting out)*. Mr. Mirovich!

MIROVICH. Mr. Mirovich! Go on, be offended! Be insulted! I'm ready to accept any challenge you care to offer.

Scene 9

Enter Cleopatra Sergeyevna.

CLEOPATRA SERGEYEVNA *(openly addressing Burgmeyer, and extending her hand)*. Hello Alexander, thank you for coming to me. Forgive me for having made you wait so long.

MIROVICH *(hardly able to speak)*. You are better already then?

CLEOPATRA SERGEYEVNA *(brightly)*. It's over... *(Again addressing Burgmeyer.)* First of all I'd like to ask you, Alexander Grigorievich, for two thousand rubles to pay a debt we contracted.

BURGMEYER. But I've just heard—it's already been paid.

CLEOPATRA SERGEYEVNA *(surprised)*. But who paid it?

KUNITSYN *(reddening and glancing at Mirovich, uncertain whether to speak or not)*. I did.

BURGMEYER *(happy at the acknowledgment, and reaching for his wallet)*. You will allow me, then, to pay you right now?

KUNITSYN *(stopping him)*. Attendez—one minute! We have other accounts to settle besides that. We'll talk about it later.

CLEOPATRA SERGEYEVNA. But Kunitsyn, why don't you want to take your money?

KUNITSYN *(again reddening)*. Do me a favor, will you? Carry on with your own discussions and don't worry about me.

BURGMEYER *(again addressing Cleopatra Sergeyevna in an uncertain voice)*. Do you have any other needs besides the payment of that debt?

CLEOPATRA SERGEYEVNA *(interrupting)*. No... well... nothing special. But Alexander Grigorievich, I would like to ask you for something far more important. I now realize how guilty I appear to you. At the time, because of one careless word of yours, I allowed feelings which I should have suppressed to grow in me, to develop to distraction! And by my folly I ruined the man for whom, more than anyone in the world, I wanted happiness. Give me a chance, Alexander Grigorievich, to make reparation. Take me back again—oh, not as a wife! No... why that would be... but as a friend, as a daughter, sister and let Mirovich still soar in the world—we are clipping his wings.

MIROVICH *(white as a corpse, wringing his hands)*. I can see now that Evgenia Nikolayevna told me the truth about your long-cherished intention to go back to your husband.

CLEOPATRA SERGEYEVNA *(again with false brightness)*. Yes, everything she said about me was true.... *(To Burgmeyer.)* Are you going to take me?

BURGMEYER. Have you ever doubted that I would, Cleopatra Sergeyevna? I am ready to fulfill any desire you have, and will consider myself fortunate in having near me a being who, no matter how little it is, feels sorry for me, instead of people ready to take almost my life from me.

CLEOPATRA SERGEYEVNA *(exerting a great effort as she approaches Mirovich)*. Goodbye, Vyacheslav, don't be angry with me, and don't curse me too much. And if you do remember me, realize that we women also have our ambitions, and that when a woman really loves someone, it isn't necessary that he should sit at her side forevermore, or that she should eternally have his caresses. On the contrary, the most precious thing for her is his peace of mind and contentment, regardless of whether they are together or apart.

MIROVICH *(obstinately and firmly)*. To tell the truth, Cleopatra Sergeyevna, with this kind of false reasoning, one can neither convince oneself of anything, or prove anything to another. You'd better reason with yourself, and understand precisely what you are undertaking.

CLEOPATRA SERGEYEVNA *(with downcast eyes)*. I am undertaking what my conscience bids me do. *(She addresses Kunitsyn hurriedly.)* You, Kunitsyn, were always good to me. I am grateful to you.... Please take the money from my husband.

KUNITSYN *(again roughly and quickly)*. Later, we'll talk about that later.

CLEOPATRA SERGEYEVNA *(looks once more at Mirovich as she goes toward the door and then suddenly clutches at her breast with both hands, and bursts out)*. Oh, my God, what is this I am doing? *(And then almost in a frenzy she turns on Burgmeyer.)* Alexander Grigorievich, take me away from here. Take me away at once!

Burgmeyer hurriedly gives her his hand, and with Kunitsyn on her other side, she is taken out.

MIROVICH *(at first making a movement as if to follow them, but stops almost at once)*. Why? For what? Our love affair has conformed to the rules. It has already gone through all its cycles. First there was the violent attraction—love! But after a while the stretched strings weakened and stopped producing charming sounds. And now these almost irresistible blows from without—the separation is inevitable.

Kunitsyn comes back. He appears shocked.

KUNITSYN *(comes directly to the proscenium)*. Well, I can now say it, using the words of Shakespeare: "My heart never knew of sorrow, but relating this sad story I will sob and weep as scowling Clifford."

MIROVICH *(addresses him in a voice choked with emotion)*. What else happened out there?

KUNITSYN *(excited out of his usual mood)*. It's terrible what happened! Cleopatra Sergeyevna completely lost control of herself. She was sobbing out loud on the street and couldn't stop. That idiot, little Burgmeyer, lost his head too. It was embarrassing to stay with her like that in the street, but he was afraid to get her into the carriage in case she'd become more disturbed. I yelled at him "Drive her. Maybe the shaking will do her good."

MIROVICH *(through twisted lips)*. She wanted it! She chose that course for herself.

KUNITSYN. No, my friend, no! No matter how you rationalize it, you're guilty in every particular. How could you keep a woman used to fastidious living in a dog-hole like this, feeding her on rotten sausage and potatoes? Any woman would leave, none could endure it. I've been telling you that money nowadays means everything. And if there's none, and it's needed, then to hell with honesty, steal some! Believe me, in practice my philosophy will always work better than yours.

MIROVICH *(angry)*. You're a complete idiot if you can't see that today I've had enough. I'm too unhappy and suffer too much to have you hectoring and bullying me....

KUNITSYN. I won't, I won't. God be with you. You're off to America then?

MIROVICH. I am.

KUNITSYN. When, soon?

MIROVICH. Most likely the day after tomorrow.

KUNITSYN. Well, I'll come and see you off! So long! *(And, not daring to approach to take leave from his friend, he goes out.)*

MIROVICH *(alone, and nodding his head with some decision)*. Great God Baal, accept two more sacrifices for your altar. Torture them, bloodthirsty God, tear out their hearts and souls with your fiery claws. Soon all will bow down to you, in this century stripped of ideals, aspirations and hopes, this century of the brazen ruble, the forged papers, the phony evidence.

CURTAIN

Translated by Andrew Donskov

ALEXANDER OSTROVSKY

LARISA
A DRAMA IN FOUR ACTS

CHARACTERS

Kharita Ignatyevna Ogudalova, a middle-aged widow; she dresses elegantly, but too young for her years.

Larisa Dmitryevna, her daughter; she dresses richly, but with restraint.

Moki Parmenych Knurov, one of the new class of powerful entrepreneurs; an elderly man with a huge fortune.

Vasily Danilych Vozhevatov, a very young man, representative of a big trading company; he dresses in the latest western style.

Yuly Kapitonych Karandyshev, a young man; a poor civil servant.

Sergei Sergeyich Paratov, an aristocrat, handsome and brilliantly endowed, in his early thirties; a shipowner.

Robinson, an out-of-work actor.

Gavrilo, proprietor of the cafe.

Ivan, a cafe waiter.

Ilya, a gypsy.

Ogudalova's footman.

Yefrosinya Potapovna, Karandyshev's aunt.

Gypsies.

ACT I

The action is set in 1880 and takes place in Bryakhimov, a sizeable town on the Volga. The town promenade, which runs along a steep bank overlooking the Volga, opening out to a small square in front of a cafe; to the right of the actors is the cafe entrance, to the left a clump of trees; in the background a low iron paling with a sweeping view of the Volga beyond—forests, villages etc.; there are tables and chairs in front of the cafe, one table to the right, close to the cafe, another to the left.

Scene 1

Gavrilo is standing in the doorway of the cafe. Ivan is tidying the tables and chairs in front of the cafe.

IVAN. Not a soul on the promenade.

GAVRILO. Always like that on holidays. We keep to the old ways here: everyone goes straight from midday service to their pies and cabbage soup, and when they've done with eating—a seven-hour snooze.

IVAN. Not seven now! Just a little doze for three or four hours. A fine old custom I should say.

GAVRILO. And they wake up when it's getting toward evening service and sit around drinking tea till they're sick of themselves....

IVAN. Sick of themselves! What do they feel like that for?

GAVRILO. You try sitting tight in front of a samovar and pouring hot water down yourself for a couple of hours and then you'll know. After they've worked up a good sweat—that's when they start getting sick of themselves.... They tear themselves away from their tea and crawl out onto the promenade to gulp some fresh air and stretch their legs a bit. And this is the time the snobs stroll about—look, there's Moki Parmenych Knurov out there limbering up.

IVAN. Every morning he paces out that promenade from one end to the other, you'd think he'd promised someone to do it. Now why should he wear himself out for nothing, that's what I'd like to know.

GAVRILO. To get some exercise.

IVAN. Exercise—what's that for?

GAVRILO. To work up an appetite. How can he get his dinner down him if he doesn't have an appetite! The kind of dinners he orders—you'd have trouble getting through them without some exercise.

IVAN. Why is it he never says anything?

GAVRILO. "Never says anything!" You're a funny sort—how can you expect someone with millions in the bank to be chatting! Who is there for him to talk to? There's two or three people in town he talks to, and that's about it, so naturally he keeps his mouth shut. That's why he doesn't stay here too long at a time; and if it wasn't for business he wouldn't be here at all. If he wants a chat he goes to Moscow or St. Petersburg, or he goes abroad, he's got more scope there.

IVAN. There's Vasily Danilych coming up the hill. He's rich too—but he talks.

GAVRILO. Vasily Danilych is young yet, he's still full of foolishness; just you wait a few years and he'll be sitting there like a statue as well.

Knurov enters from left; ignoring Gavrilo's and Ivan's bows, he sits down at a table, takes a French newspaper out of his pocket and begins to read. Vozhevatov enters from right.

Scene 2

Knurov, Vozhevatov, Gavrilo, Ivan.

VOZHEVATOV *(bowing respectfully)*. Moki Parmenych, I have the honor to bid you good day!

KNUROV. Ah, Vasily Danilych. *(They shake hands.)* And where have you been?

VOZHEVATOV. At the landing stage. *(Sits down.)*

KNUROV. Were you supposed to be meeting someone?

VOZHEVATOV. Yes, but he didn't turn up. I had a telegram yesterday from Sergei Sergeyich Paratov. I'm buying one of his steamboats.

GAVRILO. It wouldn't be the *Swallow* would it, Vasily Danilych?

VOZHEVATOV. Yes, the *Swallow*. What do you say to that?

GAVRILO. She's a fast runner, a good ship.

VOZHEVATOV. But Sergei Sergeyich let me down—didn't show up.

GAVRILO. You were expecting him on the *Flying Wonder*—but maybe he'll arrive on his own boat, the *Swallow*.

IVAN. Vasily Danilych look, there's another boat coming downstream fast.

VOZHEVATOV. As if there weren't plenty of steamers on the Volga.

IVAN. It's Sergei Sergeyich.

VOZHEVATOV. Think so?

IVAN. Certainly looks like him, sir. The *Swallow*'s paddle boxes stick out a mile.

VOZHEVATOV. You mean to say you can make out paddle boxes three miles away?

IVAN. They can be seen five miles away, sir. And she's nipping along too, you can tell the owner's on board.

VOZHEVATOV. Is it far off?

IVAN. It's just coming out from behind the island. She's really putting on the speed too.

VOZHEVATOV. Putting on speed, you say?

IVAN. Going flat out. Fantastic! Runs faster than *Flying Wonder* she does. Just eats up the miles.

GAVRILO. It's him, sir.

VOZHEVATOV *(to Ivan)*. Let me know when they start putting in.

IVAN. Yes, sir. They'll fire the cannon I suppose.

GAVRILO. Sure to.

VOZHEVATOV. What cannon?

GAVRILO. Well, he keeps his barges anchored midstream.

VOZHEVATOV. I know.

GAVRILO. And there's a cannon on one of the barges. Whenever Sergei Sergeyich is being met or seen off they always fire a salute. *(Glancing to one side, past the cafe.)* And there's a carriage coming for him sir, a cab—one of Chirkov's! He must have let Chirkov know he was coming. And that's the owner himself, Chirkov, sitting up there on the box. It must be for him, sir.

VOZHEVATOV. But how do you know?

GAVRILO. Four pacers in harness. I ask, you, who could it be for but him? Who else would he get such a team together for? Does your heart good to look at them. Like lions they are, and all on snaffle! And the harness, just look at that harness! It must be him, sir.

IVAN. And there's some gypsy up there on the box with Chirkov, all dressed up for a holiday. He's got his belt pulled so tight you'd think he was going to split in two.

GAVRILO. It must be him, sir. No one else would have such a team. It's him, sir.

KNUROV. Paratov lives in style.

VOZHEVATOV. Style, yes, you can't deny him that.

KNUROV. Are you buying the steamer cheap?

VOZHEVATOV. That's right, Moki Parmenych.

KNUROV. Of course you are, or why should you be buying? Why's he selling?

VOZHEVATOV. He doesn't get any profit out of it, I suppose.

KNUROV. I'd be surprised if he did. That's no business for the gentry. But you, you'll make a profit out of it, seeing that you're buying it cheap.

VOZHEVATOV. It suits our book; we've got plenty of cargo waiting down river.

KNUROV. Was he short of cash? Everyone knows he's a spendthrift.

VOZHEVATOV. That's his business. We can pay him cash down.

KNUROV. Yes, there's nothing you can't do with money. *(Smiling.)* Life's sweet for a man with plenty of the ready, Vasily Danilych.

VOZHEVATOV. And what's wrong with that? I should think you're the last to object to that, Moki Parmenych.

KNUROV. Well said, Vasily Danilych, well said.

VOZHEVATOV. How about a drop of something cooling, Moki Parmenych?

KNUROV. What, this time in the morning? I haven't had breakfast yet.

VOZHEVATOV. It doesn't matter. An Englishman—factory manager he was— told me that you can't beat champagne on an empty stomach for a cold in the head. And it so happens I caught a bit of a chill yesterday.

KNUROV. How did you manage to do that? It's been so warm lately.

VOZHEVATOV. Well, you see it was the champagne I caught a chill from. They serve it very cold.

KNUROV. No we'd better not; people will notice and say: the sun's hardly up and they're drinking champagne.

VOZHEVATOV. Well, just to make sure people don't say anything to our detriment, we'll drink tea.

KNUROV. Tea, that's a different matter.

VOZHEVATOV *(to Gavrilo)*. Gavrilo, bring us my special tea, you understand? My *special!*

GAVRILO. Yes, sir. *(Goes out).*

KNUROV. Don't tell me you drink a special kind.

VOZHEVATOV. Oh it's the same old champagne, only they pour it from a teapot and give us glasses with saucers.

KNUROV. Ingenious.

VOZHEVATOV. Necessity is the mother of invention, Moki Parmenych.

KNUROV. Are you going to Paris for the exhibition?

VOZHEVATOV. When I've bought the boat and sent it to pick up the cargo down river, then I'll be off.

KNUROV. I'm off in a day or two myself, they're expecting me there.

Gavrilo brings in a tray with two teapots of champagne and two glasses.

VOZHEVATOV *(pouring)*. Have you heard the news, Moki Parmenych? Larisa Dmitryevna is getting married.

KNUROV. Getting married! Are you serious? Who's the man?

VOZHEVATOV. Karandyshev.

KNUROV. Never heard such nonsense! What can have come over her? I ask you—Karandyshev! Now is he a match for her, Vasily Danilych?

VOZHEVATOV. No one says he is. But what else can she do, where is she to find a husband? Don't forget she has no dowry.

KNUROV. Even girls without dowries find good husbands.

VOZHEVATOV. Not these days. There used to be plenty of men looking for wives, enough to give the girls with no dowries a chance, but now there's not a man to spare; there are as many suitors as there are dowries; it's as simple as that. Do you think Kharita Ignatyevna would let Karandyshev have her if there were anyone better in the offing?

KNUROV. A woman of spirit.

VOZHEVATOV. She can't be Russian.

KNUROV. Why not?

VOZHEVATOV. She's so crafty.

KNUROV. How could she have made such a blunder? After all, the Ogudalovs are a decent family, and here she goes marrying her daughter to this Karandyshev— God knows where he comes from! And with those quick wits of hers—the house is always packed with bachelors.

VOZHEVATOV. Yes, they all go to her house because they have a good time there: a pretty young lady who sings and plays all kinds of instruments, a free and easy atmosphere—naturally they're drawn. But marriage, that's not something you jump into.

KNUROV. But she married off two of her girls.

VOZHEVATOV. Well yes, but I should doubt whether life has been exactly a bed of roses for either of them. The eldest was carried off by some mountain-dweller, one of those Caucasian princelings. A sight worth seeing that was, I can tell you! When he first set eyes on her he started trembling. Even burst into tears, and that's how he stood at her side for two weeks, hand on dagger and eyes flashing in case someone should try to come anywhere near her. He married her and they left, but I heard that they didn't even get as far as the Caucasus; he slit her throat on the way out of jealousy. The other one married some foreigner as well, except that afterwards he turned out not to be a foreigner at all, but just a cardsharp.

KNUROV. Ogudalova's strategy is sensible enough: she doesn't have much money, nothing to provide a dowry with, and so she keeps open house, receives everyone.

VOZHEVATOV. And she likes to have a good time herself. But her means are so limited that they're not even sufficient for that kind of life.

KNUROV. So where does she get money from?

VOZHEVATOV. The suitors pay for themselves. If the daughter takes your fancy, then dig in your purse. She'll ask the prospective husband to provide a dowry himself, and even then he won't get it!

KNUROV. It wouldn't surprise me to hear that the suitors are not the only ones who pay their way, and that your own frequent visits cost you a pretty penny.

VOZHEVATOV. I won't go bankrupt, Moki Parmenych. There's nothing to be done about it! Pleasure has to be paid for, and to spend an evening at their house is a great pleasure.

KNUROV. It is a pleasure, I won't deny it.

VOZHEVATOV. But you hardly ever go there yourself.

KNUROV. Well, it's awkward, you know. You get all sorts of riffraff there; then you run into them later and they pester you with their "good days" and idle chatter. Take Karandyshev, for example, am I really expected to know such a person?

VOZHEVATOV. Yes, their place does have something of the bazaar about it.

KNUROV. And what's the point? One badgers Larisa Dmitryevna with compliments, another with sweet nothings—such a buzz they keep up that you don't get a chance to say a word to her. It would be nice to see more of her alone, without anyone butting in.

VOZHEVATOV. You'd have to marry her for that.

KNUROV. Marry! Not everyone can do that, and not everyone wants to either. Take me, for example, I'm married.

VOZHEVATOV. Then there's nothing to be done. The grapes are fine, Moki Parmenych, but still green.

KNUROV. Is that your opinion?

VOZHEVATOV. You can see for yourself. That's not the kind of people they are, there's been temptation enough and she hasn't strayed from the straight and narrow—no, it has to be marriage, even if it's to a Karandyshev.

KNUROV. It would be nice, though, to take a little trip to Paris for the Exhibition with a young lady like that.

VOZHEVATOV. Yes, you certainly wouldn't be bored, and you'd come back refreshed. So these are the sort of schemes you've been hatching, Moki Parmenych!

KNUROV. Don't tell me that you haven't had similar schemes yourself?

VOZHEVATOV. What, me? I'm too much of a simpleton for such things. I don't have any boldness with women. It's the way I was brought up, you see—very moral and patriarchal.

KNUROV. Don't expect me to believe that! Your chances are better than mine; youth—that counts. And you won't be stingy with cash either—you're getting a boat cheap, so you can dip into the profits. I shouldn't think you'd get away with less than the *Swallow* cost you.

VOZHEVATOV. Everything has its price, Moki Parmenych. I may be young, but I won't get carried away and spend more than I need to.

KNUROV. I wouldn't wager in that. It doesn't take much to fall in love at your age. And where are calculations then?

VOZHEVATOV. No, Moki Parmenych, somehow that's a thing I haven't observed in myself at all.

KNUROV. What's that?

VOZHEVATOV. The thing people call love.

KNUROV. Very praiseworthy, you'll make an excellent merchant. All the same, you're much closer to her than the others.

VOZHEVATOV. But what's in this closeness? I sometimes pour her a glass of champagne when her mother's not looking, teach her a song or two, smuggle in novels young ladies aren't supposed to read.

KNUROV. So you're doing a bit of corrupting.

VOZHEVATOV. I'm not forcing anything on her, am I? Why should I worry myself about her morals? I'm not her guardian.

KNUROV. I still can't get over it. Surely Larisa Dmitryevna had other suitors than Karandyshev?

VOZHEVATOV. Yes, but she's rather a simple sort of girl, you know.

KNUROV. What do you mean "rather simple"? Stupid—is that what you're trying to say?

VOZHEVATOV. No, not stupid, but there's no cunning in her—not like her mother at all. The one's all tricks and flattery, while the other will suddenly, for no reason at all, blurt out the very thing she ought to keep to herself.

KNUROV. The truth, you mean.

VOZHEVATOV. Yes, the truth—and girls with no dowries can't go behaving like that. If she feels warmly toward someone she doesn't make the least attempt to hide it. Take Sergei Sergeyich Paratov. He came on the scene last year, and she couldn't take her eyes off him; and for two months he was in constant attendance, he drove away all the other suitors—and then one day he disappeared, just like that, without a trace.

KNUROV. Why did he do it?

VOZHEVATOV. Who's to say? He's an odd character. But she was so much in love with him she almost died of grief. What a sentimental creature she is! (*Laughs.*) She ran away to find him, but mama got to the station in time to bring her back.

KNUROV. And were there any suitors after Paratov?

VOZHEVATOV. A couple came running up: some gouty old man, and the steward of some princely estate who'd made his pile—you never saw him sober. Larisa had no time for either of them, but she had to be polite—mama's orders.

KNUROV. Her situation isn't enviable.

VOZHEVATOV. Yes, though it was funny in a way. Sometimes she'd go about with tears in her eyes—you could tell she wanted to have a good cry—but mama had commanded her to smile. And then this cashier turns up... starts throwing his money about, showers Kharita Ignatyevna with presents. He soon had the field to himself, but he wasn't cock-a-hoop for long. The police came and arrested him in their house. There's a fine scandal for you! *(Laughs.)* The Ogudalovs couldn't show their faces anywhere for a month. That was the last straw, and Larisa told her mother straight out: "We've been humiliated enough," she says, "and I'll marry the first man who asks for my hand, be he rich or poor." And there was Karandyshev right on hand with his proposal.

KNUROV. Where did this Karandyshev spring from?

VOZHEVATOV. He's been hanging round their place a long time, three years or more. They didn't quite chase him away, but they didn't show him much respect either. When things were quiet and there were no rich suitors in the offing, they used to keep him on a string, invite him round now and then so that the house wouldn't be completely empty. And whenever someone with money did turn up, you couldn't help feeling sorry for Karandyshev; nobody gave him a word or glance. And he would just sit there in a corner trying out various roles, darting wild glances, making out he was in despair. Once he tried to shoot himself, but nothing came of it—he just made everyone laugh. Oh, and another funny thing: one evening they had a fancy dress party—that was when Paratov was still around—so Karandyshev dressed up as a brigand, and went round swinging an axe and glaring at everyone, and at Sergei Sergeyich in particular.

KNUROV. So what happened?

VOZHEVATOV. They took the axe away and ordered him to change his costume—or out you go, that's what they said!

KNUROV. His constancy has been rewarded then. He must be a happy man.

VOZHEVATOV. Happy isn't the word—he glows like an orange. What a laugh! He's a queer fish and no mistake. He'd be well advised to get the marriage over as soon as possible, and lie low on his estate, such as it is, until the talk dies down—that's what the Ogudalovs want—but he drags Larisa out on the promenade, walks her about on his arm holding his head so high that he'll walk into someone if he's not careful. And another thing, he's started wearing spectacles, and he never used to wear them. When he bows it's hardly more than a nod; and the way he conducts himself! Before you'd hardly hear a peep out of him, but now it's I, I all the time, I want this, I want that.

KNUROV. Like a Russian peasant: just being drunk isn't enough for him, he has to smash a few things so that everyone can see it; he has to play the fool and collect a couple of beatings and that's it—he's happy and can go home to bed.

VOZHEVATOV. Yes, it seems that's going to happen to Karandyshev sooner or later.

KNUROV. Poor girl! How she must suffer just looking at him.

VOZHEVATOV. He's taken it into his head to redecorate his lodgings—

funny ideas he has. He's nailed a cheap carpet to the wall of his study, and on top of it he's hung up daggers and pistols made in Tula. You'd think he was a great hunter or something, but he's never even had a gun in his hands. He drags you back with him just to show you; and if you don't praise everything he gets offended; a vain, envious sort of fellow he is. He's had a horse sent from his village, a sorry looking nag; his coachman's practically a midget and wears a uniform made for someone twice his size. And he uses this wretched camel to take Larisa Dmitryevna around—and sits there so proudly you'd think he was being drawn by a thousand racers. He comes off the promenade and you should hear him yell to the constable, "Order my carriage to be brought up!" Well, and fine music it makes when it does roll up: every nut and bolt in it rattles out a different tune, and the springs shake like live things.

KNUROV. I can't help feeling sorry for poor Larisa Dmitryevna.

VOZHEVATOV. You're very tender-hearted this morning.

KNUROV. Can't you see that the girl was born for luxury? A precious diamond calls for a precious setting.

VOZHEVATOV. And a good jeweller.

KNUROV. You're absolutely right. A jeweller isn't just a craftsman—he must be an artist as well. Living in poverty, and with a fool of a husband into the bargain, she'll either be destroyed or sink to the common level.

VOZHEVATOV. In my opinion she'll leave him before long. At the moment it's as if all the life had gone out of her—but just you wait, she'll recover her old spirit, and then she'll take a closer look at the husband and see what manner of man he is. (Softly.) Here they are, talk of the devil.

Enter Karandyshev, Ogudalova, Larisa. Vozhevatov rises and bows. Knurov takes out his newspaper.

Scene 3

Knurov, Vozhevatov, Karandyshev, Ogudalova; Larisa sits down on a bench back-stage by the balustrade and looks out over the Volga through binoculars; Gavrilo, Ivan.

OGUDALOVA (going over to the table). Good morning, gentlemen!

Karandyshev follows her over. Vozhevatov shakes hands with Ogudalova and Karandyshev. Knurov, without a word and not getting up from his seat, gives Ogudalova his hand, nods slightly in Karandyshev's direction and buries himself in his newspaper.

VOZHEVATOV. Do sit down, Kharita Ignatyevna! (Brings up a chair.)

Ogudalova sits down.

Would you care for some tea?

Karandyshev sits down some distance away.

OGUDALOVA. Yes, I wouldn't mind a cup.

VOZHEVATOV. Ivan, bring us a cup, and some hot water.

KARANDYSHEV. What a peculiar whim to drink tea at this hour. I'm surprised at you.

VOZHEVATOV. Thirst torments me, Yuly Kapitonych, and I don't know what to drink. I'd be very grateful for your advice on the matter.

KARANDYSHEV *(looking at his watch).* It's noon now—you could down a glass of vodka, put away a cutlet and top it off with a glass of wine. That's the sort of breakfast I always have.

VOZHEVATOV *(to Ogudalova).* That's the way to live, Kharita Ignatyevna—I'm simply envious. *(To Karandyshev.)* I wouldn't mind being in your shoes, just for a day even. Vodka and wine! The likes of us can't carry on like that, we'd go out of our minds. You can do as you please. You won't squander your capital because you don't have any, but as for us, such is our bitter lot in this world, we have extremely important matters to take care of, and so we can't afford to go out of our minds.

Ivan brings in a teapot and a cup.

Here you are, Kharita Ignatyevna! *(Pours a cup and gives it to her.)* I drink my tea cold so that people won't go about saying I'm addicted to hot beverages.

OGUDALOVA. It is cold, but you've poured it a bit strong for me, Vasya.

VOZHEVATOV. Never mind. Drink it up, just for me! It'll do you no harm in the open air.

KARANDYSHEV *(to Ivan).* You there—you can come and serve dinner for me this evening!

IVAN. Yes sir, Yuly Kapitonych.

KARANDYSHEV. And put on something a bit cleaner, my good fellow!

IVAN. It'll be tails of course, sir. We know our business!

KARANDYSHEV. I say, Vasily Danilych, come and dine with me this evening!

VOZHEVATOV. I'm much obliged to you for the invitation. Am I ordered to come in tails as well?

KARANDYSHEV. As you please; don't feel constrained. Ladies will be present, though.

VOZHEVATOV *(bowing).* I obey. I hope I won't disgrace myself.

KARANDYSHEV *(goes over to Knurov).* Moki Parmenych, would you care to have dinner at my place this evening?

KNUROV *(looking him up and down with amazement).* At your place?

OGUDALOVA. Moki Parmenych, it's just the same as if it were at our house—the dinner's in Larisa's honor.

KNUROV. So, you in fact are inviting me? Very well, I'll come.

KARANDYSHEV. So, we shall expect you?

KNUROV. I've said I'll come, haven't I? *(Returns to his paper.)*

OGUDALOVA. Yuly Kapitonych is my future son-in-law, I'm giving him Larisa's hand in marriage.

KNUROV (continuing to read). That's your affair.

KARANDYSHEV. Yes, Moki Parmenych, I've decided to take the risk. Generally speaking, I've always been above prejudice.

Knurov disappears completely behind his newspaper.

VOZHEVATOV (to Ogudalova). Moki Parmenych is a hard man.

KARANDYSHEV (leaving Knurov and going over to Vozhevatov). I wish Larisa Dmitryevna to be surrounded only by the most select people.

VOZHEVATOV. You mean I belong to the select few? Thank you, I'm over-whelmed. (To Gavrilo.) Gavrilo, how much do I owe you for the tea?

GAVRILO. Two portions wasn't it, sir?

VOZHEVATOV. Yes, two portions.

GAVRILO. Well, you know yourself, Vasily Danilych, I mean you've ordered it before. It'll be thirteen rubles, sir.

VOZHEVATOV. Hm, I thought the price had gone down.

GAVRILO. How could it have, sir? Exchange rates, import duties, you know how it is, sir.

VOZHEVATOV. I'm not arguing with you. What are you pestering me for? Take your money and leave me in peace! (Gives him money.)

KARANDYSHEV. How come it's so expensive? I don't understand.

GAVRILO. For some it's expensive, for some it's not. Tea like that isn't for you.

OGUDALOVA (to Karandyshev). Oh, do be quiet and stop poking your nose in other people's affairs!

IVAN. Vasily Danilych, the *Swallow's* putting in.

VOZHEVATOV. The *Swallow's* arrived, Moki Parmenych. Would you care to have a look at her? We won't go down—we can get a good view from the hill.

KNUROV. Let's go then. I'd like to see what she looks like. (Gets up.)

OGUDALOVA. Vasya, I'll use your horse to go back.

VOZHEVATOV. Do, by all means—but send it back straight away! (Goes over to Larisa and talks to her quietly.)

OGUDALOVA (goes over to Knurov). Moki Parmenych, we've got this wedding on our hands, you wouldn't believe the fuss and bother.

KNUROV. Yes....

OGUDALOVA. And all at once there are expenses one never dreamed of. It's Larisa's birthday tomorrow. I would have liked to have given her something.

KNUROV. All right. I'll come round later. (Ogudalova goes out.)

LARISA (to Vozhevatov). Good-bye, Vasya! (Vozhevatov and Knurov go out. Larisa goes over to Karandyshev.)

Scene 4

Karandyshev and Larisa.

LARISA. I was looking across the Volga just now. Everything looks so beautiful on the far side! Let's leave for the country soon.

KARANDYSHEV. You were looking across the river, you say. And what was
Vozhevatov talking to you about?

LARISA. Oh, what business is it of yours, whatever it was!

KARANDYSHEV. Vasya you call him. You seem very familiar with this
young man!

LARISA. We've known each other since we were children; we used to play
together when we were little—and, well, I've got into the habit of calling him that.

KARANDYSHEV. You have to get rid of some of these old habits of yours.
How can you conduct yourself so freely with a stupid empty-headed boy? You
can't expect me to put up with the goings-on in that house of yours.

LARISA. We haven't done anything to be ashamed of.

KARANDYSHEV. It was no better than a gypsy camp. (*Larisa brushes away a
tear.*) Now what are you getting upset about?

LARISA. Perhaps it was a gypsy camp, but at least we had some happy times
there. Will you be able to give me anything better?

KARANDYSHEV. Of course I will.

LARISA. Why are you always reproaching me with it? Do you think I was
happy leading such a life? Mama wanted me to, so I did, like it or not, that was
the sort of life I was forced to live. To throw my past life in my face is either
stupid or cruel. Why should I have accepted you if I wasn't looking for solitude
and quiet, if I didn't want to get away from people. So please understand that,
and don't imagine that I've been won by any merits you may have—I have yet to
see what they are. I *want* to love you, yes, but it's the thought of a quiet family
life that really attracts me—such a life seems like heaven to me at the moment.
I've come to some kind of crossroads in my life; I need your support, your
approval, your sympathy; show me some kindness, some tenderness! Snatch
these moments, don't let them go!

KARANDYSHEV. Larisa Dmitryevna, I didn't mean to upset you, it just
slipped out.

LARISA. "Just slipped out"—do you know what you're saying? In other words
you didn't think. You didn't understand that your words might wound me, is
that it?

KARANDYSHEV. Of course, I had no intention...

LARISA. That's even worse. You should think just what it is you're saying.
Talk nonsense with other people if you like, but when you're speaking to me, be
careful! I feel every word that I speak myself and every word that is spoken to
me. I've become very acute, very sensitive.

KARANDYSHEV. In that case I beg you to forgive me.

LARISA. Never mind this time, but in the future please be more careful!
(*Thoughtfully.*) A gypsy camp.... Yes, I suppose that's true, but all the same some
of the gypsies in it were good, noble people.

KARANDYSHEV. And who were these noble people? Sergei Sergeyich Paratov wasn't one of them by any chance?

LARISA. No, you mustn't speak of him, I beg of you!

KARANDYSHEV. And why not, may I ask?

LARISA. You don't know him, and even if you did.... Forgive me, but it's not for you to pass judgment on him.

KARANDYSHEV. People are judged by their deeds. Can you say he behaved well toward you?

LARISA. That concerns me alone. If I don't venture to judge him, I won't allow you to either.

KARANDYSHEV. Larisa Dmitryevna, will you tell me something? Only I beg you, speak frankly!

LARISA. What is it?

KARANDYSHEV. In what way am I inferior to Paratov?

LARISA. Oh no, please don't ask me such things.

KARANDYSHEV. But why not?

LARISA. You mustn't, you mustn't ask me. What's the use of such comparisons?

KARANDYSHEV. But I'd be interested to hear what you think.

LARISA. Don't ask me, please don't.

KARANDYSHEV. But why not?

LARISA. Because the comparison won't be to your advantage. You're well enough in yourself, you're decent and honest—but beside Sergei Sergeyich you're nothing.

KARANDYSHEV. Those are just words. What's needed is proof! Examine us point by point.

LARISA. Do you know who you're trying to put yourself on a level with? How can anyone be so blind? Sergei Sergeyich is the perfect ideal of manhood. Do you understand what that means—ideal? I may be mistaken. I'm young. I still don't really understand people; but no one will ever make me change my opinion, not as long as I live!

KARANDYSHEV. I don't understand, I simply don't understand what's so special about him; I can't see anything in him, anything at all. A certain boldness, if you like, insolence....

LARISA. But do you know what his kind of boldness is like?

KARANDYSHEV. How do you mean "what it's like"? What's so remarkable about it? It's just an act, that's all.

LARISA. Well, I'll give you an example of it. A certain officer from the Caucasus, an acquaintance of Sergei Sergeyich's happened to be passing through town and came to see us. So Sergei Sergeyich says, "I hear you're a good shot." "Yes, not bad," says the officer. Sergei Sergeyich hands him a pistol, puts a glass on his own head and goes to the other end of the room. "Go ahead—he says—fire!"

KARANDYSHEV. And did he?

LARISA. Yes, and of course he shattered the glass—he went a bit pale though. Sergei Sergeyich says, "You're a fine shot all right, but you turned pale firing at a man who didn't mean very much to you. Watch me: I'll fire at a girl who is dearer to me than all the world, and I won't turn pale." He gave me a coin to hold and calm as you please, a smile on his face, fires from the same distance and hits it.

KARANDYSHEV. And you did as he said?

LARISA. How could I do anything else?

KARANDYSHEV. And weren't you afraid?

LARISA. Afraid! How could I be afraid with him?

KARANDYSHEV. He's heartless, that's why he's so bold.

LARISA. No, he does have a heart. I've seen him with my own eyes helping the poor, giving them all the money he had on him.

KARANDYSHEV. All right, let's suppose that Paratov does have certain good qualities, in your eyes at least; but what sort of a man is this merchant cub Vozhevatov, this Vasya of yours?

LARISA. Surely you're not jealous of him, are you? Really you ought to put such silly ideas out of your head. It's vulgar, and I can't stand that. I'm warning you in advance. Don't worry—I'm not in love with anyone, and don't intend to be.

KARANDYSHEV. And if Paratov were to appear?

LARISA. It goes without saying that if Sergei Sergeyich came back and if he were free, one glance from him would be enough.... Set your mind at rest, he hasn't appeared, and even if he did, it would be too late. I don't suppose we'll ever see each other again. (*From the river comes the sound of a cannon firing.*) What's that?

KARANDYSHEV. Some pigheaded merchant is disembarking from his barge, so they're firing a salute in his honor.

LARISA. It gave me such a fright.

KARANDYSHEV. Now why, I ask you!

LARISA. My nerves have gone to pieces. I looked down from this bench just now and my head began to spin. Would you hurt yourself very badly if you fell here?

KARANDYSHEV. Hurt yourself! It would be certain death—there are rocks down there. Anyway, it's such a drop that you'd be dead before you reached the ground.

LARISA. Let's go home, it's time we did.

KARANDYSHEV. Yes, and I have a dinner to arrange.

LARISA (*going to the balustrade*). Wait a moment. (*She looks down.*) Oh, oh! Don't let me fall!

KARANDYSHEV (*taking Larisa by the arm*). What childishness, let's go! (*They go out.*)

Gavrilo and Ivan enter from the cafe.

Scene 5

Gavrilo and Ivan.

IVAN. Did you hear that cannon? Our gentleman's arrived. Sergei Sergeyich has arrived!

GAVRILO. I said it was him. You can't fool me—I can tell a hawk by its flight.

IVAN. The carriage is coming up empty, that means the gentlemen are going on foot. There they are! *(Runs into the cafe.)*

GAVRILO. They're right welcome. Though Lord knows what we can give 'em.

Enter Paratov, wearing a single-breasted close-fitting overcoat, high lacquered boots and white yachting cap, and a traveling bag over one shoulder; Robinson, wearing a cape, the right flap of which is flung over his left shoulder, and a tall soft hat, which is perched on his head at a rakish angle; Knurov; Vozhevatov; Ivan comes running out of the cafe with a brush and rushes forward to brush Paratov down.

Scene 6

Paratov, Robinson, Knurov, Vozhevatov, Gavrilo, Ivan.

PARATOV *(to Ivan)*. Hey, what d'you think you're up to? I've just been on the river; the Volga's not dusty you know.

IVAN. All the same, sir, I must... it's the proper thing. We haven't seen you for a whole year, and do you think we'd.... Welcome back, sir.

PARATOV. Well, thank you. Here! *(Gives him a ruble note.)*

IVAN. We humbly thank you, sir. *(Goes off.)*

PARATOV. So you were expecting me to come on the *Flying Wonder*, Vasily Danilych.

VOZHEVATOV. Well, how was I to know you'd come flying in on our *Swallow*? I thought she always accompanied the barges.

PARATOV. Not now. I've sold them. I was intending to arrive early this morning. I wanted to race the *Wonder*; the trouble is my engineer's a coward. I keep shouting to the stokers, "Fill her up!", but he keeps stopping them. Then he pops up out of his hole: "If you throw on one more log—he says—I'm jumping overboard." He was afraid the boiler was going to burst—scribbled some figures or other for me on a piece of paper, calculating the pressure. He's a foreigner, a Dutchman, no spunk in him; with them arithmetic takes the place of a soul. But I'm forgetting to introduce my friend, gentlemen. Moki Parmenych, Vasily Danilych, allow me to present—Robinson. *(Robinson solemnly exchanges bows and shakes hands with Knurov and Vozhevatov.)*

VOZHEVATOV. What's his Christian name and patronymic?

ROBINSON. Just call me Robinson, I'll do without the rest. *(To Paratov.)* Serge!

PARATOV. What's up?

ROBINSON. It's twelve o'clock and I'm suffering.

PARATOV. Patience—we'll soon be at the hotel.

ROBINSON (indicating the cafe). Voilà!

PARATOV. Well off with you then—and may the Devil take you. (Robinson walks toward the cafe.) Gavrilo, don't on any account let this gentleman have more than one glass; he's an awkward customer.

ROBINSON (shrugging his shoulders). Serge! (Goes into the cafe. Gavrilo fol - lows him.)

PARATOV. That, gentlemen, is a provincial actor, Arkadi Shchastlivtsev by name.

VOZHEVATOV. Why does he call himself Robinson then?

PARATOV. I'll tell you; he was traveling on board some steamer—I don't know which one—in the company of his friend Neputyovy, a merchant's son. It goes without saying that they were both drunk, utterly and helplessly. They just did whatever came into their heads, and for a long time the rest of the passengers put up with it. As a final outrage they decided to put on a dramatic performance: they took their clothes off, ripped open a cushion, rolled about in the feathers and started to play at being savages; in the end the captain, at the passengers' request, put them off on a deserted island. We're racing by this island. I look—someone's waving both his hands at us at once. I give the order to stop, get into a life-boat and come upon my actor. I took him aboard, fitted him out from head to foot with my own clothes—fortunately I've got plenty to spare. I have a weakness for actors, gentlemen. And that's how he came to be called Robinson.

VOZHEVATOV. And Neputyovy—you left him behind?

PARATOV. What good is he to me? Let him cool his heels a bit. You know how it is, gentlemen—traveling's such a deadly bore, one's glad of any company one can get.

KNUROV. Quite so, quite so.

VOZHEVATOV. What a bit of luck! What a find!

KNUROV. The only drawback seems to be that he can't keep away from the drink.

PARATOV. Oh, he'll keep away from it while he's with me, gentlemen; that's something I won't put up with. He doesn't have a bean and I'm careful to keep him short of cash—when he asks me for some I shove a French conversation book into his hands—by luck I happened to have one with me: "First be so good as to learn a page of this, or else you'll get nothing." And so he sits down and learns it. A diligent student!

VOZHEVATOV. Is that the way you treat your luck, Sergei Sergeyich? You'd think such a man could be refused nothing. Is he a good actor?

PARATOV. Good Lord, no! He's had a try at every sort of role in the repertoire and been a prompter as well; these days he performs in operettas. He's all right—he keeps me amused.

VOZHEVATOV. He's a cheerful type then?

PARATOV. A fellow of infinite jest.

VOZHEVATOV. And can he take a joke against himself?

PARATOV. Oh yes, he takes no offense. If you want to forget your worries for a bit I can let you have him for a day or two.

VOZHEVATOV. That's very kind of you. If I take a fancy to him he won't lose by it.

KNUROV. Aren't you sorry to be selling the *Swallow*, Sergei Sergeyich?

PARATOV. "Sorry" isn't a word in my vocabulary. There's nothing I can't do without, Moki Parmenych; I'll sell anything you like if I find it profitable to do so. My concerns lie elsewhere these days, gentlemen. I'm marrying a girl from a very rich family—she'll bring me gold fields as her dowry.

VOZHEVATOV. A fine dowry.

PARATOV. My future father-in-law is a bigwig in the civil service—a miserable old brute, he won't hear of gypsies, sprees and suchlike; he even disapproves of people who smoke too much. It's put on your tails and *parlez français!* That's why I'm practicing with Robinson. For some reason—perhaps he thinks it sounds more impressive—he calls me "La Serge", not just Serge.. He's a scream! (*Robinson appears in the doorway of the cafe; he is chewing something; Gavrilo follows him.*)

Scene 7

Paratov, Knurov, Vozhevatov, Robinson, Gavrilo, Ivan.

PARATOV (*to Robinson*). *Que faites-vous là? Venez!*

ROBINSON (*with dignity*). *Comment?*

PARATOV. How utterly charming! What class, gentlemen! (*To Robinson.*) You must rid yourself of this disgusting habit of yours of abandoning decent society for taverns!

VOZHEVATOV. Yes, that is a habit he has.

ROBINSON. La Serge, you've gone and.... Why did you have to do that?

PARATOV. Yes, forgive me. I let them into the secret of your pseudonym.

VOZHEVATOV. We won't give you away, Robinson, old fellow—as far as we're concerned you're an Englishman.

ROBINSON. What, "Robinson, old fellow" straight away? I don't think we've drunk Bruderschaft together yet.

VOZHEVATOV. What's the difference? Why all this formality?

ROBINSON. I can't stand familiarity and I don't permit anyone to....

VOZHEVATOV. But I'm not anyone.

ROBINSON. Who are you then?

VOZHEVATOV. A merchant.

ROBINSON. Rich?

VOZHEVATOV. Rich.

ROBINSON. And generous?

VOZHEVATOV. And generous.

ROBINSON. Now, that's what I like. (*Offers Vozhevatov his hand.*) Delighted to make your acquaintance, old fellow. I permit you to be as free and easy with me as you like.

VOZHEVATOV. So we're friends then—two bodies with a single soul.

ROBINSON. And a single pocket. Christian name, patronymic? Your Christian name's enough though, we can do without the patronymic.

VOZHEVATOV. Vasily Danilych.

ROBINSON. Well then, Vasya, to celebrate our meeting you can pay my bill for me.

VOZHEVATOV. Let's have it. Gavrilo! Sergei Sergeyich, we're getting up a little outing on the river this evening—gypsy musicians in one launch and us in the other; when we get off we'll set ourselves down on a rug and brew ourselves some punch.

GAVRILO. And I've got two nice pineapples that have been sitting there waiting for you, Sergei Sergeyich; we'll cut them up in honor of your arrival.

PARATOV (to Gavrilo). Good, cut away! (To Vozhevatov.) I'm entirely at your disposal, gentlemen!

GAVRILO. Leave it to me, Vasily Danilych, I'll have everything ready! I even keep a silver saucepan for such occasions: and I'll let you have some of my people as well to look after you.

VOZHEVATOV. Good. Have everything ready by six; there'll be no penalty to pay if you pack more than we need; but if there's anything lacking—look out.

GAVRILO. We understand, sir.

VOZHEVATOV. And on the return trip we'll light different-colored lanterns on the launches.

ROBINSON. How long is it I've known him—and I'm quite fond of him already. There's a miracle for you, gentleman!

PARATOV. The main thing is to enjoy ourselves. I'm saying good-bye to bachelor life, and I want something to remember it by. You are invited to dine with me this evening, gentlemen.

VOZHEVATOV. How annoying! I'm afraid we can't make it, Sergei Sergeyich.

KNUROV. We're booked up.

PARATOV. Tell them you can't come.

VOZHEVATOV. No, we can't do that. Larisa Dmitryevna is getting married, and we're to dine at her fiancé's.

PARATOV. Larisa getting married! (Becoming thoughtful.) Ah, well.... It's her business! It's better this way really.... I haven't behaved as well as I might toward her, or rather I should say that I've behaved so badly that I shouldn't go within a mile of them; still, if she's getting married that means old scores are settled, and I can go and humbly kiss their hands—hers and Auntie's, that is. I call Kharita Ignatyevna "auntie" for short. I came very close to marrying Larisa, you know—that really would have made people laugh! Yes, I very nearly made a fool of myself. She's getting married.... Nice of her, I must say; still it does take a weight off my mind.... God grant her health and happiness! I'll pay them a visit, yes I will; it would be interesting to see how she is, very interesting.

VOZHEVATOV. Then I should think they'll invite you along too.

PARATOV. Of course, how could they manage without me!

KNUROV. I'm delighted—at least there'll be someone at table I can talk to.

VOZHEVATOV. In the meantime perhaps we'll be able to think up a few ideas for making the time pass more enjoyably.

PARATOV. Yes, gentlemen, life is short, the philosophers tell us, so we must make the best use of it we can. *N'est-ce pas,* Robinson?

ROBINSON. *Oui,* La Serge.

VOZHEVATOV. We'll do our best: you won't be bored—that we can guarantee. We'll get hold of a third launch and have a brass band playing on it.

PARATOV. Good-bye then, gentlemen! I'm off to my hotel. Robinson—quick march!

ROBINSON *(raising his hat).* Let joy abound! Let Bacchus reign!

ACT II

A room in Ogudalova's house; there are two doors: the first—through which people enter—at the back, the other to the left; to the right is a window; the room is hand - somely furnished and contains a piano, on top of which lies a guitar.

Scene 1

Ogudalova alone. She goes over to the door left holding a jewel box.

OGUDALOVA. Larisa! Larisa! *(Larisa offstage: "I'm dressing, mama!")* Just look at the present Vasya's brought you! *(Larisa offstage: "I'll look at it later!")* What lovely things—five hundred rubles they must have cost. "Leave it in her room early tomorrow morning—he says—and don't tell her who it's from." As if the scamp didn't know that I'd simply have to tell you. I asked him to sit down for a bit, but he couldn't stay, he's taking some foreigner about, showing him the town. But he's such a joker—you never know whether he's serious or just putting you on. "This foreign gentleman has to be shown all our famous drinking establishments"— that's what he said. He wants to bring him here too. *(Glancing out the window.)* And here's Moki Parmenych! Stay there, I'd better have a word with him alone.

Enter Knurov.

Scene 2

Ogudalova and Knurov.

KNUROV *(in the doorway)*. Anyone else there?
OGUDALOVA. Nobody, Moki Parmenych.
KNUROV. Good, that suits me fine.
OGUDALOVA. I can't tell you how happy I am to see you! It's terribly good of you to come, Moki Parmenych. Really I'm all of a dither... I don't know where to put you.
KNUROV. Don't worry. I'll find a seat myself. *(Sits down.)*
OGUDALOVA. You must excuse Larisa, she's just changing. I'll tell her to hurry up.
KNUROV. No, why disturb her?
OGUDALOVA. To what do we owe the honor?
KNUROV. You know I like to have a stroll before dinner, so, well, I just thought I'd drop by.
OGUDALOVA. I can assure you, Moki Parmenych, that you make us very happy; I simply can't find words to express it.
KNUROV. So you're giving Larisa Dmitryevna away?

OGUDALOVA. Yes, Moki Parmenych, I am.

KNUROV. So you found someone who'd take her without a dowry then.

OGUDALOVA. That goes without saying, Moki Parmenych. Where should I get money from for a dowry?

KNUROV. And this suitor of yours—does he have means?

OGUDALOVA. Means! He's as poor as a church mouse.

KNUROV. I see. And do you think you're acting wisely giving Larisa Dmitryevna to a poor man.

OGUDALOVA. I'm sure I don't know, Moki Parmenych. It's her decision entirely.

KNUROV. Well, and this young man—what about him? Is he acting wisely in your opinion?

OGUDALOVA. Well, I suppose he's behaving admirably.

KNUROV. Admirably! I can't see anything to admire. Of course he's no fool if you look at it from his point of view. Who is he, after all? A nobody! And now the whole town's talking about him, he's worming his way into society—why, he even had the impertinence to invite me to dinner. But here's the rub—how is he going to support a wife like that? I'll wager he hasn't given it a thought. And that's what you and I ought to have a little talk about.

OGUDALOVA. By all means, Moki Parmenych!

KNUROV. What do you think of your daughter—what sort of girl is she?

OGUDALOVA. Well I really don't know what to say; all I can do now is to listen to you.

KNUROV. Larisa Dmitryevna doesn't have anything down-to-earth about her—she doesn't cope easily with day-to-day life... how shall I put it? She doesn't have the pettiness to scrimp and scrape.

OGUDALOVA. No she doesn't, you're right.

KNUROV. Why, she's an ethereal being then.

OGUDALOVA. Ethereal, Moki Parmenych!

KNUROV. She's made for glitter!

OGUDALOVA. For glitter, Moki Parmenych!

KNUROV. Well, and this Karandyshev of yours—can he provide her with it?

OGUDALOVA. Heavens, no!

KNUROV. She won't be able to stand a poverty-stricken existence in a small town. What's in store for her? She'll fade away and finish up with consumption the way they all do.

OGUDALOVA. What are you saying, what are you saying! God forbid!

KNUROV. It'll be a good thing if she has the sense to leave her husband and return to you.

OGUDALOVA. But that would be a misfortune, Moki Parmenych; what would we live on, the two of us?

KNUROV. Well it needn't be such a misfortune, you know. The protection of a rich and powerful man....

OGUDALOVA. How wonderful if such a protector could be found.

KNUROV. It depends on you. In situations like these it's essential to have a friend, someone respectable and trustworthy.

OGUDALOVA. Oh you're right, it is essential.

KNUROV. You may very well say to me, she hasn't even got married yet and it'll be a long time before she and her husband part. Well, perhaps it will be a long time—who knows?—but, on the other hand, it may be quite soon. So I thought it not inadvisable to let you know, in case you should think of taking some unfortunate step, that there is no sacrifice I am not willing to make for Larisa Dmitryevna's sake. Why do you smile?

OGUDALOVA. I'm so happy that you're well disposed toward us, Moki Parmenych.

KNUROV. Perhaps you're thinking that such offers are not made without ulterior motives?

OGUDALOVA. Oh, Moki Parmenych!

KNUROV. Take offense if you will, turn me out of your house!

OGUDALOVA (in confusion). Oh Moki Parmenych!

KNUROV. Find someone who will promise you tens of thousands with no thought of gain, and then abuse me. But I wouldn't give myself the trouble of looking if I were you—because you won't find anyone. But I'm getting away from the subject—I didn't come to talk about such matters. What's that box you have there?

OGUDALOVA. You see, Moki Parmenych, I was wanting to give my daughter a present.

KNUROV (examining the contents of the box). I see....

OGUDALOVA. But these things are so expensive, I can't afford them.

KNUROV (giving her back the box). Well, it's not worth worrying about; there are more important matters. You must order Larisa Dmitryevna a decent wardrobe—what am I saying, "decent"? I mean really first-class. A wedding dress and all the rest of it.

OGUDALOVA. Oh yes, Moki Parmenych. Of course.

KNUROV. I couldn't bear to see her wearing any old thing. Order from the best place in town and don't worry about the cost, don't penny-pinch! You can send the bills to me: I'll pay for everything.

OGUDALOVA. I simply can't find words to thank you.

KNUROV. That's what I came to see you about. (Rises.)

OGUDALOVA. But I so much wanted to give my daughter a little surprise tomorrow. A mother's heart, you know....

KNUROV (picking up the box). Let's have a look. How much are they?

OGUDALOVA. What would you value them at, Moki Parmenych?

KNUROV. What's there to value? A mere bagatelle. Three hundred rubles, no more. (Takes money out of his wallet and gives it to Ogudalova.) Good-bye! I'm going to stroll about a bit more. I'm counting on a good dinner this evening. We'll see each other there. (Goes to the door.)

OGUDALOVA. Thank you so much for everything, Moki Parmenych—for everything! (Knurov goes out. Larisa enters holding a basket.)

Scene 3

Ogudalova. Larisa.

LARISA *(puts the basket down on the table and examines the box)*. Is that Vasya's present? Rather pretty. It's very nice of him.

OGUDALOVA. "Rather pretty!" Those things cost a lot of money. You don't seem very pleased.

LARISA. I can't say they give me any particular joy.

OGUDALOVA. Be sure to thank Vasya—just whisper "thank you" in his ear. And Knurov too.

LARISA. What am I supposed to be thanking Knurov for?

OGUDALOVA. Do as I tell you. I know what for.

LARISA. Oh mama, always these secrets and cunning tricks.

OGUDALOVA. "Cunning tricks" she says! You won't last long in this world without cunning, believe me.

LARISA *(takes up her guitar, sits down by the window and begins to sing)*. "O mother mine, O mother dear, Thy infant weeps—hast thou no tear?" Yuly Kapitonych wants to stand as a justice of the peace.

OGUDALOVA. What a splendid idea! In what district?

LARISA. Zabolotye.

OGUDALOVA. But good heavens, isn't that right in the middle of the forest? What on earth does he want to go and choose somewhere so remote for?

LARISA. There aren't so many candidates—so he'll stand a very good chance of getting elected.

OGUDALOVA. Well, I suppose it's all right—after all, people do live in these places.

LARISA. I don't care if it is in the forest—anything to get away from here.

OGUDALOVA. Yes, I suppose there is something to be said for living in the back of beyond—your Karandyshev will show up better there. I dare say he'll be the top man in the district; I'm sure you'll get used to him by and by.

LARISA. I like him perfectly well now—there's nothing wrong with him that I can see.

OGUDALOVA. Oh yes, the answer to the maiden's prayer.

LARISA. Of course, there are better men, I'm well aware of that.

OGUDALOVA. But we have to take what we can get and be grateful.

LARISA. The way I feel now, he'll do as well as anyone....

OGUDALOVA. Well, all I can say is that I'm pleased you like him—I thank heaven for it! It's not for me to speak ill of him in front of you—but there's no reason for us to keep up a front with each other either—you're not blind.

LARISA. Yes, I am, blind and numb, and I'm glad of it. For a long time now I've been going about in a sort of dream. Yes. I must go away, I must tear away from this place. I won't give Yuly Kapitonych a moment's peace until he agrees to go. Summer will be over soon, and I want to go for long walks in the forest picking berries and mushrooms.

OGUDALOVA. So that's what you got yourself a basket for. Now I understand. You should get one of those wide-brimmed straw hats, then you'll be a real shepherdess.

LARISA. I'll get a straw hat too. *(Sings).* "Ah tempt me not in vain...." It'll be peaceful there, quiet.

OGUDALOVA. Just you wait till September comes—it won't be so quiet then; the wind'll be moaning at your window.

LARISA. I won't mind that.

OGUDALOVA. You'll have the wolves to serenade you too.

LARISA. Whatever it's like it'll be better than here. At least my heart will be at rest.

OGUDALOVA. Don't think I'm trying to put you off. By all means go and rest your heart or whatever! But just bear in mind that Zabolotye isn't Italy. It's my duty to say that or you'll blame me afterwards and say I didn't warn you.

LARISA. Thank you.... But I don't care if it is wild and windy and miles from anywhere; after what I've been through here any quiet backwater will seem paradise. I can't understand why Yuly Kapitonych keeps putting off our departure.

OGUDALOVA. Do you think he feels like retiring to the country? He wants to cut a fine figure here. It's not surprising—an absolute nobody, and suddenly he has an entry into society.

LARISA *(sings).* "Ah tempt me not in vain...." How annoying, I just can't get the tune.... *(Looking out of the window.)* Ilya! Ilya! Come in a moment! I want to take some songs with me when I leave for the country—I'll play and sing to while away the time.

Scene 4

Ogudalova, Larisa. Ilya.

ILYA. Best wishes of the season! God grant you health and happiness! *(Puts his cap down on the chair by the door.)*

LARISA. Ilya, give me the tune of "Tempt me not in vain." I keep going wrong. *(Hands him the guitar.)*

ILYA. In a jiffy, miss! *(Takes the guitar and tunes it.)* It's a fine song; sounds best with three voices though—we need a tenor to take the second verse.... A real beauty that song is. But we've had a stroke of bad luck, real terrible luck.

OGUDALOVA. What was that?

ILYA. Well, we had this Anton who sang tenor.

OGUDALOVA. Yes, I remember him.

ILYA. Just the one tenor we had—all the rest are basses. And fine basses they are too! But the only tenor we had was Anton.

OGUDALOVA. Well then?

ILYA. He can't sing with us no more, and there ain't nothing we can do about it.

OGUDALOVA. Isn't he well?

ILYA. No, he's well, right as rain.

OGUDALOVA. What's the matter with him then?

ILYA. Bent right over he is, a walking corner, a regular letter "T"—two weeks he's been like it. What a bit of bad luck! It costs money these days to take on an extra singer—but how can we sing without a tenor? He goes to the quack, and the quack says, "It'll loosen up in a week or two, you'll be as straight as a rod." But it's now that we're needing him.

LARISA. For heaven's sake, sing!

ILYA. In a jiffy, miss. The second string needs tuning. Yes, what a cruel bit of luck! When you're singing in a choir you have to stand up and throw your chest out, but bent double he is.

OGUDALOVA. What brought it on?

ILYA. Foolishness, that's what.

OGUDALOVA. What foolishness?

ILYA. The sort of foolishness we're all liable to. I says to him, "Now don't you go overdoing it, Anton!"—but he don't savvy.

OGUDALOVA. Neither do we.

ILYA. Well it's like I said: he goes on a binge, I says to him, "Now you're overdoing it, Anton!"—but he don't savvy. What a terrible bit of bad luck! And these days you can't get a man for less than a hundred rubles—that's the plight we're in: we're expecting this here gent and Anton goes and gets hisself bent double. A fine upstanding gypsy he was too—and now just look at him! *(Sings in a bass voice.)* "Tempt me not.... *(A voice at the window: "Ilya, Ilya come here! Hurry up!")* "Why? What do you want?" *(Voice from the street: "You can't mean it!")* I don't have time now, miss—our gent's arrived! *(Puts down the guitar and picks up his cap.)*

OGUDALOVA. What gentleman is this?

ILYA. Oh such a fine gentleman—we've been waiting and waiting for him; a year we've been waiting—that's the sort he is! *(Goes out.)*

Scene 5

Ogudalova, Larisa.

OGUDALOVA. Who could it be? He must be rich, Larisa—a bachelor too I should think, if the gypsies are so pleased to see him. It's obvious he spends a lot of time with them. Oh, Larisa, are we letting a suitor slip through our fingers? Why were we in such a hurry?

LARISA. Oh, Mama, haven't I suffered enough? Haven't we been humiliated enough?

OGUDALOVA. Now aren't we being dramatic! Don't think you can frighten me with words like "humiliation," my girl! We're poor people—humiliation's our daily bread. It's better to experience while you're young, so that you can have a decent life afterwards.

LARISA. No, I can't, I can't—it's too painful.

OGUDALOVA. You don't get anything if you're not prepared to fight for it.

LARISA. You want me to put on a front, to lie.

OGUDALOVA. That's right—put on a front, lie as much as you like. Don't expect luck to run after you if you run away from it. *(Karandyshev enters.)*

Scene 6

Ogudalova, Larisa, Karandyshev.

OGUDALOVA. Yuly Kapitonych, here's Larisa getting all ready for the country. She's even got herself a basket to go mushrooming with.

LARISA. Yes, please let's leave soon—nothing would please me more.

KARANDYSHEV. What's all the hurry? I don't understand.

LARISA. I want to get away from here.

KARANDYSHEV *(vehemently)*. Who are you running away from? Who's on your heels? Or you're ashamed of me, is that it?

LARISA *(coldly)*. No, I'm not ashamed of you. You haven't given me any reason to be so far.

KARANDYSHEV. Then why run away, why hide yourself? Give me time to arrange things, to collect myself, to come down to earth! I'm content. I'm happy. Let me savor my happiness to the full.

OGUDALOVA. Let you show off, you mean.

KARANDYSHEV. Yes—show off, as you like. I won't deny it. I've had to put up with a great many affronts in my life, my pride has been wounded on more than one occasion; and now I want to boast and show off a bit—as I have every right to do.

LARISA. When do you propose to leave town then?

KARANDYSHEV. Once the wedding's over—any time you like, the very next day if you wish. But I insist that the ceremony be held here, so that people have no reason to say that we're skulking because you married beneath you, and that I'm just a straw you clutched at as you were drowning.

LARISA. There's a good deal in that last remark of yours, Yuly Kapitonych, and that's the truth.

KARANDYSHEV *(angrily)*. Well, it's true I'll ask you to keep to yourself! *(Tearfully.)* For God's sake, have some pity on me! At least let other people think that you really love me, that you accepted me willingly.

LARISA. What for?

KARANDYSHEV. How can you ask that? Can't you understand that a man has his pride?

LARISA. Pride! You only think about yourself! Everyone loves only himself! When is someone going to show me some love? You don't know what you're driving me to!

OGUDALOVA. That's enough, Larisa, what's the matter with you?

LARISA. Mama, I'm afraid, I'm afraid something's going to happen, just listen to me; if the wedding must be held here, then let it be a quiet one with as few people as possible.

OGUDALOVA. Now I don't want to hear any more such nonsense! Either a proper wedding or none at all! I am Ogudalova, and penny-pinching isn't my style. You'll outshine any bride that's even been seen in this town, I'll see to that!

KARANDYSHEV. Yes, I too shall spare no expense.

LARISA. Well, I won't say any more. I see that for you I'm just a doll; you'll play with me a bit, break me in pieces and throw me away.

KARANDYSHEV. The dinner I'm giving today is going to cost me a pretty penny, let me tell you.

OGUDALOVA. This dinner seems quite unnecessary to me—just money down the drain.

KARANDYSHEV. I wouldn't begrudge the money if it cost me twice or three times as much.

OGUDALOVA. Nobody wants this dinner.

KARANDYSHEV. I want it.

LARISA. But why, Yuly Kapitonych?

KARANDYSHEV. For three years, Larisa Dmitryevna, I have born the open mockery of your acquaintances—now my turn has come to laugh at them!

OGUDALOVA. Whatever next? You want to provoke a quarrel, is that it? In that case Larisa and I will stay away.

LARISA. Oh please, don't insult anybody.

KARANDYSHEV. You say that—but doesn't it matter if I'm insulted? Well, you needn't worry, there won't be any quarrel: everything will be very peaceful. I shall propose a toast in your honor and thank you publicly for the happiness which you have conferred upon me—for not treating me like other people, for prizing me at my true worth and believing in the sincerity of my feelings. And that will be my entire revenge!

OGUDALOVA. We could do without that too.

KARANDYSHEV. No, those coxcombs have sickened me with their bragging. They didn't amass their riches themselves, so why do they boast of them? Fifteen rubles they spend on a pot of tea!

OGUDALOVA. Ah, you're still after poor Vasya. are you?

KARANDYSHEV. Not just Vasya—one's as bad as the next. Just look at what's going on out there. You'd think everyone had a birthday. The cabbies are all in high good humor, galloping through the streets shouting to each other: "The young gentleman's come, the young gentleman's come!" The waiters at the inns are wreathed in smiles, they run out into the street, from inn to inn, yelling to each other, "The young gentleman's come, the young gentleman's come!" The gypsies have gone out of their minds, all clamoring at once, waving their arms about. You can hardly get near the hotel there are so many people. Four gypsy girls decked out in all their finery have driven up in a carriage to welcome him. A glorious sight, a triumph! But this same gentleman, so I hear, squandered all his property, sold his last steamer. So who's all this fuss about then? A bankrupt, a debauchee, a man devoid of principles. And the town greets him like a conqueror. There's a lesson to be drawn from that!

OGUDALOVA. Who is it then?

KARANDYSHEV. Your precious Sergei Sergeyich Paratov.

OGUDALOVA. Ah, so it's him!

LARISA. Please, please let's leave for the country immediately!

KARANDYSHEV. Now we shall certainly stay.

OGUDALOVA. What's the matter with you—why should you run away from him? He's not a bandit!

LARISA. Why don't you listen to me? Can't you see that you're destroying me?

OGUDALOVA. You're being absurd.

KARANDYSHEV. What are you afraid of?

LARISA. I'm not afraid for myself.

KARANDYSHEV. For whom then?

LARISA. For you.

KARANDYSHEV. Oh, you need have no fear on my behalf! I won't allow myself to be insulted. Just let him try to provoke me, and he'll soon....

OGUDALOVA. You don't know what you're saying. May heaven protect you! He isn't Vasya, you know. You'd better watch your step with him or you'll regret it.

KARANDYSHEV *(at the window)*. If you'll be so good as to look out of the window you'll see his carriage drawing up; four pacers in a row, and a gypsy sitting up on the box with the coachman. Pulling the wool over people's eyes. Let him have his fun, you say—he's doing no one any harm. Well I think it's idiotic, disgusting.

LARISA *(to Karandyshev)*. Please let's go to my room. You receive him, mama, and please make it clear that his visits are unwelcome!

Larisa and Karandyshev go out. Paratov enters.

Scene 7

Ogudalova, Paratov.

PARATOV *(adopting a mock-earnest tone throughout the scene)*. Auntie, your hand!

OGUDALOVA *(extending her hand)*. Oh, Sergei Sergeyich! Oh, my dear boy!

PARATOV. You wish to enfold me in your embrace? By all means! *(They embrace and kiss.)*

OGUDALOVA. What wind blows you here? Just passing through, I suppose?

PARATOV. No, I came here for a reason, and my first business is to call on you, Auntie!

OGUDALOVA. I'm delighted. How are you, how are things with you?

PARATOV. I can't complain, Auntie. I manage to enjoy myself—but things aren't so good.

OGUDALOVA *(looking at Paratov intently)*. Sergei Sergeyich, tell me, my dear boy, why did you just disappear like that?

PARATOV. I had a telegram with bad news, Auntie.

OGUDALOVA. Bad news?

PARATOV. Yes, in my absence my stewards had managed to bring my estate to the brink of ruin. Thanks to them, my land, my goods and chattels, even my boats, almost came under the auctioneer's hammer. So, off I rushed to pull my chestnuts out of the fire.

OGUDALOVA. And, of course, you soon put everything in order.

PARATOV. I'm afraid not; I patched things up, but there are still some holes. But don't worry, Auntie, I keep my spirits up—I haven't lost my cheerful disposition.

OGUDALOVA. I can see you haven't.

PARATOV. What we lose on the swings we gain on the roundabouts, Auntie, that's the way things go.

OGUDALOVA. And where are your roundabouts? Do you have some new money-making schemes up your sleeve?

PARATOV. Money-making schemes aren't for the frivolous upper classes—that's why we finish up in debtors' prison, Auntie. No, I've decided to sell my freedom.

OGUDALOVA. I understand: you want to marry money. And what price do you put on your freedom?

PARATOV. Half a million, dear lady.

OGUDALOVA. A tidy sum.

PARATOV. I can't go below that, Auntie, there wouldn't be any profit in it—you know I'm expensive.

OGUDALOVA. That's my boy.

PARATOV. Take me or leave me.

OGUDALOVA. Spoken like a man! It does my heart good to look at you.

PARATOV. You flatter me indeed. Your hand, if you please. *(Kisses her hand.)*

OGUDALOVA. And are there any prospective buyers?

PARATOV. They won't be hard to find.

OGUDALOVA. May I ask a tactless question?

PARATOV. That depends—I blush easily, you know.

OGUDALOVA. Enough of your joking now! Are you engaged or not? And if you are—who is she?

PARATOV. You can cut my throat, but I won't tell you.

OGUDALOVA. Oh, very well.

PARATOV. I'd very much like to pay my respects to Larisa Dmitryevna. May I see her?

OGUDALOVA. Why not? I'll send her in. *(Picks up the jewel box.)* By the way, Sergei Sergeyich, tomorrow is Larisa's birthday, and I so much wanted to give her these—but I'm afraid I just can't afford them.

PARATOV. Auntie, Auntie! I bet you've hooked a few with that one already. I remember your tactics.

OGUDALOVA *(takes Paratov by the ear)*. Oh, you wicked boy!

PARATOV. I'll bring a present tomorrow that'll put this one in the shade.

OGUDALOVA. I'll go and call Larisa. *(Goes out. Larisa enters.)*

Scene 8

Paratov, Larisa.

PARATOV. You weren't expecting me?

LARISA. I'd given up expecting you. I waited and waited, but there came a time when I couldn't wait any more.

PARATOV. Why was that?

LARISA. I couldn't believe you'd come any more. You left so suddenly, and you never wrote me a single letter.

PARATOV. I didn't write because I had nothing good to tell you.

LARISA. That's what I thought.

PARATOV. And now you're getting married.

LARISA. Yes.

PARATOV. May I ask you a question? Did you wait for me long?

LARISA. Why should you want to know that?

PARATOV. I'm not asking out of idle curiosity, Larisa Dmitryevna, but rather in a spirit of scientific inquiry. I want to know how long it takes for a woman to forget a man she once loved passionately: a day, a week, month..... Was Hamlet right when he said to his mother "Ere those shoes were old," etcetera.

LARISA. I shan't answer your question, Sergei Sergeyich; you may think of me as you please.

PARATOV. I shall always think of you with respect, but in the light of your behavior I can't help having a lower opinion of women in general.

LARISA. What behavior are you talking about? You don't know anything.

PARATOV. Those "tender loving glances," those murmured confidences, every word breaking off in a sigh, those vows! And in a month all this is repeated to someone else like a lesson learned by heart. Oh, frailty!

LARISA. What do you mean?

PARATOV. Thy name is woman!

LARISA. How dare you insult me in this way? How can you know whether or not I love another man? Are you so certain of it then?

PARATOV. No, not certain, but I assume it must be so.

LARISA. And you rebuke me so cruelly on a mere assumption?

PARATOV. But you are getting married, aren't you?

LARISA. But what forced me into it? You don't know what my life here is like—to be wretched and to have to smile, mouth pleasantries, put up with the attentions of would-be suitors I can't stand the sight of. And the constant scandals—what can I do but get away from this house, away from this town?

PARATOV. Larisa, so you....

LARISA. So I what? What is it you're trying to say?

PARATOV. Forgive me! I've done you wrong. So you haven't forgotten me, you still...love me? (*Larisa makes no reply.*) Be frank with me!

LARISA. Of course, I do. What else did you expect me to say?

PARATOV (*kisses Larisa's hands tenderly*). You've made me happy, very happy.

LARISA. That's all you wanted to hear. You're a proud man.

PARATOV. I can give you up. I'm forced to by circumstances. But to give up your love would be very hard.

LARISA. I see.

PARATOV. If you had transferred your affections to another man I would have been deeply wounded—and that's something I would have found it hard to forgive you.

LARISA. And now?

PARATOV. And now I shall cherish the happiest recollections of you all my life, and we shall part the best of friends.

LARISA. So it doesn't matter if a woman weeps her heart out as long as she continues to love you?

PARATOV. It can't be helped, Larisa Dmitryevna! There's no equality in love, and I can't help it if the world was made that way. Someone has to cry sometimes—that's love.

LARISA. The woman has to, you mean.

PARATOV. Well, you can hardly expect a man to.

LARISA. Why not?

PARATOV. It's very simple, if a man cries he gets called an old woman, and the human mind can't invent anything a man fears more than that.

LARISA. So, if love were equal on both sides there'd be no tears. Does that ever happen?

PARATOV. Yes, it does, now and then—except that kind of love always makes me think of a piece of confectionery, a meringue or something.

LARISA. Sergei Sergeyich, I shouldn't have told you what I did; I hope you won't abuse my frankness.

PARATOV. Good lord, what do you take me for! If a woman is unattached, then it's a different matter. I am a man of principle, Larisa Dmitryevna, for me marriage is sacred. That's one point on which I won't tolerate freethinking. Tell me, your future husband of course has many good qualities?

LARISA. No—just one.

PARATOV. That's not much.

LARISA. But a precious one.

PARATOV. And what exactly may this quality be?

LARISA. He loves me.

PARATOV. Truly, as you say, a precious quality. Very useful in the home.

Enter Ogudalova and Karandyshev.

Scene 9

Paratov, Larisa, Ogudalova, Karandyshev and presently a footman.

OGUDALOVA. Allow me to introduce you, gentlemen! *(To Paratov).* Yuly Kapitonych Karandyshev! *(To Karandyshev.)* Sergei Sergeyich Paratov!

PARATOV *(shaking hands with Karandyshev).* We've met before. *(Bowing.)* I am a person with large mustaches and small talents, and crave your indulgence. I'm an old friend of Kharita Ignatyevna's and Larisa Dmitryevna's.

KARANDYSHEV *(guardedly).* How do you do.

OGUDALOVA. Sergei Sergeyich is like one of the family.

KARANDYSHEV. How nice.

PARATOV *(to Karandyshev).* You're not a jealous sort of person?

KARANDYSHEV. I trust that Larisa Dmitryevna will give me no cause for jealousy.

PARATOV. But jealous people are that way whether they have cause or not.

LARISA. I can promise that Yuly Kapitonych will have no reason to be jealous on my account.

KARANDYSHEV. No, of course not, but if....

PARATOV. Oh yes, I can imagine—it would be a very alarming spectacle.

OGUDALOVA. What on earth's come over you gentlemen? You'd think jealousy was the only possible topic of conversation.

LARISA. We're leaving for the country soon, Sergei Sergeyich.

PARATOV. Leaving these delightful parts?

KARANDYSHEV. What do you find so delightful about them?

PARATOV. Oh, it's a matter of taste—one man's meat is another man's poison.

OGUDALOVA. Very true, very true—some like town life, others prefer the country.

PARATOV. Every man to his taste, Auntie—some like pineapple, some like pig gristle.

OGUDALOVA. Oh, you naughty man! How is it you know so many proverbs?

PARATOV. I mix a lot with barge haulers, Auntie—that's the way to learn Russian.

KARANDYSHEV. Learn Russian from barge haulers!

PARATOV. And why not?

KARANDYSHEV. Well, because among us they are considered....

PARATOV. Who is this "us"?

KARANDYSHEV. When I say "among us," I mean among educated people—not barge haulers.

PARATOV. Very well then, what do you consider barge haulers to be? As a shipowner I'm prepared to stand up for them—in fact you might say I'm a bit of a barge hauler myself.

KARANDYSHEV. We consider them to be the embodiment of ignorance and ill breeding.

PARATOV. Go on, Mr. Karandyshev, go on!

KARANDYSHEV. That's all I have to say.

PARATOV. Oh no it's not. The main thing is missing, an apology.

KARANDYSHEV. You want me to apologize!

PARATOV. Yes, I'm afraid you must—there's no way out.

KARANDYSHEV. But why should I? I was merely stating a conviction which I hold sincerely.

PARATOV. Aha... It's no good trying to wriggle out of it.

OGUDALOVA. Gentlemen.... Gentlemen, please!

PARATOV. Don't worry, I'm not going to call him out: your bridegroom won't come to any harm. I'll just teach him a little lesson. It's a rule of mine never to forgive anyone anything, just in case they forget themselves and start taking liberties.

LARISA *(to Karandyshev).* What's the matter with you? I order you to apologize immediately.

PARATOV. I think it's time I made it clear what manner of man I am. If I'm out to teach someone a lesson, I'll sit at home for a week thinking up a suitable punishment.

KARANDYSHEV *(to Paratov).* I don't understand....

PARATOV. In future learn to understand first and open your mouth afterwards!

OGUDALOVA. Sergei Sergeyich, I go down on my knees before you; for my sake, forgive him!

PARATOV *(to Karandyshev).* You'd better thank Kharita Ignatyevna. I forgive you this time. Just be careful who you're dealing with in future, my dear fellow! "I'll creep up on you unawares, and when I've got you—say your prayers!"

Karandyshev opens his mouth to reply.

OGUDALOVA. Don't argue with him, or we'll quarrel in good earnest. Larisa, have some champagne brought in, and pour them each a glass. Let them drink in honor of their reconciliation. *(Larisa goes out.)* And please don't let's have any more quarrelling. I'm a peaceable woman. I like everything to be nice and friendly.

PARATOV. I'm a peaceable sort myself. I wouldn't harm a fly; I'm never one to start anything, I can assure you.

OGUDALOVA. Yuly Kapitonych, you're young yet, you should mind your p's and q's and control your temper. Why not invite Sergei Sergeyich to dinner tonight. We'd love him to be there. So, invite him!

KARANDYSHEV. Yes, I was going to myself. Sergei Sergeyich, would you care to dine at my place this evening?

PARATOV *(coldly).* I'd be delighted. *(Enter Larisa, followed by a servant carry - ing a tray on which are a bottle of champagne and two glasses.)*

LARISA *(pours).* Gentlemen, please drink up. *(Paratov and Karandyshev each takes up a glass.)* I want you to be good friends.

PARATOV. Your wish is my command.

OGUDALOVA *(to Karandyshev).* And you follow Sergei Sergeyich's example!

KARANDYSHEV. Naturally Larisa Dmitryevna's word is law as far as I'm concerned. (*Vozhevatov enters.*)

Scene 10

Ogudalova, Larisa, Paratov, Karandyshev, later Robinson.

VOZHEVATOV. Where there's champagne we're sure to turn up. We have a nose for it! Kharita Ignatyevna, Larisa Dmitryevna, will you allow a fair-haired stranger to enter?

OGUDALOVA. What fair-haired stranger?

VOZHEVATOV. You'll see. Come in, blondie! (*Robinson enters.*) I have the honor to present my new friend, Lord Robinson.

OGUDALOVA. How do you do.

VOZHEVATOV. Kiss the ladies' hands! (*Robinson kisses Ogudalova's and Larisa's hands.*) And now, milord, you can come over here!

OGUDALOVA. Why do you order your friend about like that?

VOZHEVATOV. He's unused to the company of ladies, and so he's terribly shy. He's spent most of his life traveling by land and sea, and not long ago he was all but reduced to a state of savagery on a desert island. (*To Karandyshev.*) Allow me to introduce you. Lord Robinson—Yuly Kapitonych Karandyshev!

KARANDYSHEV (*shaking hands with Robinson*). Have you been out of England long?

ROBINSON. Yesss.

VOZHEVATOV (*to Paratov*). I've taught him about three words of English, about as many as I know myself, to tell the truth. (*To Robinson.*) What do you keep eying the wine for? Kharita Ignatyevna, may he have a glass?

OGUDALOVA. Of course.

VOZHEVATOV. You know, the English drink wine all day, beginning in the morning.

OGUDALOVA. You really drink wine all day?

ROBINSON. Yesss.

VOZHEVATOV. They eat three breakfasts and then dine from six to twelve.

OGUDALOVA. Can that be possible?

ROBINSON. Yes.

VOZHEVATOV (*to Robinson*). Pour away then!

ROBINSON (*filling his glass*). Eef yoo pleeze! (*They drink.*)

PARATOV(*to Karandyshev*). Why not ask him to dinner, too? We go everywhere together, I can't do without him.

KARANDYSHEV. How should I address him?

PARATOV. Nobody calls them by their names—just lord, milord.

KARANDYSHEV. He's not really a lord is he?

PARATOV. Of course not, but that's what they like. If you like, you can just call him Sir Robinson.

KARANDYSHEV. Sir Robinson, I beg you to do me the honor of dining with me this evening.

ROBINSON. Ay zenk yoo.

KARANDYSHEV *(to Ogudalova).* I have to go now, Kharita Ignatyevna—a number of things require my urgent attention. *(Bowing to the company.)* I'll be expecting you, gentlemen. I take my leave of you. *(Goes out.)*

PARATOV *(picking up his hat).* Yes, and it's time we were on our way. We must rest after our journey.

VOZHEVATOV. And get ready for dinner.

OGUDALOVA. Don't be in such a hurry. Don't all leave at once. *(Ogudalova and Larisa follow Karandyshev into the hall.)*

Scene 11

Paratov, Vozhevatov, Robinson.

VOZHEVATOV. Was the bridegroom to your liking?

PARATOV. I can't imagine him being to anyone's liking. And he can't keep his mouth shut either, the damned fool!

VOZHEVATOV. Don't tell me there was a scene?

PARATOV. We had a few words. He tried to get on his high horse with me. But just you wait. I'll play a little joke on you my friend. *(Striking his forehead.)* Ah, a brilliant thought! Well, Robinson, you've got some hard work ahead, prepare yourself!

VOZHEVATOV. What's the idea?

PARATOV. Here it is…. *(Listening intently.)* They're coming! I'll tell you later, gentlemen. *(Enter Ogudalova and Larisa.)* I'll take my leave.

VOZHEVATOV. Good-bye! *(They bow themselves out.)*

ACT III

Karandyshev's study. The room is pretentiously but tastelessly furnished; a rug adorns the wall above the sofa, and on it a number of guns are arranged. Three doors: one in the center, two to the side.

Scene 1

Yefrosinya Potapovna, Ivan (who enters from door on left).

IVAN. We're needing some lemons.

YEFROSINYA POTAPOVNA. Lemons, what lemons, you rascal?

IVAN. Messina lemons.

YEFROSINYA POTAPOVNA. And what should you be needing them for?

IVAN. After dinner some gentlemen take coffee, some take tea—so we have to have them for the tea.

YEFROSINYA POTAPOVNA. You'll be the death of me, you will. Give them cranberry juice, what's the difference. You'll find a decanter in there; and just you be careful, it's very old, the stopper'd fall out if it wasn't held with sealing wax. Let's go, I'll give it to you myself. *(Goes out center, Ivan follows. Ogudalova and Larisa enter left.)*

Scene 2

Ogudalova, Larisa.

LARISA. Oh Mama, I didn't know where to hide my face.

OGUDALOVA. It's just what I would have expected from him.

LARISA. The food was terrible, you couldn't eat it. And he goes and invites Moki Parmenych as well! What's the matter with him?

OGUDALOVA. Yes, he certainly gave them a meal they won't forget.

LARISA. Oh God, how dreadful! It's worse feeling ashamed for someone else than for yourself. It's not our fault, but I'm ashamed, so ashamed. I wish I could run away and hide. And he doesn't seem to be aware of anything. He even seems to be enjoying himself.

OGUDALOVA. How could he possibly be aware of anything? He's never been invited to dine anywhere decent in his life. He imagines he's astounding everyone with his luxurious fare. And haven't you noticed what's happening? They're deliberately getting him drunk.

LARISA. Oh God, oh God, make him stop, make him stop!

OGUDALOVA. How can I? He's not a child, it's time he managed without a nanny.

LARISA. He's not stupid. How is it he doesn't see?

OGUDALOVA. Not stupid, but vain. They're teasing him, praising the wines, and he's happy; they keep filling his glass and only pretend to drink themselves.

LARISA. I'm afraid, I'm so afraid. Why are they doing this?

OGUDALOVA. Oh, just for a laugh.

LARISA. But don't they realize that they're torturing me?

OGUDALOVA. I suppose someone must want you to be tortured. You see how it is, Larisa; this is only the beginning, and already you're in torment. What's it going to be like later?

LARISA. It's no good, everything's settled now. There's nothing I can do now but regret.

Enter Yefrosinya Potapovna.

Scene 3

Ogudalova, Larisa, Yefrosinya Potapovna.

YEFROSINYA. Finished eating already? Wouldn't you like some tea?

OGUDALOVA. We won't, if you don't mind.

YEFROSINYA. And what about the menfolk? What are they up to?

OGUDALOVA. They're sitting in there chatting.

YEFROSINYA. You'd think they'd want to leave the table, seeing that they're finished. What more do they want? The trouble I've had with this dinner, the fuss and bother, the expense! These cooks are barefaced robbers; he comes marching into the kitchen like a conquering hero; and just you try telling him anything!

OGUDALOVA. Well, and why should you need to tell him anything? If he's a good cook he'll know his own business.

YEFROSINYA. I'm not talking about that. I wouldn't say a word if it was my own stuff, sent up from the country, but we paid good money for it, and I hate to stand by and see it wasted. I ask you, he wants sugar and vanilla and isinglass; but vanilla costs money, and isinglass is even costlier. Well, I wouldn't mind him putting in a little bit just to keep people happy, but you'd think it was water the way he uses it! My blood runs cold just watching him.

OGUDALOVA. Well, of course, if you're trying to economize.

YEFROSINYA. Economizing's got nothing to do with it. The man's simply taken leave of his senses. Now take sturgeon, for example, a sturgeon tastes the same whether it's big or small, doesn't it? But the price isn't the same, let me tell you! A dozen at fifty kopecks would have been plenty, but he's been paying fifty kopecks apiece.

OGUDALOVA. Well, as far as the ones we had at dinner were concerned, it wouldn't have done them any harm to swim around in the Volga until they grew up a bit.

YEFROSINYA. Oh, yes. I grant you, you can pay a ruble apiece, or even two rubles. Let folks that are rolling in money pay that if they like. If it's for some big-wig, or a bishop say, well that's right and proper, but, I ask you, who's this for?

And he wanted to buy expensive wine too, a ruble a bottle or more, but, Lord be praised, a merchant, an honest man, came to the rescue: take the lot at sixty kopecks a bottle, he says. and we'll stick on some labels, any ones you fancy. He let us have some good stuff too: I tried a glass; it smelled of cloves and rose petals and something else beside. How could anyone say it was cheap with all that in it? And sixty kopecks a bottle, that's not cheap, you know; still, it was a good buy. More than that we couldn't afford. We have to live on our earnings. Now a neighbor of ours got married not long back, and you just should have seen all the bedding that arrived; pillows there were, and mattresses. They kept carrying them in until I thought they'd never stop; all down it was too, not a feather in it; and then came furs: fox, marten, sable! Yes, all that went into his house, and so if he feels like spending he can. Then take the clerk next door. He gets married and all the dowry he collects is an old upright piano. You're not going to make a fortune with that now, are you? And we've got no reason to go acting grand either.

LARISA (to Ogudalova). I'd like to run away and never come back.

OGUDALOVA. Unfortunately, that's not possible.

YEFROSINYA. If you're not feeling well you're welcome to sit in my room. When the men arrive they'll smoke the place out so you can hardly breathe. What am I doing standing about! I'd better go and count the silver and see that it's put under lock and key. There's no trusting folk these days.

Ogudalova and Larisa go out right, Yefrosinya center. Paratov, Knurov and Vozhevatov enter left.

Scene 4

Paratov, Knurov, Vozhevatov.

KNUROV. I'm going to my club for some dinner, gentlemen. I haven't eaten a thing.

PARATOV. Stay a bit longer, Moki Parmenych!

KNUROV. Never in my life has such a thing happened to me. People with some standing in society are invited to dinner, and there's nothing to eat. He's a fool, gentlemen.

PARATOV. We won't argue with you about that. One must give him his due; he's a fool indeed.

KNUROV. He has to be the first to get drunk, too.

PARATOV. You see, I'm putting a little scheme of mine into operation. I thought I'd shake him up a bit and see what happens.

KNUROV. So you had it all planned?

PARATOV. We had agreed on a plan of action. And it's exactly on such occasions that Robinson comes in useful, gentlemen.

VOZHEVATOV. Worth his weight in gold!

PARATOV. In order to get one's host drunk one has to drink with him; but how could one possibly drink the concoction he is pleased to call wine? But

Robinson was positively nurtured on wines of the Château Yaroslavl variety, and can drink them without turning a hair. He drinks everything, praises everything, tries one thing and then another, compares them, smacks his lips with the air of a connoisseur, but naturally he refuses to drink unless our host joins him; and naturally our host falls for it. And not being much of a drinker he was soon well away.

KNUROV. Well, that's all very amusing, but I'm starving, gentlemen, and that's no joke at all.

PARATOV. You'll be able to fit dinner in later. Stay a bit longer and we'll ask Larisa Dmitryevna to sing something for us.

KNUROV. That's a different matter. But where is Robinson?

VOZHEVATOV. They're still drinking in there. (*Robinson enters.*)

Scene 5

Paratov, Knurov, Vozhevatov, Robinson.

ROBINSON (*collapsing onto a sofa*). Help, save me! Well, Serge, you'll have to answer for this at the Last Judgment.

PARATOV. What's the matter? Are you drunk?

ROBINSON. Drunk! Now, I ask you, when have I ever complained about that? Drink! That would be heaven. I couldn't ask for anything better. It was with that noble intention that I came here, indeed, I live on earth with it; it is the aim of my life.

PARATOV. Then what's the matter?

ROBINSON. I've been poisoned—help, help!

PARATOV. What were you drinking mostly, wine?

ROBINSON. How should I know. Am I a chemist or something? No apothecary could tell what was in it.

PARATOV. But what was the label on the bottle?

ROBINSON. It said Burgundy on the bottle, but it tasted more like some sort of cough syrup. I shall pay dearly for this, I can feel it.

VOZHEVATOV. That happens when they make wine. They put in too much of one thing or another. A man isn't a machine, you know; anyone can make a mistake. Perhaps they went a bit heavy on the toadstools.

ROBINSON. What are you in such a good humor about? A man's at death's door and you stand there grinning.

VOZHEVATOV. There's nothing for it, Robinson! You'll have to die.

ROBINSON. Nonsense, I don't agree to die. I'm just worried that I might be maimed for life.

VOZHEVATOV. You'll lose an eye at least, and don't say I didn't warn you.

KARANDYSHEV (*offstage*). Hey there, bring us some more burgundy.

ROBINSON. There, you hear him, burgundy again! Save me, I'm done for! Serge, you at least should have pity on me! Remember that I'm in the flower of my years and great things are expected of me. Must art be deprived of....

PARATOV. There, there, don't cry, I'll cure you. I know just what you need. Your illness will disappear like magic.

Enter Karandyshev with a box of cigars.

Scene 6

Paratov, Knurov, Vozhevatov, Robinson, Karandyshev.

ROBINSON *(looking at the carpet on the wall)*. What's that you've got there?
KARANDYSHEV. Cigars.
ROBINSON. No, I mean hanging up there? They're dummies aren't they?
KARANDYSHEV. What do you mean, dummies? Those are Turkish guns.
PARATOV. So now we know whose fault it is the Austrians can't get the better of the Turks.
KARANDYSHEV. What do you mean? I don't understand these jokes. If you'll forgive me saying so, you're talking nonsense. How can it be my fault?
PARATOV. You brought up all their useless old guns, and they were so grief-stricken that they went out and equipped themselves with good English ones.
VOZHEVATOV. Yes, yes, it's all your fault! You've been unmasked. The Austrians won't thank you for that, I can tell you.
KARANDYSHEV. But what makes you think they're useless? Take this pistol, for example. *(Takes pistol from the wall.)*
PARATOV *(taking it from him)*. This one?
KARANDYSHEV. Careful, it's loaded!
PARATOV. Have no fear! Loaded or unloaded, the danger's the same; it won't fire in either case. You can shoot me at five paces—go ahead.
KARANDYSHEV. Oh no, I can't do that. This pistol may come in handy some day.
PARATOV. Yes, for knocking nails into walls. *(Throws the pistol down on the table.)*
VOZHEVATOV. You shouldn't say such a thing. In the words of the old Russian proverb: "In a tight corner you can shoot with a stick."
KARANDYSHEV *(to Paratov)*. Would you like a cigar?
PARATOV. They must be terribly expensive; at least seven rubles a hundred I should think.
KARANDYSHEV. Yes, something like that; they're a fine brand, a very fine brand.
PARATOV. I know that brand: Regalia Cabagissima Dos Amigos. I keep them for my friends, but I don't smoke them myself.
KARANDYSHEV *(to Knurov)*. Do have one.
KNUROV. I don't want your cigars. I'll smoke my own.
KARANDYSHEV. They're an excellent cigar, I assure you.
KNUROV. If they're so good, smoke them yourself.
KARANDYSHEV *(to Vozhevatov)*. Would you like one?
VOZHEVATOV. They're too expensive for me. I'd get spoilt. Such things are too good for the likes of us.

KARANDYSHEV. Do you smoke, Sir Robinson?

ROBINSON. Me? What a question! Give us half a dozen! *(Selects six cigars, takes a piece of paper out of his pocket and wraps them up carefully.)*

KARANDYSHEV. But why don't you light up now?

ROBINSON. Oh no, I can't do that. These cigars deserve to be smoked in the open air amidst the beauties of nature.

KARANDYSHEV. Why's that?

ROBINSON. Because if you were to smoke them in a decent house, you'd be liable to get a beating; and that's something I don't care for.

VOZHEVATOV. You don't enjoy a beating?

ROBINSON. No, I've had a strong aversion to it ever since my childhood.

KARANDYSHEV. What a card he is! A card, gentlemen—isn't that so! You can tell at once he's an Englishman. *(Loudly.)* But where are our ladies? *(Still louder.)* Where are the ladies?

Ogudalova enters.

Scene 7

Paratov, Knurov, Vozhevatov, Robinson, Karandyshev, Ogudalova.

OGUDALOVA. The ladies are here, don't worry. *(Quietly, to Karandyshev.)* What do you think you're doing? Just take a look at yourself.

KARANDYSHEV. Do you think I can't take care of myself? Look at them; they're all drunk, and I'm just merry. Today I rejoice, today I triumph.

OGUDALOVA. Go ahead and triumph, but not so loudly. *(Going over to Paratov.)* Sergei Sergeyich, please stop trying to make Yuly Kapitonych look like a fool. It's very painful for us; you're insulting both me and Larisa.

PARATOV. Now, Auntie, would I dare insult you?

OGUDALOVA. Don't tell me you haven't put that silly quarrel out of your head? You ought to be ashamed of yourself!

PARATOV. Really, Auntie, how can you say such things! I'm not one to bear malice. Just to make you happy I'm ready to put an end to the quarrel once and for all. Yuly Kapitonych!

KARANDYSHEV. What can I do for you?

PARATOV. Would you like to drink Bruderschaft with me?

OGUDALOVA. Now that's the spirit. Thank you!

KARANDYSHEV. Bruderschaft did you say? Certainly, I'd be delighted.

PARATOV *(to Ogudalova)*. And ask Larisa Dmitryevna to come in! Why is she hiding from us?

OGUDALOVA. Very well, I'll get her. *(Goes out.)*

KARANDYSHEV. What shall it be—burgundy?

PARATOV. No, not burgundy, if you don't mind! I'm a simple man.

KARANDYSHEV. What then?

PARATOV. It seems to me that brandy would be just the thing. Do you have any?

KARANDYSHEV. Of course, I have. There's nothing lacking in this house! Hey there, Ivan, bring us some brandy.

PARATOV. No need to fetch it. We'll drink it in there. Only tell them to let us have some tumblers. I've no use for these little glasses.

ROBINSON. That's a drink I know how to deal with. We're old friends.

Paratov and Karandyshev go out left.

Scene 8

Knurov, Vozhevatov, Robinson.

ROBINSON (*looking through the door*). That's the end of Karandyshev. I began, and Serge will finish him off. They're filling their glasses and now they're standing there, glasses upraised, a tableau vivant. Just look at the smile on Serge's face! He reminds me of Bertram in *Robert le Diable*. (*Sings from "Robert le Diable."*) "You are my saviour"—"I am your saviour"—"And protector"—"And protector." And now they're tossing it back. They're embracing. (*Sings.*) "O happy hour"—"You're in my power." Hey, Ivan's taking the brandy away, he's taking it away! (*Loudly.*) Hey, what do you think you're doing, leave it! It's what I've been waiting for all day. (*Runs off. Ilya enters center.*)

Scene 9

Knurov. Vozhevatov, Ilya. Later Paratov.

VOZHEVATOV. What's up, Ilya?

ILYA. Our bunch is all ready, they're waiting outside. When are we leaving?

VOZHEVATOV. We'll all go together in a minute. Just wait there.

ILYA. Good. Everything'll be as you say.

Paratov enters.

PARATOV. Ah, there you are Ilya. Ready?

ILYA. Ready, Sergei Sergeyich!

PARATOV. Do you have a guitar with you?

ILYA. I didn't think to bring one, Sergei Sergeyich.

PARATOV. We must have a guitar, do you hear?

ILYA. I'll run and get one straight away, Sergei Sergeyich. (*Goes out.*)

PARATOV. I mean to ask Larisa Dmitryevna to sing for us; and then we'll go across the river.

KNUROV. It won't be much of a jaunt without Larisa Dmitryevna. If only.... That's a pleasure one would be prepared to pay well for.

VOZHEVATOV. If Larisa Dmitryevna went with us, I'd give all the rowers an extra ruble each out of sheer joy.

PARATOV. Now isn't that strange, gentlemen. I was thinking just the same thing; our minds must work in the same way.

KNUROV. But do you think there is a possibility?

PARATOV. The philosophers tell us that nothing in this world is impossible.

KNUROV. But we don't need Robinson, gentlemen. We've had our fun with him, and enough's enough. If he comes with us he'll just get blind drunk and generally objectionable. No, this trip is serious business, and we can do without his company. *(Pointing to the door.)* Just look at him soaking up the brandy in there.

VOZHEVATOV. We won't take him then.

PARATOV. He's sure to manage to tag along somehow.

VOZHEVATOV. Wait a minute, gentlemen, and I'll get rid of him. *(Calls through the doorway.)* Robinson!

Robinson enters.

Scene 10

Paratov, Knurov, Vozhevatov, Robinson.

ROBINSON. What do you want?

VOZHEVATOV. How would you like to go to Paris?

ROBINSON. What do you mean, Paris. When?

VOZHEVATOV. This evening.

ROBINSON. But I thought we were going for a trip across the Volga.

VOZHEVATOV. It's up to you. You go on the Volga, I'll go to Paris.

ROBINSON. But I don't have a passport.

VOZHEVATOV. Leave that to me.

ROBINSON. All right then, yes.

VOZHEVATOV. We'll leave together from here then; I'll take you back to my place; wait for me there. Get yourself some rest. I have to call on one or two people on business.

ROBINSON. It would have been interesting to hear the gypsies sing though.

VOZHEVATOV. And you an artiste too! You ought to be ashamed of yourself. How could anyone with any pretensions to culture like gypsy songs? Now an Italian opera or a gay operetta—that's different. That's the sort of thing you ought to be hearing. I bet you've played in them yourself.

ROBINSON. Well, of course I have! I've played in *Songbirds.*

VOZHEVATOV. What part?

ROBINSON. The notary.

VOZHEVATOV. There you are then, an artiste like you and not visit Paris. After you've been to Paris, just think of the parts you'll be able to get!

ROBINSON. Your hand on it!

VOZHEVATOV. You'll come?

ROBINSON. I will!

VOZHEVATOV *(to Paratov)*. You should have heard him singing *Robert*. What a voice!

PARATOV. What a sensation we'll be at the Nizhni Novgorod fair!

ROBINSON. If I go, that is.

PARATOV. What's this.

ROBINSON. I see enough ignorance around me without going to fairs.

PARATOV. Oho, now listen to him!

ROBINSON. These days educated people travel to Europe, they don't waste their time hanging about fairs.

PARATOV. And which of Europe's domains and cities are you intending to honor?

ROBINSON. Paris, naturally. I've been intending to go there for a long time.

VOZHEVATOV. The two of us are leaving this evening.

PARATOV. So that's it! Well I hope you enjoy the trip. Yes, you really ought to pay Paris a visit. You're just what they've been waiting for all these years. But where's our host?

ROBINSON. He's in there. He said he was preparing a surprise for us.

Ogudalova and Larisa enter right; Karandyshev and Ivan left.

Scene 11

Ogudalova, Paratov, Knurov, Vozhevatov, Robinson, Karandyshev, Ivan, later Ilya, Yefrosinya Potapovna.

PARATOV *(to Larisa)*. Why did you desert us?

LARISA. I'm not feeling very well.

PARATOV. I've just drunk Bruderschaft with your fiancé. Now we're friends forever.

LARISA. Thank you for that. *(Presses Paratov's hand.)*

KARANDYSHEV *(to Paratov)*. Sergei, old fellow!

PARATOV *(to Larisa)*. You see the familiar footing we're on. *(To Karandyshev.)* What can I do for you?

KARANDYSHEV. Someone's asking for you out there.

PARATOV. Who is it?

IVAN. Ilya, the gypsy.

PARATOV. Tell him to come in here then. *(Ivan goes out.)* I do hope, gentlemen, that you won't mind me inviting Ilya to join our company. He's my dearest friend; anyone who opens the doors of his house to me must be prepared to let my friends in, too. That's my rule.

VOZHEVATOV *(quietly, to Larisa)*. I know a new song.

LARISA. A good one?

VOZHEVATOV. You'll love it: "A fine thread I spin for my lady's soft slippers."

LARISA. That's pretty.

VOZHEVATOV. I'll teach you it. *(Ilya enters carrying a guitar.)*

PARATOV *(to Larisa)*. Larisa Dmitryevna, it lies in your power to make each one of us happy. Sing for us, anything you like! I haven't heard you sing for a whole year, and perhaps I'll never hear you again.

KNUROV. Allow me to second that request!

KARANDYSHEV. No, gentlemen, I'm afraid Larisa Dmitryevna won't be singing today.

PARATOV. How do you know she won't? Maybe she will.

LARISA. You'll have to excuse me, gentlemen. I'm in no mood for it today, and in no voice for it either.

KNUROV. Please, just for us. Anything you like.

KARANDYSHEV. If I say she won't, she won't, and that's that.

PARATOV. Perhaps she'll change her mind. We'll ask her nicely, we'll get down on our knees.

VOZHEVATOV. I'm willing. I've got flexible joints.

KARANDYSHEV. No, no, it's no good asking. It's out of the question; I forbid it.

OGUDALOVA. What's this! It's a bit early yet to be throwing your weight around.

LARISA. You forbid it? In that case, gentlemen, I will sing. *(Karandyshev goes and sits in a corner, glowering.)*

PARATOV. Ilya!

ILYA. What shall we sing for them, miss?

LARISA. "Tempt me not."

ILYA. We need a third voice. Ah, the shame of it, what a tenor he was! And it was all his own stupid fault. *(They sing a duet.)*

> Ah tempt me not in vain
> With tender words of old,
> Nor seek to wake again
> A heart long since grown cold.

Each in his own way shows that he is moved. Paratov sits with his head in his hands. Robinson joins in the second verse softly.

> Your vows are all untrue,
> Your love not what it seems.
> I cannot dream anew
> The old deceiving dreams.

ILYA *(to Robinson)*. Thank you, sir. You saved the day.

KNUROV *(to Larisa)*. To see you is a great pleasure, but to hear you is a greater one still.

PARATOV *(gloomily)*. I think I'm going out of my mind. *(Kisses Larisa's hand.)*

VOZHEVATOV. To hear her and die. What more could one ask! *(To Karandyshev.)* And you wanted to deprive us of this pleasure.

KARANDYSHEV. I admire Larisa Dmitryevna's singing no less than you do, gentlemen. We'll drink her health in champagne this very minute.

VOZHEVATOV. Now you're talking.

KARANDYSHEV *(loudly)*. Bring us some champagne!

OGUDALOVA *(quietly)*. Shhh! What are you shouting for?

KARANDYSHEV. I'm in my own home, aren't I? I know what I'm doing. *(Loudly.)* Let's have some champagne!

Yefrosinya Potapovna enters.

YEFROSINYA. What are you talking about, champagne. One thing one minute, another the next.

KARANDYSHEV. Don't interfere in what doesn't concern you! Do as you're told!

YEFROSINYA. You can go and get it yourself! I've run my legs off, I have; and what's more, I've hardly had a bite to eat since this morning. *(Goes out.)*

Karandyshev goes out left.

OGUDALOVA. Listen, Yuly Kapitonych.... *(Follows Karandyshev out.)*

PARATOV. Ilya, go and make sure our boats are ready! We'll be along in a minute. *(Ilya goes out center.)*

VOZHEVATOV *(to Knurov)*. Let's leave him alone with Larisa Dmitryevna. *(To Robinson.)* Look out, Robinson, Ivan's taking the brandy away.

ROBINSON. I'll kill him. I'd sooner part with my life.

Knurov, Vozhevatov and Robinson go out left.

Scene 12

Larisa, Paratov.

PARATOV. You wonderful, adorable girl. *(Gazes passionately at Larisa.)* How I was cursing myself when you were singing.

LARISA. Why?

PARATOV. Do you think I'm made of stone? Do you think it's easy to lose a jewel like you?

LARISA. If you are losing me, who's to blame?

PARATOV. I am, of course, and much more than you realize. I can't help despising myself.

LARISA. But why—tell me!

PARATOV. Why did I run away from you? Why did I give you up?

LARISA. Well, and why did you?

PARATOV. You may well ask me! Cowardice, of course, what else? I had to try and retrieve my financial situation. But to hell with that! I did worse than gamble away my fortune. I lost you. I'm suffering myself, and I've caused you to suffer.

LARISA. Yes, I can't deny it. You made my life wretched for a long time.

PARATOV. Wait, wait a little before you start accusing me. I haven't become utterly vile and contemptible. I wasn't born into trade; noble feelings still stir within me. A few more moments like this, yes... a few more moments....

LARISA *(softly)*. Go on.

PARATOV. And I'll throw all calculation to the winds, and no force on earth will tear you from me; not unless it kills me first.

LARISA. What do you want?

PARATOV. To see you, to listen to you... I'm leaving tomorrow.

LARISA *(bowing her head)*. Tomorrow.

PARATOV. To listen to your enchanting voice, to forget the whole world and to dream of one bliss, and one only....

LARISA. And what is that?

PARATOV. The bliss of being your slave, of being at your feet.

LARISA. But how may that be?

PARATOV. Listen to me; we're going on the river, come with us!

LARISA. But what about the others? How can I? What will happen here?

PARATOV. And what is this "here"? Do you know who'll be arriving at any moment? Auntie Karandysheva and young ladies in silk dresses they've had dyed especially for the occasion. And do you know what they'll talk about? Salting mushrooms.

LARISA. When are you going?

PARATOV. Now.

LARISA. Now?

PARATOV. Now or never.

LARISA. Let's go.

PARATOV. So, you'll come on the river with us then?

LARISA. Whatever you like.

PARATOV. How fine, how truly noble. My wonderful, adorable girl! Queen of my heart!

LARISA. You will always be my king.

Enter Ogudalova, Knurov, Vozhevatov, Robinson, Karandyshev and Ivan, who carries a tray with glasses of champagne.

Scene 13

Ogudalova, Larisa, Paratov, Knurov, Vozhevatov, Robinson, Karandyshev, and Ivan.

PARATOV *(to Knurov and Vozhevatov)*. She'll come.

KARANDYSHEV. Gentlemen, I propose a toast to Larisa Dmitryevna. *(Everyone raises his glass.)* Gentlemen, just now you were entranced by Larisa Dmitryevna's talent. Your praise is nothing new to her; since her childhood she has been surrounded by admirers who never tired of paying her compliments. Yes, she does indeed have many talents, but it is not for them I wish to praise her. Larisa Dmitryevna's greatest gift, and one which has never been properly appreciated, gentlemen, is... is....

VOZHEVATOV. He's getting mixed up.

PARATOV. No, he'll be all right, he's got it off by heart.

KARANDYSHEV. ...is the ability to single out true worth. Yes, Larisa Dmitryevna is well aware that all that glitters is not gold. She has been surrounded by brilliant young men, but she has not been taken in by their tinsel; she has sought out a man distinguished not by brilliance, but by worth....

PARATOV (approvingly). Bravo, bravo!

VOZHEVATOV AND ROBINSON. Bravo, bravo!

KARANDYSHEV. Yes, gentlemen, I am proud. I have the right to be proud! She has understood me, valued me at my true worth and given me preference over all others. Forgive me, gentlemen, perhaps not everyone will relish what I have said, but I considered it my duty to thank Larisa Dmitryevna publicly for the honor she has done me. Gentlemen, I propose a toast to my fiancée and drink to her myself!

PARATOV, VOZHEVATOV, ROBINSON. Hurrah!

PARATOV (to Karandyshev). Is there any wine left?

KARANDYSHEV. Of course there is! I'll go get some.

PARATOV. We have another toast to drink.

KARANDYSHEV. And what's that?

PARATOV. A toast to that most fortunate of mortals, Yuly Kapitonych Karandyshev.

KARANDYSHEV. Oh, yes. And you're going to propose it? Yes Serge, that's splendid. I'll go and rustle up some wine. (Goes out.)

KNUROV. Well, enough's enough. I'll go and have a bite to eat and meet up with you later. Good-bye! (Bows to the ladies.)

VOZHEVATOV (indicating center door). Why not go this way, Moki Parmenych! It leads straight to the hall, and no one will see you.

Knurov goes out.

PARATOV (to Vozhevatov). We're leaving too. (To Larisa.) Get ready. (Larisa goes off right.)

VOZHEVATOV. Without waiting for the toast?

PARATOV. It's better this way.

VOZHEVATOV. But why?

PARATOV. Funnier. (Larisa enters; she is carrying a hat.)

VOZHEVATOV. You're right—it is. Robinson! We're off!

ROBINSON. Where to?

VOZHEVATOV. Home, to pack for Paris.

Robinson and Vozhevatov bow and go out.

PARATOV (quietly, to Larisa). Let's go. (Goes out.)

LARISA. Good-bye, Mama!

OGUDALOVA. What's this! Where are you going?

LARISA. Either you will have cause for rejoicing or you can drag the river for me.

OGUDALOVA. Lord have mercy on us! What are you saying?

LARISA. There's no escaping fate. I can see that now. (*Goes out.*)

OGUDALOVA. So that's what it's come to at last—everyone taking to his heels. Oh, Larisa! Should I follow her.... No, what's the point? There are plenty of people with her, at all events. And here—well, if she throws him over it's no great loss.

Enter Karandyshev and Ivan with a bottle of champagne.

Scene 14

Ogudalova, Karandyshev, Ivan, later joined by Yefrosinya Potapovna.

KARANDYSHEV. Gentlemen, I.... (*Looking about the room.*) Where are they? Can they have left? Very polite, I must say—but so much the better! How did they manage to get away so quickly. Taken offense, have they? Well I'm not surprised—good riddance to them. We'll stay and have a quiet family evening. But where's Larisa Dmitryevna? (*Goes to door right.*) Auntie, is Larisa Dmitryevna with you?

YEFROSINYA (*entering*). Don't ask me where your precious Larisa Dmitryevna is.

KARANDYSHEV. What is all this, what's going on? Ivan, where have the gentlemen and Larisa Dmitryevna got to?

IVAN. I suppose Larisa Dmitryevna must have left with the gentlemen. Seeing as how the gentlemen were meaning to take a trip on the river; a picnic it was going to be.

KARANDYSHEV. What do you mean, on the river?

IVAN. They hired boats, sir. Crockery and wine; we supplied all that. Sent it off some time ago, and a waiter too, everything proper like.

KARANDYSHEV (*sits down and buries his head in his hands*). My God, what's happening!

IVAN. There's gypsies with them too, and music. Everything proper like.

KARANDYSHEV (*hotly*). Kharita Ignatyevna, where is your daughter?

OGUDALOVA. All I know is that I brought my daughter to your house, Yuly Kapitonych; you tell me where my daughter is!

KARANDYSHEV. You did it deliberately, it was all plotted beforehand.... (*Tearfully.*) How cruel, how unspeakably cruel!

OGUDALOVA. Your celebrations were a bit premature.

KARANDYSHEV. Yes, that was ridiculous. I'm a ridiculous man. I know perfectly well that I'm ridiculous. But are people condemned to death for being ridiculous? All right, laugh at me, laugh in my face! Dine at my table, drink my wine, mock me, laugh at me. I deserve it. But to crush a man's chest, tear out his heart, throw it on the ground and stamp on it just because he's ridiculous! (*Groans.*) How can I go on living?

YEFROSINYA. Now that's enough of that, stop it! There's nothing to take on about.

KARANDYSHEV. And these people aren't brigands, but respected members of society. Friends of Kharita Ignatyevna's.

OGUDALOVA. I don't know anything about it.

KARANDYSHEV. Yes, you hunt in a pack, you always stick up for each other. But let me tell you this, Kharita Ignatyevna—even the meekest man can be driven to desperation. Not all criminals are rogues; law-abiding men can resort to crime too when there's no other way out. If all that's left to me in this world is either to hang myself out of despair or to avenge myself, then I shall choose vengeance. Fear, pity, law no longer exist for me now; I feel as if I'm suffocating with rage. I'll avenge myself on every one of them. I swear I will, unless they kill me first! (Snatches up the pistol from the table and rushes out.)

OGUDALOVA. What was that he picked up?

IVAN. A pistol.

OGUDALOVA. Run, run! Follow him, make them stop him!

ACT IV

Scene 1

Robinson with a billiard cue in one hand and Ivan (who sticks his head through the door of the cafe).

IVAN. May I have that cue sir, if you don't mind.

ROBINSON. No, you can't have it. Why won't you give me a game?

IVAN. How can you expect anyone to play with you when you won't pay up?

ROBINSON. I'll settle with you later. Vasily Danilych has all my money. He took it with him. Don't you believe me?

IVAN. How come you didn't go on the picnic with him?

ROBINSON. I dropped off, and he didn't dare disturb me—so he had to go alone. Give us a game.

IVAN. No sir, it wouldn't be fair. I put down cash and you don't; if you win you take it, and if you don't you won't pay up. Put down your money, then we'll see.

ROBINSON. Do you mean to say I don't have any credit here then? That's strange. I've never been treated like this in any town; I've been everywhere in Russia, and I've always lived mainly on credit.

IVAN. That, sir, I can well believe. You can order anything you like and we'll bring it to you; knowing the kind of gentlemen Sergei Sergeyich and Vasily Danilych are, we're obliged to give you credit; but for billiards you need ready money.

ROBINSON. Now why didn't you tell me that before? All right—take the cue and bring me a bottle...of what, now?

IVAN. The port isn't bad, sir.

ROBINSON. I don't drink any old stuff, you know.

IVAN. You shall have the best, sir.

ROBINSON. And tell them to cook me... what's it called, you know....

IVAN. We could roast you some snipe, sir; would that do?

ROBINSON. Ah that's it, snipe.

IVAN. Yes, sir. *(Goes out.)*

ROBINSON. So they thought they'd play a joke on me; well, that's capital. I'll play a joke on them too. I'm so heartbroken that I'll run up a bill for twenty rubles; let them pay it. They imagine I need their company—but they're mistaken; all I need is credit—as long as I've got that I won't get bored on my own; I can play solo very cheerfully. All I need to make my happiness complete is someone to borrow money from....

Ivan enters with a bottle.

IVAN *(putting down the bottle).* The snipe are on order sir.

ROBINSON. You know I was thinking of renting a theater here.

IVAN. A promising undertaking, sir.

ROBINSON. I don't know who I'll get to run the buffet. Do you think your employer would be interested?

IVAN. I should think he would, sir!

ROBINSON. Naturally he'll have to provide first-class service. I shall insist on that. And naturally I shall expect a substantial advance immediately.

IVAN. He's too old a hand for that one. You won't get any advance out of him; he's been caught that way twice before.

ROBINSON. Twice, you say? Yes, in that case....

IVAN. He's not going to fall for it a third time.

ROBINSON. People these days! I really don't know what things are coming to; wherever you go the place has been cleaned out—no pickings left for anybody. Well, it doesn't matter, I don't really need it. You needn't mention it to him, or he may think I wanted to deceive him. I have my pride, you know.

IVAN. Yes sir, of course. You should have seen Mr. Karandyshev just now when all his guests upped and left. Furious he was—talked about killing some-one, and left the house with a pistol in his hand.

ROBINSON. A pistol? I don't like the sound of that.

IVAN. He'd had a drop too much. He'll get over it, I should think. He's been up and down the promenade a couple of times—here he comes now.

ROBINSON (timidly). You did say he had a pistol? He wanted to kill some-one. Not me, I hope?

IVAN. I couldn't say, sir. (Exit.)

Karandyshev enters. Robinson tries to hide behind his bottle.

Scene 2

Robinson, Karandyshev, later Ivan.

KARANDYSHEV. Where are your friends, Mr. Robinson?

ROBINSON. What friends? I have no friends.

KARANDYSHEV. What about those gentlemen who brought you to dinner with them?

ROBINSON. How can you call those friends? Just fleeting acquaintances.

KARANDYSHEV. Do you happen to know where they are at the moment?

ROBINSON. I couldn't tell you. As a matter of fact, I've been trying to get away from that crowd; I'm a law-abiding man, you know, a family man.

KARANDYSHEV. A family man, you say?

ROBINSON. Oh yes, very much so. For me a quiet life in the bosom of one's family is the most precious thing in the world; any kind of unpleasantness or quarrelling I just can't stand; I'm very fond of a chat as well, as long as the conversation is intelligent and polite—about art, or something like that. And, well, with a man of honor such as yourself I don't mind having a little drink to pass the time. Would you like to join me?

KARANDYSHEV. No, I wouldn't.

ROBINSON. As you wish. The main thing is that there should be no unpleasantness.

KARANDYSHEV. But you must know where they are.

ROBINSON. They're having a gay old time somewhere. What else could they be doing?

KARANDYSHEV. I heard they'd gone across the river.

ROBINSON. That may very well be.

KARANDYSHEV. Didn't they ask you to go with them?

ROBINSON. Oh no, you see, I'm a family man.

KARANDYSHEV. When are they coming back then?

ROBINSON. I shouldn't think they know that themselves. Round about dawn, I suppose.

KARANDYSHEV. Round about dawn?

ROBINSON. Perhaps earlier.

KARANDYSHEV. Well, I'll wait for them in that case; there are a few things I'd like to clear up with them.

ROBINSON. If you want to wait, you'd do better to wait at the landing stage; what would they come here for? They'll go straight home from the landing stage. They'll have had enough eating and drinking by then, I should think.

KARANDYSHEV. But what landing stage? There are lots of landing stages.

ROBINSON. Any one you like, but not here, you won't see them here.

KARANDYSHEV. Very well, I'll do as you say. *(Shakes hands with Robinson.)* Would you like to keep me company?

ROBINSON. Er no, I'm afraid that's impossible, me being a family man. *(Karandyshev goes out.)* Ivan, Ivan! *(Ivan enters.)* Lay the table in my room and take the wine in there!

IVAN. You'll find it stuffy in there, sir. What do you want to go shutting yourself up for.

ROBINSON. The evening air is bad for my health; my doctor forbids it. Oh, and if that gentleman should ask for me, tell him I'm out. *(Goes into the cafe.)*

Gavrilo comes out of the cafe.

Scene 4

Gavrilo, Ilya, gypsies.

GAVRILO. Have a good trip?

ILYA. Ay, that we did, never better!

GAVRILO. And the gentlemen, were they merry?

ILYA. Ay, they had a gay old time, laughing and joking. They're on their way now. It's likely they'll spend the whole night drinking.

GAVRILO *(rubbing his hands)*. All right then, get seats for yourselves. I'll order the women to be given tea; and you get along to the buffet and grab yourselves a bite!

ILYA. Tell 'em to give the old girls a drop of rum with their tea. They like that.

Ilya, gypsies, Gavrilo go into cafe. Knurov and Vozhevatov enter.

Scene 5

Knurov and Vozhevatov.

KNUROV. I think the drama's beginning.
VOZHEVATOV. Looks like it.
KNUROV. I noticed the tears in her eyes.
VOZHEVATOV. They come easily enough with her.
KNUROV. Say what you will, her situation isn't enviable.
VOZHEVATOV. Oh, it'll all work out in the end.
KNUROV. I rather doubt that.
VOZHEVATOV. Karandyshev will rant and rave a bit, then he'll be his usual self again.
KNUROV. Yes, but she won't. After all, you don't throw your fiancé over practically the day before the wedding without some solid reason. Think about it yourself. Sergei Sergeyich comes here for a single day, and for his sake she abandons the man she was supposed to spend the rest of her life with. That means she's putting her hopes on Paratov; why else should she have anything to do with him.
VOZHEVATOV. So, you think he's been leading her on again?
KNUROV. Stands to reason. And he must have made definite promises. Why else should she trust a man who's betrayed her once before.
VOZHEVATOV. Well! I can't say that surprises me. Sergei Sergeyich isn't one to let anything stand in the way of something he wants. A bold fellow.
KNUROV. Well, however bold he may be, he's not going to give up a fiancée with a million for Larisa Dmitryevna's sake.
VOZHEVATOV. I should think not! Nothing less likely!
KNUROV. Well then, you must see where the poor girl stands.
VOZHEVATOV. What's to be done about it? It's not our fault—we're just spectators.

Robinson appears on the cafe porch.

Scene 6

Knurov, Vozhevatov, Robinson.

VOZHEVATOV. Ah, milord! What did you dream of?
ROBINSON. Fools with money; the same as I see when I'm awake.
VOZHEVATOV. And how have you been passing your time here, my ragged philosopher?
ROBINSON. Royally! I'm living on the fat of the land—and on credit too, at your expense. What could be better!

VOZHEVATOV. You're to be envied. And how long do you intend to revel in these delights?

ROBINSON. What a very odd question to ask. What advantage would I gain from giving them up?

VOZHEVATOV. Perhaps memory plays me false, but I don't seem to remember giving you carte blanche.

ROBINSON. You offered to take me to Paris. Isn't that the same thing?

VOZHEVATOV. No, it isn't the same thing at all. If I've given a promise, I keep it; for me a promise is sacred. Ask anyone—have I ever failed to keep my word?

ROBINSON. And while you're getting ready to go to Paris, am I supposed to live on air?

VOZHEVATOV. There was nothing about that in our understanding. Anyway, we can go to Paris now if you like.

ROBINSON. It's late now; I tell you what, Vasya, let's go tomorrow.

VOZHEVATOV. All right then, tomorrow. Come to think of it, why don't you go alone. I'll pay your expenses there and back.

ROBINSON. How can I go alone? I don't know the way.

VOZHEVATOV. They'll take you.

ROBINSON. Listen, Vasya, my French isn't all that fluent. I keep meaning to learn it properly, but somehow I never seem to have the time.

VOZHEVATOV. What should you need to speak French for?

ROBINSON. Well, I mean, to be in Paris and not speak French?

VOZHEVATOV. But it's not necessary at all; no one speaks French there.

ROBINSON. The capital of France, and he says no one speaks French there! Do you take me for an idiot?

VOZHEVATOV. What's all this about capitals? You haven't gone off your head, by any chance? What Paris do you think we're talking about? There's a tavern in the town square called the Paris—and that's where I was going to take you.

ROBINSON. Bravo, bravo!

VOZHEVATOV. And you thought I meant the real one? You should have thought about it a bit first. And you think yourself so clever too! I ask you, what on earth should I take you to Paris for? To put you in a cage and exhibit you to the public?

ROBINSON. You've been well schooled, Vasya, well schooled; you'll do well in commerce, no doubt about that.

VOZHEVATOV. Yes, pretty well I should think; I'm told people think me promising.

KNUROV. Don't waste your breath on him, Vasily Danilych. I was wanting to have a few words with you on a certain matter.

VOZHEVATOV (going over to him). At your service.

KNUROV. I've been thinking about Larisa Dmitryevna. It seems to me that her situation is now such that as true friends we are called upon to take an active interest in her welfare. You might even say we are morally obliged to do so.

VOZHEVATOV. This is the time for someone to whisk her off to Paris. Is that what you mean?

KNUROV. Yes, I suppose you could put it like that. It comes to much the same thing.

VOZHEVATOV. Well, what's the trouble? Who's in your way?

KNUROV. You are; you're in my way and I'm in yours. Perhaps competition doesn't worry you? I don't lose any sleep over it either; but all the same it is awkward; much better to have a clear field.

VOZHEVATOV. It's no good trying to buy me off, Moki Parmenych.

KNUROV. No need for that. We can arrange things some other way.

VOZHEVATOV. Here's the best way. *(Takes a coin from his pocket and puts his hand over it.)* Heads or tails?

KNUROV *(thoughtfully)*. If I say "heads" I'll lose. You're sure to be heads. *(Resolutely)*. Tails.

VOZHEVATOV. You win. So, I'll have to go to Paris alone. Never mind. I'll have fewer expenses.

KNUROV. Well just remember the saying, "Don't make promises, but if you make them, keep them." As a merchant you ought to know what that means.

VOZHEVATOV. I can assure you that you do me an injustice. I know very well that a merchant's word is his bond. I'm dealing with you now, not Robinson.

KNUROV. Here comes Sergei Sergeyich with Larisa Dmitryevna! Let's go inside and leave them undisturbed.

Knurov and Vozhevatov disappear into the cafe. Paratov and Larisa enter.

LARISA. Oh, I'm so tired. It took all my strength to get up that hill. *(Sits down backstage on a bench by the balustrade.)*

PARATOV. Ah, Robinson, it's you! Are you leaving for Paris shortly?

ROBINSON. Who would I go with? Now with you, La Serge, I'd go anywhere; but I wouldn't go with a merchant. No, I'm finished with merchants.

PARATOV. What's this I hear?

ROBINSON. Ignoramuses!

PARATOV. You astound me! And when did you make this discovery?

ROBINSON. I always knew. I was always a supporter of the aristocracy.

PARATOV. That does you credit, Robinson. But you haven't chosen a very good time for a show of pride. You must adapt yourself to circumstances, my poor friend. The age of the enlightened patron is gone; we witness the triumph of the bourgeoisie; these days art is weighed in the scale against gold. The true golden age has arrived at last! Still, you mustn't complain. Some of those Medicis might very well have made you eat blacking or rolled you down a hill in a barrel for their amusement. Don't go away; I shall be needing you.

ROBINSON. I'd go through fire and water for you! *(Goes into the cafe.)*

PARATOV *(to Larisa)*. Allow me to thank you for the pleasure—no, that's not the word—for the happiness you have given us.

LARISA. No, no, Sergei Sergeyich, I don't want fine words from you. Just tell me one thing: am I or am I not your wife?

PARATOV. The most important thing now is to get you home. There'll be time to talk things over tomorrow.

LARISA. I'm not going home.

PARATOV. But you can't stay here. To go on a river trip with us during the day, there's nothing so shocking about that; but to spend the night carousing here in town, and with men whose reputations aren't exactly spotless, that'll really be giving the gossips something to talk about.

LARISA. Let them talk, what do I care? As long as I'm with you it doesn't matter where I am. You took me away; you must take me back home.

PARATOV. You'll be going in my carriage. Isn't that much the same thing?

LARISA. No, it isn't. You took me away from the man I was going to marry; Mama saw us leave, she won't worry however late we come back. She trusts you, so she is calm; she will wait for us, wait to give us her blessing. I must either return with you, or not go home at all.

PARATOV. What do you mean "not go home at all"? Where else can you go?

LARISA. The wide world has room enough for the wretched, the orchard here, the river down there. Any branch will do to hang myself; or there's the river. It's easy to drown if you have the strength of will.

PARATOV. Very noble and tragic! You can and must live. Who will deny you his love and respect? Why, that fiancé of yours, a smile and a kind word and you'll be able to twist him round your finger.

LARISA. You don't know what you're saying. If I can't love my husband, I must at least respect him; and how can I respect a man who puts up with insults and ridicule. No, that's all over; he no longer exists for me. I have only one fiancé—you.

PARATOV. Forgive me, and don't be offended, but really, you hardly have the right to make such claims on me.

LARISA. No right! Have you forgotten? Then I'll go over it all again from the beginning. A year I suffered, a year I was unable to forget you. Life become empty, meaningless; in the end I decided to marry Karandyshev, almost the first man that came along. I thought that the responsibilities of family life would fill my life and reconcile me to it. Then suddenly you appeared and said "Give up everything, I am yours." Can you deny that? I believed your word, I thought that my suffering had won this from you.

PARATOV. That's all very fine, but we'll talk about it tomorrow.

LARISA. No, today, now.

PARATOV. You demand it?

LARISA. I do.

Knurov and Vozhevatov can be seen in the doorway of the cafe.

PARATOV. Very well. Listen to me, Larisa Dmitryevna. You admit that one is sometimes carried away in the heat of the moment?

LARISA. Yes, it happens to me sometimes.

PARATOV. No, I didn't express myself well; can you understand that a man might be bound hand and foot by unbreakable chains and yet be so carried away that he forgets everything in the world, forgets the reality that oppresses him, forgets even his chains?

LARISA. Happy the man who can do that.

PARATOV. It's a very pleasant state of mind. I don't deny it, but it doesn't last. The madness of passion soon passes, and what remains are chains and common sense that tells us that these chains are unbreakable.

LARISA. Unbreakable chains! *(Quickly.)* You're not married?

PARATOV. No.

LARISA. All other chains are of no account. We shall carry them together. I'll share the burden and bear the heavier part myself.

PARATOV. I'm engaged to be married.

LARISA. Ah!

PARATOV *(showing her his ring)*. Here is the golden chain which will bind me for the rest of my life.

LARISA. Why didn't you tell me? Cruel, wicked! *(Sinks down into a chair.)*

PARATOV. Do you think I was in a state to think of such things? One look at you and nothing else existed for me.

LARISA. Look at me! *(Paratov looks into her eyes.)* "Eyes as clear as heaven..." Ha, ha, ha! *(Laughs hysterically.)* Go away from me! I've had enough. From now on I'll look after myself. *(Leans her head on her hand.)*

Knurov, Vozhevatov and Robinson appear on the cafe porch.

Scene 8

Paratov, Larisa, Knurov, Vozhevatov, Robinson.

PARATOV *(going toward the cafe)*. Robinson, go and get my carriage! It's waiting near here somewhere. You're taking Larisa Dmitryevna home.

ROBINSON. La Serge! He's here, he's going about with a pistol.

PARATOV. Who is this "he"?

ROBINSON. Karandyshev.

PARATOV. Well, what's that got to do with me?

ROBINSON. He'll kill me.

PARATOV. What a terrible loss to the world. Do as you're ordered! No arguments, I don't like that, Robinson.

ROBINSON. I tell you he'll kill me if he sees me with her.

PARATOV. He may kill you or he may not, but if you don't carry out my orders I certainly shall. *(Goes into the cafe.)*

ROBINSON *(shaking his fist after him)*. Barbarians! Brigands! Fine company I've fallen into! *(Goes out.)*

Vozhevatov goes over to Larisa.

LARISA *(looking at Vozhevatov)*. I feel as if I'm falling and there's nothing I can hold on to.

VOZHEVATOV. Larisa Dmitryevna, my dear friend. It's no good, there's nothing we can do.

LARISA. Vasya, we've known each other since we were children, we're almost like brother and sister; tell me what I must do, advise me!

VOZHEVATOV. Larisa Dmitryevna, I respect you and would gladly....
There's nothing I can do. You must believe me.

LARISA. I'm not asking anything of you. All I want is sympathy. Weep with
me at least, if there's nothing else you can do.

VOZHEVATOV. There's nothing I can do, nothing.

LARISA. You too have your chains?

VOZHEVATOV. Shackles, Larisa Dmitryevna.

LARISA. What are they?

VOZHEVATOV. A merchant's sworn word. *(Goes into the cafe.)*

KNUROV *(goes over to Larisa).* Larisa Dmitryevna, listen to what I have to
say, and don't be offended. The last thing I want is to offend you. I desire only
your good and the happiness you so thoroughly deserve. How would you like to
go to Paris with me for the exhibition? *(Larisa shakes her head.)* And financial
security for the rest of your life? *(Larisa makes no reply.)* You need have no fear of
scandal. There will be no censure. There are bounds beyond which censure dare
not pass; I can afford to keep you in such luxury that even the most censorious
will gape in amazement and be at a loss for words. *(Larisa turns her head away.)*
You're overwrought. I won't insist on an answer now. Think it over! If you
decide to give my offer favorable consideration, please inform me; and from that
moment on I shall be your most devoted servant and no desire, no caprice of
yours will be too eccentric or too costly to be fulfilled to the letter. For me even
the impossible is little. *(Bows respectfully and goes into the cafe.)*

Scene 9

Larisa alone.

LARISA. Earlier on I looked down there through the railings and my head
began to spin. I nearly fell. And if one does fall death is certain! *(Thinks.)* To
jump, that would be it! No, no need to jump.... just stand by the railings and
look down, your head spins and you fall.... Yes, that would be better. *(Goes to the
railing and looks down. She bends, grasps the railings firmly, then steps quickly back.)*
Oh, oh, how dreadful! *(Almost falling, grabs hold of the arbor nearby.)* My head's
going round and round. I'm falling, falling, oh! *(Sits down at the table by the
arbor.)* No, no, it's no good. *(Through tears.)* Parting with life isn't as easy as I
thought. I don't have the strength, it seems. Oh God, how wretched I am! And
yet there are people who don't find it so hard. I suppose they just can't go on living, nothing attracts them any more, nothing is dear to them, there's nothing
they regret leaving behind. But what am I saying.... is anything dear to me, do I
have anything left to live for? Why can't I bring myself to do it? What is it that
keeps me hanging over the abyss? What stops me? *(Thinks.)* No, not Knurov...
luxury, glitter... no... no... all that doesn't even tempt me.... *(Shuddering.)* To be a
kept woman... oh no... I simply lack the strength of will. Pitiful weakness: to
cling to life, any kind of life, when life has become impossible and pointless.
What a pathetic creature I am. If only someone would kill me.... How good it
would be to die...while I still have nothing to reproach myself with. Or to fall ill

and die.... Yes, I think I'm falling ill, I'm in such pain. To have a long illness, to grow calm, to make one's peace with the world, to forgive everyone and die.... I feel terrible, my head's spinning. *(Rests her head on her hand and remains in a state of semi-consciousness.)*

Enter Robinson and Karandyshev.

Scene 10

Larisa, Robinson, Karandyshev.

KARANDYSHEV. You say you were ordered to take her home?
ROBINSON. Yes, ordered to.
KARANDYSHEV. And you say they insulted her?
ROBINSON. Most grievously.
KARANDYSHEV. She has no one to blame but herself: she deserved to be punished for what she did. I told her the sort of people they were, and how could she have failed to notice how different they are from me, but no one but me has the right to judge her, still less to insult her. Perhaps I'll forgive her, perhaps I won't, that's my affair; in any case it's my duty to come forward and defend her. She has no brothers, no close friends; I and I alone must guard her honor and punish those who insult her. Where is she?
ROBINSON. She was here. There she is!
KARANDYSHEV. I must talk with her alone; your presence is unwanted. Leave us.
ROBINSON. With the greatest pleasure. I'll tell them I've delivered Larisa Dmitryevna into your keeping. I have the honor to take my leave. (*Karandyshev goes over to the table and sits down opposite Larisa.*)

Scene 11

Larisa and Karandyshev.

LARISA *(lifting her head).* If only you knew how you disgust me. Why have you come here?
KARANDYSHEV. Where else should I be?
LARISA. I don't know. Wherever you like, as long as it isn't where I am.
KARANDYSHEV. You are mistaken; I must always be near you so that I can protect you. You have been insulted, and I am here to avenge you.
LARISA. As far as I'm concerned the worst insult is that you should offer me your protection; apart from that I don't remember any insults.
KARANDYSHEV. You are unjust to yourself. Knurov and Vozhevatov are spinning a coin to see which one gets you. Isn't that an insult? A fine set of friends you have. How can they respect you? They don't look upon you as a woman, as a human being, a human being has the right to order his own fate.

They look upon you as a thing. If you are a thing, of course it's a different matter. A thing belongs to whoever wins it, a thing is hardly capable of taking
offense.

LARISA *(deeply hurt).* A thing, yes, that's it, a thing. They're right. I'm a
thing, not a human being. That's something I have just proved to myself. I am a
thing, I know it! *(Hotly.)* At last a word has been found to fit me, and you have
found it. Go away. I beg you to leave me in peace.

KARANDYSHEV. Leave you? How can I—whose mercy would I be leaving
you to?

LARISA. A thing must have an owner. I'll go to my owner.

KARANDYSHEV *(passionately).* You must come with me, you belong to me.
(Grasps her by the arm.)

LARISA *(pushing him away).* Oh, no! Things have their price.... Ha. ha. ha....
I'm much, much too expensive for you.

KARANDYSHEV. You don't know what you're saying! Who would have
thought I would ever hear such shameless words from you!

LARISA *(weeping).* If one has to be a thing, there is one consolation: to be
expensive, to be very expensive. Do me one last service, go send Knurov to me.

KARANDYSHEV. You can't mean that, you can't.

LARISA. Very well, I'll go myself.

KARANDYSHEV. Larisa Dmitryevna! Stop! I forgive you. I forgive you
everything.

LARISA *(smiling bitterly).* You forgive me? Thank you very much. But I can't
forgive myself for getting tied up to a nonentity like you.

KARANDYSHEV. Let's get away, let's get away from this town. I'll do anything you want.

LARISA. Too late. I begged you to take me away from the gypsy camp and
you wouldn't do it; it seems I'm fated to live and die with the gypsies.

KARANDYSHEV. Make me a happy man, I beg of you!

LARISA. Too late. I've seen the glitter of gold now and the sparkle of diamonds.

KARANDYSHEV. For your sake I'm prepared to make any sacrifice, to suffer any humiliation.

LARISA *(with disgust).* Go away. You're too shallow, too insignificant for me.

KARANDYSHEV. Tell me, how can I win your love? *(Falls on his knees).* I
love you. I love you.

LARISA. You're lying. I looked for love and couldn't find it anywhere.
People saw me as a pleasant way of passing the time. They still do. No one ever
cared to look into my heart, no one ever gave me sympathy or a kind word. The
world has been a cold place for me. I'm not to blame. I looked for love and
couldn't find it. It doesn't exist, so what's the good of looking for it? In future I'll
look for gold. Go away, I shall never belong to you.

KARANDYSHEV *(getting up).* You mustn't change now. *(Slips his hand
inside his coat.)* You shall be mine!

LARISA. Anyone's but yours!

KARANDYSHEV *(violently).* You won't?

LARISA. Never.

KARANDYSHEV. Then be nobody's! *(Fires the pistol at her.)*

LARISA *(clutching her breast)*. Ah! Thank you for that! *(Sinks into a chair.)*

KARANDYSHEV. What have I done, what have I done.... I must be mad. *(Lets the pistol fall.)*

LARISA *(tenderly)*. My dearest, what a kindness you have done me! Put the pistol here, here on the table. I did it myself... myself... Ah, what a kindness! *(Picks up the pistol and puts it on the table.)*

Paratov. Knurov. Vozhevatov, Robinson. Gavrilo and Ivan enter from the cafe.

Scene 12

Larisa and the above.

ALL. What's happening, what's happening?

LARISA. I did it myself... no one's to blame... I did it myself. *(Gypsies strike up a song offstage.)*

PARATOV. Tell them to be quiet, tell them to be quiet!

LARISA *(her voice gradually weakening)*. No, no, what for?... Let people enjoy themselves if they want to...why should I be in anyone's way? Live, all of you, live! You must live and I must... die.... I don't reproach anyone, no one has done me any wrong.... You're all good people... I love you... I love you all. *(Kisses her hand to them.)*

Loud chorus of gypsies.

                              CURTAIN

FYODOR SOLOGUB

VANKA THE STEWARD AND JEHAN THE PAGE
A Drama in Thirteen Parallel Scenes

CHARACTERS

Russian Scenes:
Prince
Princess
Vanka
An Old Servant
Swarthy Wench
Drinking-House Strumpets
Tipplers
Servants of the Prince
Executioners
Filthy Tartar

French Scenes:
Count
Countess
Jehan
Agobard, a Retainer
Raymonda, a Maidservant
Starling
Merry Maidens
Pages
Servants of the Count

Author's Note
This drama, in its Russian part, is taken from songs assembled in the book *Folksongs of Great Russia*, edited by Professor A.N. Sobolevsky, volume 1, St. Petersburg, 1895 (first 47 variants, pp. 1-84).

Scene 1

The broad courtyard of the prince's palace. Thronged with motley menials of the prince who await their master. The prince comes out onto the porch; with him the princess. All bow low while the prince and princess advance majestically. Vanka shoulders his way through the crowd and falls at the prince's feet.

VANKA. Long life to you Prince and fair Princess!

PRINCE. What brings you hither, my fine fellow?

VANKA. Once upon a time I lived with my father, his sole son and heir. I was my mother's darling and the apple of my father's eye. Being a dashing young fellow, my greatest delight was a wild spree, a long evening tramp, or a dark night's ride. Geese and swans I'd go ahuntin', and fine gray-feathered ducklings too. But then father married me off against my will and my wishes. Big dowry, paltry bride.

PRINCE. 'Twas ever so—a sack of money with a wife, a scrawny bedmate yours for life.

VANKA. Being a fine fellow, I left my scrawny jinx of a wife, traveled many lands, and came at last to your princely palace. I throw myself at your feet, and pledge my loyalty in your service.

Bows low to the ground.

PRINCE. And will you serve me faithfully?

VANKA. I shall serve you truly and faithfully, in your sight and out of it.

PRINCE. Then live here, my fine young fellow, and serve us as a groom.

VANKA. For that I thank you most humbly. I am well content with your princely grace and favor. May God grant you and your fair princess everlasting good health. *(Bows low.)*

Courtyard of the count's castle. In the courtyard servants and pages. The count and countess come out onto the porch. All bow low before them, and they graciously acknowledge the bows. Jehan steps out of the crowd. He bends his knees before the count.

JEHAN. Most gracious Count, most gracious Countess, look favorably upon me, a penniless youth, the son of noble and honorable parents.

COUNT. Fair youth, who are you and whence?

JEHAN. My name is Jehan, my nickname the Fair. I stem from Gogenau. My father is an old warrior and your true vassal, Robert the Hawk. My father taught me to wield arms, from my mother I learned to play the lute and to sing diverting and pleasing songs to ladies and damsels, and a goodly monk of the monastery of Gogenau, brother Thomas, did not spare his labors or the whip to instruct me in reading and writing. My parents have sent me forth into the world so that I should enter the service of a renowned lord; and behold I bow low before you.

Oh, Count, most gracious lord, I entreat you to take me into your service. I promise to serve you faithfully and zealously, with all my strength and capacity, taking no thought for my own life for the good and advantage of my lord and his fair and gracious lady, whose charms are as radiant as the sun's, if it be possible for one sun to shine in the presence of one still more luminous.

COUNT. The boy has a way with words and commends himself most impressively.

COUNTESS. It seems to me that he will make a goodly page.

COUNT. We'll see. And in the meantime, let him serve under the guidance of our groom Adalbert.

JEHAN. May the Lord bless you with victories and glory, gracious Count. May the Lord bless you with happiness and love, gracious Countess.

Bows low and kisses the skirt of the count's cloak, and the hem of the countess's dress.

Scene 2

A chamber in the princely dwelling. The prince and princess sit alone.

PRINCE. My darling Princess, Annushka, light of my life, who is most worthy and pleasing in your eyes?

PRINCESS. You are most worthy, you are most pleasing. You are dearer to me than the bright sun, the clear moon. Among princes, among boyars, among our merchant visitors, among the simple folk there is none to compare with you, my love, in knightly prowess. And your eyes are like a hawk's, your brows are sable, and your curls fall blacker than dark night. And no one is to be found wiser than you—a word from you is worth a ruble.

PRINCE (*complacently*). Yes, that's the way I'm known to be. I should be taken as an example.

They kiss.

PRINCE. And among my courtiers who is worthy, who is deserving of favor?

PRINCESS. Worthy among your courtiers is Vanka, the groom. He has lived with us for a year, has not drunk of bitter wine, has not tasted of sweet mead.

PRINCE. Then Vanka shall become a steward. (*Shouts.*) Vanka!

Shouts are heard offstage.

Vanka, Vanka! Where's Vanka? The prince is calling Vanka. Run and fetch Vanka quickly, you little rogue. Vanka! Where's he got to, the little devil? Vanka, you devil, you goblin, get a move on, you block of oak, the prince is calling you. Come on, you clumsy lout, the prince is waiting, he's getting right angry. Give him a punch to make him run livelier. Run, run, Vanka, get a move on—the prince in person is going to bestow honor upon you. Well, what are you dawdling about for, come on! Get a move on. Get a move on!

Someone pushes Vanka into the royal chamber. Vanka comes flying in, sprawls headlong. Picks himself up, shakes out his hair and bows gravely.

VANKA. So I'm right on the spot as they say, Vanka on the spot.

PRINCE. You're a smart one, Vanka. God sheds his grace on you, you dashing young fellow, and I, the prince, am mightily well disposed toward you. I'm taking you out of the grooms and putting you, dashing young fellow that you are, among the stewards.

VANKA. For that, Prince and young Princess, I humbly thank you. *(Bows low.)* Your hand, I pray. *(Kisses the prince's hand.)* Gracious Princess, your hand, I pray. *(Kisses the princess's hand.)*

PRINCE. See that you don't steal, guard our chattels with your life.

VANKA. So shall it be, I swear it. *(Bows low.)*

PRINCE. But if you are a faithful servant, Vanka, you shall find much favor with me.

VANKA. I need not say I am glad to serve your princely highness, I need not say. *(Bows low.)*

PRINCE. And now, Vanka, be off with you.

VANKA. I wish you long life, Prince and fair Princess. I am your faithful servant.

Bows low, goes out and spits.

PRINCESS. A tactful young man.

PRINCE. I am hopeful that he will not steal.

PRINCESS. He's not that kind, he won't steal.

The prince and princess kiss.

A room in the count's castle. The count and countess are sitting alone.

COUNT. Light of my eyes, soul of my soul, my sweet Jehanne, who in this world is most dear to you?

COUNTESS. My beloved lord, when I lived at home, my dear parents were dearer to me than anyone else in the world. But of course I didn't know you then.

COUNT *(smiling)*. And then?

COUNTESS *(coquettishly)*. And then there was my dear old nanny. But, of course, I didn't know you then.

COUNT. And then?

COUNTESS. I saw many handsome, valorous knights, but you, my beloved lord and master, are handsomest and most valorous of all. Your chest is broader than the chest of the knight Romauld of Normandy, victor of eleven tournaments. Your voice is more resounding than the voice of the sexton of Rouen cathedral. And your caresses are more ardent and sweeter... *(Blushes and falls silent. The count twirls his mustache complacently. The countess gives him a timid glance and smiles radiantly. They kiss.)*

COUNT. I wish to reward in your name the man among my servants who has won favor with his zeal.

COUNTESS. The boy Jehan, who serves in the stables, is so full of zeal that it is diverting to look at him. He blows and spits on my stirrup, and rubs it with his sleeve to make it gleam like pure gold.

COUNT. Let Jehan be made a page.

Strikes the foot of the candelabra with his dagger. Enter Agobard, his old retainer.

COUNT. Agobard, you old dog, send in Jehan, the boy from the stables, the pretty one they call the Fair. And let him put fresh clothes on the wash, in case he makes this place smell of what it shouldn't.

AGOBARD. But the boy Jehan is right here—he took it into his head to come all dressed up, without a hair out of place.

COUNT. What does he want then?

AGOBARD. Just a silly whim! The gracious countess won't want even to look at it.

COUNTESS. But what is it, dear Agobard?

COUNT. Inquisitive daughter of Eve!

AGOBARD. Utter nonsense! I did my best to chase him away, but he keeps begging so pathetically. He's caught a starling, you know, put it in a cage and taught it to twitter a few words; he wants to present it to our gracious lady. Really, such nonsense!

COUNTESS *(joyfully)*. How utterly diverting! Agobard, you darling old dog, call him at once, and let him bring the starling.

AGOBARD *(muttering, opens the door and shouts)*. Hey you, boy, come here. And let's see you bow lower, you blunder-headed dunce!

Jehan enters, bows low, approaches the count and countess and sinks on his knees before the countess. He is holding a cage, in the cage a starling.

STARLING *(squawks)*. Long life!

The count laughs thunderously, the countess dissolves in gleeful laughter. Jehan and Agobard laugh.

JEHAN *(when the laughter has somewhat quieted)*. Gracious lady...

STARLING *(squawks)*. The count is terrible to his enemies!

Again everyone laughs, the count and countess, sitting on their high-backed chairs, Agobard standing at the door, and Jehan on his knees before the countess. They laugh a long time. The laughter finally subsides.

JEHAN. Gracious lady, deign to accept this worthless tribute from the most zealous, though the humblest of your servants.

STARLING *(squawks)*. Fair Countess! *(Everyone laughs as before.)*

COUNTESS. Thank you, sweet Jehan, your gift is very pleasing to me. The starling will hang caged in the room where I sew.

COUNT. You're a nimble one, sweet Jehan. Something will come of you, I can see that. I release you from service under our groom Adalbert, and appoint you our page. Bernard the page is grown up now and has started chasing girls. Time for him to bear arms. And instead of him you will serve at the table of my beloved spouse, Countess Jehanne.

Jehan joyfully bows before the count.

AGOBARD *(muttering)*. A great, great honor for a mere boy! He should stand a bit lower at table—there are many pages older than he.

COUNT *(laughing)*. The old grumbler has had a really good grumble. Well, and you, boy, see that you serve me faithfully.

JEHAN. Gracious Count, my devotion knows no bounds, and my zeal contends with my devotion as to which of the two is stronger and more ardent.

Kisses the graciously extended hands of the count and countess.

COUNT. See to it that the countess's plates are even cleaner than her gilded stirrup. Only don't blow and spit on them. (*The count and countess laugh. Jehan blushes.*)

COUNT. That old dog Agobard will instruct you in etiquette, what to do and how to do it. Obey him and prick up your ears, for I give short shrift.

JEHAN. Where there is anger, there is grace. And if I should be at fault in anything, my gracious lord, I am aware of the consequences. The likes of us don't get through life without a beating.

COUNT. And for loyalty and zeal you shall be rewarded.

JEHAN. Not for reward, but for honor and conscience shall I serve. (*Bows low.*)

COUNT. And now, little ragamuffin, be off with you.

Jehan bows low, straightens himself and goes out. The countess looks tenderly at her husband, placing a hand on his knee. She speaks sweetly.

COUNTESS. Jehan, come here now. (*To the count.*) May I? (*The count nods silently. Jehan approaches and bows.*)

COUNTESS. Jehan, I hope you don't smell too much of the stables?

JEHAN. Gracious lady, I bathed in the stream. Then your maidservant, who is very pretty, although she possesses but a hundredth part of your beauty, young Raymonda, sprinkled a few drops of rosewater into a pitcher and with this water rubbed my entire body, from my neck to my heels.

COUNTESS. How kind of Raymonda.

Laughs. The count guffaws. Jehan blushes.

AGOBARD *(mutters)*. That Raymonda and that boy should both be given a taste of the whip.

COUNTESS. All right, all right, old dog, don't growl. Jehan, if you are so fragrant, come much closer to me. As a reward for the starling I wish to kiss your scarlet lips. *(To the count.)* May I, my good lord?

COUNT. To you it is permitted, my sweet Jehanne. You are my faithful little wife.

AGOBARD *(mutters).* A great, great honor for a mere lad! If I had my way, Raymonda and he...

JEHAN *(bowing low).* The gracious countess rewards me beyond my deserts.

Draws close. The countess grasps his neck with her left hand, takes his chin in her right hand, laughs and kisses him on the lips with such tenderness that Jehan blushes scarlet. The count guffaws.

COUNTESS *(tenderly).* That's for the starling.

STARLING *(squawks).* Long life!

Jehan bows low, modestly covers his face with his sleeve and runs off. The count guffaws.

COUNT. An obliging and nimble boy.

COUNTESS. They say he has a good voice.

COUNT. Keep a sharp eye on him, old dog. Something will come of him. And see that he learns to fight as befits a warrior, and that he has a firm grasp of everything pertaining to cavalry and infantry.

COUNTESS *(sighing, whispers).* Battles and wounds. Some are killed, others are mutilated.

COUNT. A long peace is dear only to women and cowards.

Agobard goes off. The count and countess kiss.

Scene 3

A garden of the princely dwelling. The princess walks back and forth, sniffing flow - ers, and stealing glances at Vanka. Vanka is strolling nearby, preening himself and whistling.

PRINCESS. Vanka, oh Vanka!

VANKA *(approaching).* What is your pleasure, Princess?

The princess laughs flirtatiously. Vanka pretends not to respond.

PRINCESS. Vanka, oh Vanka!

VANKA. What is your pleasure, Princess?

PRINCESS. It's a bit too warm for me today, Vanka.

VANKA. Take off your sarafan, Princess.

PRINCESS. Hee-hee.

Vanka flirts. The princess pretends not to respond.

PRINCESS. To the devil with you. Hee-hee.

Moves away capriciously.

PRINCESS. Vanka, oh Vanka!
VANKA. What is your pleasure, Princess?
PRINCESS. Something is itching where I can't reach it, I need to be scratched between my shoulder blades.
VANKA. Get up against the birch tree, Princess, and rub your back against it.

The princess laughs flirtatiously. Vanka pretends not to respond.
VANKA. Princess, oh Princess!
PRINCESS. What do you want, Vanka?
VANKA. Come closer to me, I'll warm up your back with my fist so that it stops itching.

The princess giggles and strikes an affected pose. Vanka strolls around her and spits.

PRINCESS. Vanka, oh Vanka!
VANKA. What is your pleasure, Princess?

The princess giggles. Vanka contrives to give the princess a slap on the back with the palm of his hand.

PRINCESS *(squeals piercingly)*. Ee-ee-eekh! You devil, you fiend, what a wallop!
VANKA *(guffawing)*. What a sweet little morsel you are.
PRINCESS. Gave me such a wallop that I feel even hotter.
VANKA. Take off that sarafan then, it's as easy as pie.
PRINCESS *(giggling and covering her face with her muslin sleeve)*. They'll see.
VANKA. There's no one here to see.
PRINCESS. Vanka, oh Vanka!
VANKA. What is your pleasure, Princess?
PRINCESS. What a sweet little morsel you are, Vanka. Hee-hee!

Vanka guffaws. The princess flirts.

PRINCESS. What's the point of stewing in the sun! I just can't take any more of it. Let's go, Vanka, to my chambers, my private chambers.
VANKA *(laughing)*. And will you give me some young wine?
PRINCESS. I will set it before you.
VANKA. And will you give me sweet mead?
PRINCESS. I will give it to you.
VANKA. And will you treat me to a heart-shaped honey-cake?

PRINCESS. I will indeed.

VANKA. And will you kiss my sugar-sweet lips?

PRINCESS. That's the way it has to be, I will kiss them.

VANKA. And will you take off your sarafan?

PRINCESS. Stop pestering me, I'll take it off.

VANKA. And the rest?

PRINCESS. You don't give up, do you, Vanka—yes, I'll take it off because I'm feeling very hot, I just can't stand it any more!

Both laugh.

VANKA. And will you dance for me with nothing on?

PRINCESS. All right then, I'll dance, whatever happens.

VANKA. Take my hand, my right hand, the hand of a dashing young man, and lead me to your private chambers.

They go off together.

A garden near the count's castle. The countess, holding in her hand a white fan, walks past the rose bushes. Jehan stands behind the bushes watching the countess ten - derly and discreetly.

COUNTESS. Jehan!

JEHAN. Here I am, Countess, eternally prepared to serve you and the count.

COUNTESS. The count is hunting, we are alone. *(Throws Jehan a languid glance. Jehan blushes).* Dear Jehan!

JEHAN. What is your command, gracious lady?

COUNTESS. The sun is so high and sultry, the sky is cloudless, the sons of Aeolus are asleep, and even the windy zephyr lies hidden in the bushes by the river. It is so stifling and hot, my eyes are misty and my restless heart whispers— can you guess what it whispers?

JEHAN. Gracious Countess, the language of the heart is dark but clear to the ear of a young man.

COUNTESS. Naughty Jehan, you seem to have imagined something.

Jehan smiles tenderly and slyly. The countess blushes.

COUNTESS. Jehan, why are you staring at my bosom? I didn't uncover it for you, but for the sweet sighs of my white fan.

JEHAN. Pardon me, gracious Countess. (*Goes off to one side and casts surrepti - tious and passionate glances at the countess.*)

COUNTESS. Jehan, why won't you help me? Have you forgotten that my wish is your command?

JEHAN. What is your command, gracious lady?

COUNTESS. The clasps of my belt are pricking my fingers—unfasten the belt, it's stifling me.

JEHAN *(carrying out her command, kisses the countess's hands and sighs).* This belt has had its moments of happiness. Cruel belt! Its embraces have wearied the gracious lady.

COUNTESS. Impudent Jehan, can it be that you dream that your arms could encircle me in its stead? How naughty of you!

Strokes his cheek. Jehan blushes and smiles tenderly.

JEHAN. Sweet Countess, Jehanne!

COUNTESS. What do you have to say, Jehan? Speak up, speak up, don't be afraid. If you say something you shouldn't, I promise not to be too angry.

JEHAN. I am your faithful servant, sweet lady Jehanne. I am prepared to replace your belt with my hands, your dress with my body.

COUNTESS. What a naughty boy you are!

Blushes and giggles. Jehan looks at her with a bold and lustful gaze.

COUNTESS. What a naughty little boy you are, Jehan!

JEHAN *(softly)*. Sweet Jehanne!

COUNTESS. So that's the kind of naughty boy you are!

Jehan goes down on one knee and kisses the countess's hands.

COUNTESS. When the same spot is kissed over and over again it becomes very hot.

JEHAN. Sweet Jehanne, your body is as fragrant as a lily of paradise *(kisses her shoulders)*.

COUNTESS. You certainly know how to kiss, you bad boy!

JEHAN *(sighing)*. The unbearable barrier of clothing!

COUNTESS *(giggling)*. And what do you suggest?

JEHAN. No one will see here except for the sun on high and your devoted page Jehan.

COUNTESS. Jehan, you know, you really are a handsome fellow. Certainly you are!

JEHAN. So they say, milady.

He laughs. The countess tickles and pinches him. Jehan, twisting in her arms, caresses her breasts with tender movements of his hands and shoulders. At every touch the countess blushes and gives little shrieks.

COUNTESS. I've grown quite weary in the sun, in this garden, where the shadow of the trees is pierced by the serpentine kisses of the monster that rules the heavens. How wicked he is, that dragon! It's said that he is covered from head to foot with golden scales. Jehan, accompany me to my bedchamber and stay with me for a while.

JEHAN. I am glad to serve my gracious mistress.

COUNTESS. You can sing me a little song.

JEHAN. Even two if you like, and as many as the countess will command. And you, sweet Jehanne, will you play to me on the lute?

COUNTESS. How can one refuse you, sweet Jehan! I shall play the lute for you.

JEHAN *(sighs)*. The unbearable barrier of clothing.

COUNTESS *(ingenuously)*. But there won't be any of that there.

JEHAN. Gracious lady, deign to lean on my arm lest you grow tired—the staircase is close by—and up its dark and cool flights I shall carry you in my arms into the quiet of your bedchamber, sweet Jehanne!

They go out together.

Scene 4

The princess's bedroom. Vanka is sitting proudly at the desk playing high and mighty; the princess waits on him, she places several goblets of mead and tasty morsels on the table.

PRINCESS. I, a princess, set the table, I, a princess, fill the cups, I, a princess, make the bed. I wine and dine the dashing young buck, wine and dine, bow low. Eat, drink your fill, Vanka, eat and make my life a treat. *(Bows low.)*

VANKA *(indifferently)*. Bow down to my feet. My fairest one, fairest of flowers, my fair Princess Annushka.

PRINCESS *(bowing low)*. I can't gaze my fill on your youthful beauty.

VANKA. Lay the mattress stuffed with down on the bed, on the bed's new planks, lay the cushions neatly at the headboard, pull up the sable blanket.

The princess nimbly and gracefully does as she is told. She stands and waits. Vanka eats, champing loudly, drinks, smacking his lips loudly; having eaten and drunk his fill, he belches loudly and makes the sign of the cross over his mouth.

PRINCESS *(ingratiatingly)*. Your dear soul is conversing with God.

VANKA. It turns out you're a fool, Princess—you have sweetly given me to eat and drink, I politely belch you thanks, and my dear soul has nothing to do with it. Well is the bed ready or not?

PRINCESS. Ready, Vanka, ready. *(Bows low.)*

VANKA. Take me by my white hands, lead me to the plank bed, lay me down, dashing young fellow that I am, on a mattress of down.

The princess does as she is told.

VANKA. Stupid woman, you've forgotten to take off my boots.

The princess bows low and removes Vanka's boots.

VANKA. Take off your sarafan. *(The princess takes off her sarafan and bows low.)*

VANKA. Bare your white body, bare your frisky feet. *(The princess strips naked and bows low.)*

VANKA. Dance. *(The princess bows low and dances.)*

VANKA. Sing. *(The princess dances and sings.)*

VANKA. That'll do. Lie down beside me. *(The princess bows low and climbs onto the bed.)*

VANKA *(shouts).* There's a woman for you! More like sugar than a woman!

PRINCESS. Hee-hee, my longed for one! My bright hawk! Damn that mug of yours, how did you capture me?

VANKA *(proudly).* With my flesh.

The bedchamber of the countess. Jehan carries in the countess in his arms and seats her in an armchair.

COUNTESS. You're so strong, Jehan! You carried me up the dark and chilly flights of the staircase as if I were as light as a feather. What do you wish as a reward for your zeal?

JEHAN. To hold you, Countess Jehanne, to hold you in my arms, to feel the trembling of your white breast against my heart—oh my sweet Jehanne, that would be a sublime bliss with which the delights of the garden planted by God Himself are not to be compared.

COUNTESS. Between two rivers, Jehan, was it not so?

JEHAN. Between two arms, as between the two rivers bounding my paradise I enjoyed a bliss brief but incomplete. The rushing wind of swift running would ofttimes lift a curtain easily stirred and no longer held in place by the cruel barrier of a stern belt, a curtain that hides heavenly beauties. I now stand, a poor page, before a thin curtain, but one that has been lowered, and again an intolerable barrier has arisen between the trembling of my desires and the delight of my paradise. *(Jehan presses himself to the countess. The countess slowly removes his caftan.)*

COUNTESS. As you see, you naughty boy, I myself am your servant. If you wish, I'll pour you some wine. Would you like me to pour you some wine?

JEHAN. If that amuses the gracious countess, then I, her faithful servant, am prepared for an hour to be the lord and master of sweet Jehanne.

COUNTESS. A kind master?

JEHAN. If you wish, gracious Jehanne, even a cruel one.

COUNTESS. What a saucy boy you are! But will you dare?

JEHAN. If the gracious countess wishes, then I will dare.

The countess pushes the half undressed Jehan from her knees. Pours two goblets of wine. Gives one of them to Jehan.

JEHAN. To the health of the gracious count. *(They drink.)*

COUNTESS. What are you standing there for? No one will see—here's a soft couch, lay yourself down on it and I'll feast my eyes on you.

JEHAN *(lowering himself).* My shoes are grimy and the soles are covered with sand.

COUNTESS. You're already demanding my services, you naughty boy!

Bends over and pulls off his shoes.

COUNTESS. Now lie down.

Jehan lies down, the countess looks at him and laughs. Jehan blushes. The countess quickly strips him.

COUNTESS. Drink, my sweet Jehan.

They drink.

COUNTESS. Your cheeks are red from the wine.
JEHAN. Not from wine, sweet Jehanne, but from desire.
COUNTESS. What do you want?
JEHAN. Your kisses.

The countess laughs and kisses him.

COUNTESS. You're a silly boy, Jehan—surely that isn't all you want?
JEHAN. No, it isn't.
COUNTESS. What do you want?
JEHAN. The falling away of these intolerable barriers.

The countess laughs and undresses.

COUNTESS. You and I, Jehan, are as stupid as Adam and Eve. Shouldn't we summon the wise serpent?
JEHAN. The serpent's already here, Jehanne. There he is looking in the window. Surely you can hear what he's whispering?
COUNTESS *(laughing)*. I can hear. He's tempting me to bite this apple. *(Gives him a little bite on the cheek.)*
JEHAN. Oh, Jehanne, that's my cheek! He's joking, the wicked serpent. That's not what he's whispering to me.
COUNTESS. What is it then, Jehan?
JEHAN. He's whispering to me: take her by her black braids, turn her over on the couch and do with her as you will. *(Gently takes the countess by the hair and pulls her downward. The countess pretends to be frightened.)*
COUNTESS *(screaming)*. Jehan, Jehan, don't pull so hard. I'll lie down by myself, by myself.... *(Falls down beside Jehan on the couch. Jehan laughs and embraces her.)*
COUNTESS. You frightened me, you horrid boy.
JEHAN. Sweet Jehanne, that was the serpent's advice, and he knows how these things are done.
COUNTESS. Sweet Jehan, even the pagan Tartar and the untamed Muscovite know how to take a woman by force. Love requires boldness but loathes force.
JEHAN. Oh, my sweet naked preacher of sermons. You are as wise as you are beautiful.

COUNTESS. My beloved! My bright hawk! Oh you young reprobate, how did you capture me, Jehan?

JEHAN. With love, my sweet Jehanne, with love. Jehanne! Jehanne! My beloved! Jehanne!

Embraces and caresses her passionately.

COUNTESS. Jehan, Jehan, Jehan!

Scene 5

The garden. The princess is looking out of the window. Vanka is strolling beneath, spitting and whistling.

PRINCESS. Vanka, Vanka, you rogue, what have you brought me to? I was a faithful wife to my husband, but how am I to look him in the eye?

VANKA *(spitting)*. You'll look him in the eye all right. All you skirts are hot for a man.

The garden. The countess lets fall her kerchief from the window. Jehan picks it up, kisses it and hides it.

COUNTESS. Jehan, Jehan, you horrid boy! What have you done to me! I was a faithful wife to the count, but how am I to look him in the eye?

JEHAN. Look him boldly in the eye, my sweet Jehanne. You don't think you're the only one he caresses, do you?

COUNTESS. But Jehan I *am* his wife.

JEHAN. You will remain his faithful wife.

COUNTESS. To betray one's husband is a great sin.

JEHAN. Pray to God, repent and be silent. God will forgive, the priest will give you a dispensation, the count won't find out.

COUNTESS. Yes that's true, Jehan. The best thing is to kiss—now while we have the chance.

Scene 6

The princess's room. Vanka and the princess sit at a table regaling themselves and conversing.

PRINCESS. Vanka, Vanka, you dashing young gallant, keep away from the royal drinking house.

VANKA. Look what she's thought up now! Not to go to the drinking house. A fool, that's what you are, even if you are a princess.

PRINCESS. I'm a fool and you're a clever one, but you'd better listen to me. You're so clever, but you have just one thing on your mind. I'm a silly bit of skirt, but I've seventy-seven things on mine.

VANKA. How come?

PRINCESS. The prince will find out.

VANKA. No chance.

PRINCESS. For sure he'll find out.

VANKA. Well I'll be damned!

PRINCESS. And the prince will yell out like a wild beast: "Now you my servants, my faithful servants! Go to the open country, dig two deep pits, drive in two spruce posts, set up two oaken cross-beams on them, hang a silken noose from them, get your hands on the dashing young gallant and bring him straight here, then you can string up my faithful servant Vanyushka!" My young gallant will be swinging in the noose; princess Annushka will end her days imprisoned in a tower.

Vanka scratches himself a long time, falls into deep thought, and spits hard and far.

VANKA. There, there, my little Annushka, the prince's very own wife, my sweet lady love! I won't go to the drinking house, I won't drink new wine, or strong-brewed mead!

The countess's bedchamber. The countess and Jehan are sitting at a table. Two bowls of fruit and wine are set before them.

COUNTESS. Sweet Jehan, don't keep company with young rakes, don't go to taverns with them, don't drink wine with them.

JEHAN. Dear Jehanne, but how can I hold aloof from my comrades! I'll be called proud and made a mockery of. And how can I refuse to drink wine! It gladdens the spirit.

COUNTESS Silly boy! You don't take any heed, don't even want to know why I ask this of you.

JEHAN. There's no counting ladies' whims.

COUNTESS. You'll get dead drunk, Jehan.

JEHAN. And I'll start bragging, that's how it goes.

COUNTESS. And you'll start babbling all sorts of nonsense.

JEHAN. It's true, dear Jehanne—we get tipsy and then anything can come into our head. Yes, wine gives a man many things—laughter, jokes and tears and pranks and fibs and songs.

COUNTESS. You'll start bragging.

JEHAN. But aren't I a handsome fellow? You must admit I've got something to boast about. And the glances of the gracious lady have fallen upon me.

COUNTESS. There you are, silly boy, that's what you'll be bragging about. You'll be boasting about me. *(Weeps.)*

JEHAN. Sweet Jehanne, how could you think such a thing! Could I really be so dishonorable! Could I disgrace your sweet name! I'd rather die than commit so vile a deed!

COUNTESS. Is that true, sweet Jehan? Oh I long to believe you, but I can't help being frightened. We women are so timid and you men are so tremendously brave: you speak before you have time to think. You men...

JEHAN. You are right, dearest Jehanne. Caution is not among a young warrior's virtues.

COUNTESS And then the two of us will be lost.

JEHAN. Why?

COUNTESS. The count will learn of it.

JEHAN. How can he? After all, he doesn't share our revels.

COUNTESS. They'll inform him.

JEHAN. Our friends?

COUNTESS. Friendship changes easily to enmity. And what is friendship! Even epics have a lot to say of betrayal and treachery between friends.

JEHAN (pensively). Yes, friends! I know how that is. You're a clever girl, Jehanne! You know everything and you understand everything.

COUNTESS. The count will give orders for you to be hanged and for my head to be cut off—and what's even worse, I might be punished with birch rods and put in a nunnery. That would be like being buried alive. And the count will marry someone else.

JEHAN. My sweet Jehanne, my beloved! From now on I won't keep company with young rakes, or drink wine with them.

Scene 7

In the early morning at the gate of the prince's garden stands the Swarthy Wench. Vanka comes from the gate, radiant and joyful—and he whistles loudly, spitting into the distance. And when he notices the Swarthy Wench he frowns slightly.

SWARTHY WENCH (piteously). I'm perishing with cold, chilled to the bone. I, the maiden fair, the swarthy one standing behind the white stone wall, awaiting the brave young gallant, none other than the valorous Vanka, the prince's steward.

VANKA (proudly). You've been wasting your time, waiting for nothing, vainly stamping your nimble feet. Go your way before you get a beating.

SWARTHY WENCH (sweetly). Vanka, oh, Vanka, the man I have longed for, come to me, Vanka!

VANKA (roughly). Get away from me, you hateful creature!

SWARTHY WENCH (reproachfully). You loved me once, but now you turn your back on me.

VANKA (furiously). Leave me in peace, you disgusting creature!

SWARTHY WENCH (threateningly). I'll give you something to remember me by. You'll be sorry, but it will be too late.

They go their separate ways.

Morning at the gate of the count's garden. Raymonda is waiting. Jehan comes through the gate.

RAYMONDA. It's cold this morning, and I've been waiting for you, dear Jehan.
JEHAN. Why did you get up so early? You're standing barefoot in the dewy grass—look out, you'll catch your death of cold. Go home to your warm chamber.
RAYMONDA. Sweet Jehan, warm me with a tender kiss.
JEHAN. Raymonda, I'm not in the mood for kissing.
RAYMONDA. Jehan, my sweet, come and see me tonight.
JEHAN. Raymonda, I can't come tonight.
RAYMONDA. Where is the love you used to feel? Or have you forgotten my caresses?
JEHAN. Snow melts, water runs away and yesterday is forgotten.
RAYMONDA. But you will remember!

They go their separate ways.

Scene 8

A street. Vanka is alone. He has a somber air, hanging his head, deep in thought, talking to himself.

VANKA. It's a prison, a prison—the prince's court! Somehow I want to see my father and mother, to see that skinny and unlucky wife of mine—I can't forget how she wept like a river, her tears rolling like two streams, she started sobbing like a thunderstorm.

Enter first Drinking-House Strumpet. She steals up to Vanka and claps him on the shoulder. Vanka starts and cries out.

VANKA. To hell with you!
FIRST STRUMPET. Steward Vanka, the prince's faithful servant, what are you doing standing there lost in gloom, hanging your unruly head? What other trouble do you have in store? Is it no one to kiss, is that it?

Giggles, presses against Vanka.

FIRST STRUMPET. Let's be off, let's be off, my dashing young gallant, let's go to the royal drinking house for a spree.
VANKA *(pushing her away)*. To the devil with you.

She giggles and goes off. Vanka watches her, smirks cheerfully, spits,—and again falls into deep thought. Enter Second Strumpet. She steals up to Vanka and claps him on the back. Vanka starts and cries out.

VANKA. May you be torn to pieces.
SECOND STRUMPET. Vanka, ah Vanka! Why are you so down in the mouth? Is it that you don't have anyone to put your arms around? Well, don't

you upset yourself about that. *(Giggles, dances and cries out.)* Hey there, Vanka, grab me by my white hands, let's go to the royal drinking house, guzzle new wine, and drink heady mead, a sweet brew.

VANKA *(sullenly.)* To the devil with you!

She goes out giggling. Vanka watches her go, smirking.

VANKA. Get along with you, strumpet.

Becomes pensive. Enter Third Strumpet; steals up to Vanka and shoves him in the back, making him jerk forward, stumble and fall. She giggles, he picks himself up cursing.

VANKA. May the earth open and swallow you up! May you fall into a bottomless pit!

THIRD STRUMPET. Vanka, little Vanka, dashing young gallant, why are you hanging your head! Don't you have a sweetheart? *(Presses herself to him, embraces him, whispers something. Vanka guffaws, watching her go, and yells.)*

VANKA. You're a fine one. Be off with you! Well, well, well! There's a wench for you! A right precious peach! *(Becomes pensive. Scratches the nape of his neck for a long time. Suddenly yells.)* I'm going to the drinking house. *(Runs off.)*

A street. Jehan is alone. He is lost in thought, head bowed. He is talking to himself.

JEHAN. Boring! I feel like going on a spree with the lads. They've all gone to that merry tavern at the sign of the Golden Hind, where the maidens are so merry. The way they sing! The way they play!

Enter First Merry Maiden. Steals over to Jehan and suddenly tickles him. Jehan starts and cries out.

JEHAN. Oh, you silly girl, you gave me a fright!

FIRST MERRY MAIDEN. Jehan darling, page of the glorious count, why are you so gloomy? Has some misfortune befallen you? Or don't you have anyone to kiss? Let's go the the Golden Hind. It's very lively there.

JEHAN. I don't want to.

FIRST MERRY MAIDEN. You don't want to? Well, we'll manage without you.

She goes off. Jehan watches her, smiling and is lost in thought. Enter Second Merry Maiden. Steals over to Jehan, covers his eyes with the palms of her hands and laughs. Jehan nimbly frees himself.

JEHAN. You too, you little minx.

SECOND MERRY MAIDEN. Jehan, darling. Such a sour face? Or don't you have anyone to fondle? *(Lifts the edge of her skirt, straightens her garter.)* Give me your arm, we'll go to the Golden Hind, we'll drink, sing and make love.

JEHAN. Go by yourself, I don't want to.

SECOND MERRY MAIDEN. Well, if you don't want to, you don't have to. But do come if you change your mind. *(Exits.)*

JEHAN *(follows her with his eyes, smiling, and whispers).* You're a merry one!

He becomes lost in thought. Enter Third Merry Maiden. She stops in front of Jehan and fixes her eyes on him. Jehan gives a start.

JEHAN. A third one! What do you all want of me?

THIRD MERRY MAIDEN. Jehan, Jehan, most exquisite of pages. Why do you hang your head like that? Has your sweetheart been unfaithful? That'll do— jealousy and moping are a waste of time. *(Coquettishly, she whispers something in his ear.)*

JEHAN. Be off with you. I don't want to listen.

THIRD MERRY MAIDEN. So, you're not interested! All right then, stay on your own and stagnate in that individualism of yours. What we like is a kind of jolly togetherness!

Exits. Jehan laughs and follows her with his eyes.

JEHAN. Those sweet maidens will cheer up the gloomiest man in the world. *(Stands for a long time, lost in thought. Suddenly shouts.)* I will go to the Golden Hind! *(And runs out.)*

Scene 9

A drinking house. A variety of topers, from drunken sots to princely retainers, who hold themselves apart, and visitors from far off. At this point no one is yet more than half-sozzled. The Drinking-House Strumpets sit at the window, in the hope of spotting Vanya's arrival.

STRUMPETS. Vanka the Steward is making his arrival at the royal drinking house.

> A green caftan adorns his shoulders.
> The hat on his head is of crushed velvet.
> The boots he's pulled on are Morocco leather.
> His golden signet burns like a fever.
> Slender the cane his right hand twirls.
> And round that cane a crimson bow.
> His russet curls fall to his shoulders.

His clear eyes burn with fire. Here comes our Steward, like a young falcon in flight.

DRUNKARDS. Hey, you strumpets, what have you set eyes on there in the window? Vanka the Steward won't even take a glance at you. He won't even be spitting on you. *(Vanka enters the drinking house and sits apart by himself, swagger -*

ing. The strumpets all go to him; they don't take so much as a glance at the others.)

FIRST STRUMPET. Vanka, oh Vanka, you dashing young gallant. I've poured you a goblet of young wine, and added sweetest mead. You, who are the prince's servant! Down this goblet of young wine. *(Bows low. Vanka drinks and pretends indifference.)*

SECOND STRUMPET. And now will I pour Vanka the Steward, the dashing young gallant, another flagon of goodly brew; Oh Vanka faithful steward, drink deep of the heady brew. *(Bows low. Vanka drinks and pretends indifference.)*

THIRD STRUMPET. And now will I, bold drinking-house strumpet, pour you a third flagon of sweetest mead, and bring it to you with low bow—and you, brave Vanka the Steward, drink deep of this sweetest mead.

DRINKING-HOUSE STRUMPETS. A right drinking-house befuddlement has taken hold of our dashing young gallant.

DRUNKARDS. Good is the drinking-house draft. Makes the head go round.

FIRST STRUMPET. I spent the night, a lively drinking-house strumpet, with a clerk; I listened, lively one that I am, to his caressing words; I asked for money and the drunken sot sent me off with the greatest honor.

All laugh merrily.

SECOND STRUMPET. And I spent the night, bold drinking-house strumpet, with a Hanseatic visitor; bold creature that I am I accepted a piece of soap; I asked for money, and the little Fritz said: I can't understand your lingo.

All laugh merrily and sprawl all over the counters.

THIRD STRUMPET. And this bold drinking-house strumpet spent the night with a generalissimo, a bad one at that; he gave me a bent penny, and I asked him, brave strumpet that I am, for a little something more, and they led me off, bold creature that I am, with slaps for accompaniment.

They all roll about the floor in a fit of laughter.

STRUMPETS. And what do you have to boast about Vanka?

VANKA *(swaggering)*. The Lord has been good to me, a dashing young gallant, and the prince gracious to me. I sit at the same table as the prince, and I drink, eat with the same spoon, and partake of vodka from the same glass.

STRUMPETS. Oh yes Vanka! Vanka's such a fellow. Drinks from the same glass as the prince, and vodka too.

VANKA *(weeping)*. Well have we drunk, well have we eaten; lived in luxury, we have, and have worn clothes from the prince's shoulders and have led the princess by the hand and have lain with the princess.

DRUNKARDS. Vanka, oh Vanka, our dearest little brother, dashing Vanka, steward to the prince, who is your mistress?

VANKA. I dare not say.

STRUMPETS. Vanka, oh Vanka, our longed for friend, dashing one, steward to the prince, who calls you darling? Who is it calls you the darling of her heart?

VANKA *(weeping with emotion)*. Princess Annushka holds me close to her sweet heart in love; Annushka and I are like husband and wife.

PRINCE'S SERVANTS. These are incomprehensible fairy tales. Did you dream it up, brave youth? We should inform the prince. A wretched fellow's worthless bragging.

VANKA *(weeping)*. Brothers, all has been drunk, all has been eaten, in beauty and goodness done, and I have led the princess by the hand and have lain with the princess on her bolster.

PRINCE'S SERVANTS. It would fine to report such doings to the prince. It would not bring us loss, but gain. The prince would be greatly vexed. Grab Vanka by his yellow curls, by his white hands.

They seize Vanka and lead him away. He drunkenly wriggles in their arms; at times he seems to beat them off, mumbling something incomprehensible.

STRUMPETS. Have mercy, faithful servants of the prince, don't take Vanka off to the prince, lay him down to sleep with us in our little hut. Vanka wasn't really bragging, it was just the wine in him talking big. He wove a story that wasn't true at all. Which couldn't possibly be true.

PRINCE'S SERVANTS. No, he's in the trap, my friends, he won't get out. He swaggered about right in front of us, and now we'll have our little game with him.

The Drinking-House Strumpets fall flat at the feet of the prince's servants, they beg forgiveness for Vanka, and weep piteously.

STRUMPETS. Ah, prithee, faithful servants of the prince, take pity on Vanka, the prince is sure to condemn him without mercy, to put him to death.

PRINCE'S SERVANTS. That's just what the dog deserves. There's no punishment good enough for such a Judas. Burying him alive wouldn't be enough.

They push the Strumpets away and lead Vanka off. The Strumpets dissolve in tears.

STRUMPETS. If only we could have escaped this evil! Why did this dashing young gallant have to start sniveling and bragging? And the prince's executioners were there, right butchers they are! And they seized our dashing young gallant on the spot. Even his closest friends did him evil!

The Golden Hind drinking house. All kinds of folk sit about and make merry: townsfolk, passers-by, schoolboys. The count's pages sit at a table to one side. Merry maidens sit with the pages, keeping an eye cocked to the window.

MERRY MAIDENS. And here he comes, Jehan. Just passing? No, seems to be coming here. How smart he looks. A green caftan made of the finest cloth.

PAGES *(enviously)*. It's all right for him to get dressed up! He's in the count's good graces.

MERRY MAIDENS. A red velvet cap! And little bells sewn to all the seams of his clothes, making a pretty jingle. Oh, how long and pointed are the curling tips of his shoes!

PAGES. Playing the dandy—but when he came to the castle, he was barefoot, his clothes in tatters, and carried a pair of worn-out shoes over his shoulders.

MERRY MAIDENS. He has black hose with red stripes. How smoothly they fit his shapely legs! And who gave him those golden buckles? They say...

PAGES. Well, what do they say? What do they say?

MERRY MAIDENS. Oh nothing! Just nonsense. People say all kinds of things! How beautifully Jehan's auburn curls cluster beneath his velvet cap! How his eyes shine. What a handsome fellow he is! It's not surprising that... Let it go...

PAGES. Handsome, but not for you. You'd think he's the only handsome fellow around! There are a few even more handsome than he is.

Jehan enters the tavern, goes over to the pages, smiling cheerfully.

JEHAN. So here I am, my friends! Greetings to you, dear comrades! And you too, my merry beauties!

PAGES. Welcome, dear Jehan! How splendid that you've come. We're so happy to see you! Now we'll really have a feast.

MERRY MAIDENS. Good day to you, sweet Jehan. Come and sit here, right in the middle of us! We'll do our best to see things aren't dull.

JEHAN. Well, I'm not one of those who finds things dull. *(Takes a seat with the merry maidens.)*

FIRST MERRY MAIDEN. Jehan, sweet, gorgeous Jehan, I've poured you a goblet of white wine—drink it to the glory of youth full of joy and free of care. *(Presents Jehan with the goblet, he smiles and sinks into his chair. Jehan kisses the maiden and takes the goblet from her.)*

JEHAN. Friends, here's to our joyful and carefree youth! *(Drinks. The pages repeat his toast and drink.)*

SECOND MERRY MAIDEN. I've poured our sweet, beloved Jehan a second goblet of red wine. Drain it, faithful page to the count, to the bright cloudless merriment that joins young friends. *(Smiling and making a deep reverence, she presents the goblet to Jehan. Jehan takes it and kisses the maiden tenderly.)*

JEHAN. Friends, here's to that bright and cloudless mirth that joins us in firm bond.

The pages repeat the toast. All drain their goblets.

THIRD MERRY MAIDEN. Well, I, a merry maiden among merry maidens, I will pour you a third goblet of sweet and heady wine, and give it to you standing on my knees—drink it for her who is sweeter than mead, to one more radiant than life and stronger than death, drink to our sovereign mistress Love! *(Goes down on her knees before Jehan and presents him with the goblet. Jehan takes it and tenderly embraces the maiden, giving her a big kiss.)*

JEHAN. Friends, let us empty this goblet to her who is sweeter than mead, more radiant, more precious than life, and stronger than death, a toast to our sovereign mistress—Love!

The pages repeat the toast. All drink.

MERRY MAIDENS. Jehan has gotten drunk. His head is sinking onto the table. He has drunk too much wine at a sitting.

JEHAN *(bestirs himself)*. Who says I'm drunk? Not true! I'm ready to drink as much again, and again, and again, ad infinitum!

PAGES. The innkeeper here keeps good wine. It really goes to your head. These are merry maidens indeed. Friends, let us act as do all drunkards—let us boast in front of each other. Whoever can outbrag the rest will be our leader. That's fine! Who's to start? Let the girls begin. All right, girls, get down to it.

FIRST MERRY MAIDEN. Not long ago I spent the whole night with his worship the burgomaster. He didn't demand too much of me, and in the morning he gave me a silver shilling and some red velvet for a dress.

All laugh merrily.

SECOND MERRY MAIDEN. I spent last night with the knight Heinrich. He was very loving and tender, and in the morning he gave me gold and a splendid cape that he'd taken from a passing merchant the May before.

All laugh merrily.

THIRD MERRY MAIDEN. The night before last I spent with an abbot, Father Hieronymus. I was absolutely worn out! Only the monks get so passionate in their caresses. Toward morning he remembered that we had sinned, and fell to whipping himself and me with a leather belt—himself lightly enough on his priestly robes, and me with all his might all over my bare body. Then he forgave me my sins, and that was all. So I came home without any sins, but without any money or presents either; I had plenty of bruises, though.

All laugh merrily.

MERRY MAIDENS. Now you, Jehan—what are you going to brag about?

JEHAN *(tongue-tied)*. God has mercy on me, and the count is kind. During the count's dinner I stand behind the gracious countess's seat. The count has ordered me clothes of the best cut and the finest cloth.

MERRY MAIDENS *(flattering)*. Oh, Jehan! What a fellow Jehan is! Serves himself at the countess's table. Bravo, Jehan! Who wouldn't fall in love with such a gallant.

JEHAN *(moved to tears)*. I have a beloved and she calls me darling, her sweetheart.

PAGES. Jehan, our dearest fried, and who is this beloved?

JEHAN. I cannot tell you, dear friends. No one may know. It is a great secret.

MERRY MAIDENS. Jehan, longed-for, sweet, handsome fellow, who is it who calls you her sweetheart? Tell us, have your boast! We know you'll outbrag all the rest.

JEHAN (moved to tears). Countess Jehanne, the soul of my soul, presses me to her burning heart.

PAGES. Utter nonsense! Could you have seen this in a dream, Jehan? We should tell the count—we are his faithful servants after all. Jehan insults our master with his bragging.

JEHAN (weeping). How joyful my life is. How sweet are the kisses of my darling Jehanne! How intoxicating her embraces and caresses in the quiet of her bedchamber! Oh, if only you could see how heavenly her white body is.

PAGES. We cannot endure such defamation. Our lord must be told of this. We cannot allow the name of our gracious countess to be dishonored before the people. We must seize him and take him to judgment to our count.

They grab Jehan and lead him away.

MERRY MAIDENS. Have pity on Jehan, sweet dear pages, and don't take him to your count, give him to us and we will lay him down to sleep. It wasn't Jehan bragging so—drunkenness spoke with his lips, of things that could not have happened.

PAGES. No, we won't let him go. We must take him for the count to pronounce judgment. There were strangers here. They may have heard his bragging. Rumors of what happened here will reach the count. Then we would be executed too—why did we listen and make no report?

The merry maidens get down on their knees weeping, they kiss the hands of the pages, pleading on Jehan's behalf.

MERRY MAIDENS. Have pity on Jehan, don't destroy him, have compassion for his youth! The count will hang him without mercy.

The pages push the Merry Maidens away and lead Jehan off. The Merry Maidens weep.

MERRY MAIDENS. Oh, why did such a misfortune befall us! Stupid Jehan, what a thing to brag about. You should have told us alone, fine company to blab in! Oh, they've seized Jehan, led him away! His own comrades are betraying him.

Scene 10

The prince sits drinking mead. Before him, an old servant stands and the Swarthy Wench is hanging about.

OLD SERVANT. There is a saying: long of hair, short of wit. There isn't a brainy woman living.

PRINCE. Oh, but my princess has brains, brains to spare. She's quiet and meek, gracious to the serfs and treats me with honor.

SWARTHY WENCH *(standing in the doorway)*. Hail to you, Prince. Don't order me to behead or hang a man, order me to speak the truth. I've come to denounce Vanka the Steward.

PRINCE. Then speak to me, faithful servant! Tell me the honest truth. If you tell the truth, I will be grateful to you, if you speak falsely, I'll have them lop off your head.

SWARTHY WENCH. O hail unto you, Prince! You drink, eat, make merry, boast of your fine princess, but know nothing, you have no notion! Your sweet princess is not honorable, that sweet princess of yours is not faithful! I tell you she lives with the unfledged steward, with Vanka—she lives with him in wanton love.

The prince kicks her away. The Swarthy Wench goes flying head over heels.

The count is alone. He is examining the weapons of his ancestors. Enter Raymonda, bowing low.

COUNT. What do you want, Raymonda? *(Raymonda approaches with another bow.)*

COUNT *(impatiently)*. Well, say what you have to say....

RAYMONDA *(in a whisper)*. Jehan and I—aren't we a match?

COUNT. That may well be.

RAYMONDA. Kissing and caressing was all he thought of...

COUNT You should have kept an eye on him.

RAYMONDA. But why did he deceive me with a married woman? Why did he raise his eyes to a lady of exalted station?

COUNT. Pages are not forbidden to sigh for a lady's beauty.

RAYMONDA. But sighing isn't what he's at—he has been fortunate.

COUNT *(angrily)*. And who may this lady be?

RAYMONDA. Gracious Count, dare I say?

They are silent. The Count gives a sign. Raymonda goes out.

Scene 11

In the prince's palace. The prince sits on a fretted oaken chair frowning angrily. Servants stand along the walls, looking fearfully. An old servant approaches the prince, bows to the ground, and gives a polite little cough.

PRINCE. Our most loyal and devoted servant, what do you require? You've come to me at an evil hour.

OLD SERVANT. O hail unto you, our prince and father! Your princely servant, Vanka the Steward, whom you love and pity is now sitting in a stately tavern, drinking new wine, quaffing mead, and bragging about the lovely princess Anna, about your princely excellency; I'm living with princess Anna he says, like husband and wife; God is good to me, and Annushka is most gracious toward me; I've been paying court to her these past three years.

PRINCE *(barks out in a loud voice)*. I reckon I still have in my service, as we put it, our terrible Russian headsman. Let him put up his block of white oak, let him sharpen his axe. I reckon I still have faithful servants! Let them take Vanka the Steward, the fond love of my young princess, and let them bring him to terrible judgment:

Shouting in the courtyard: "They're bringing him!" Whispering in the palace: "The prince didn't like what he heard. He's terribly angry with our young fellow. What was said didn't suit the prince in the least. His princely highness is wrath with our dashing young gallant. The prince's heart is mightily inflamed. His hot blood is seething." Vanka is brought in. The court buzzes with whispers: "They're taking Vanka the Steward to the courthouse. His green caftan is torn to tatters. His Morocco boots are down at the knees. His auburn curls are rumpled. His bright eyes are swollen with tears."

VANKA *(bowing low)*. Hail to you, O Prince, our father! For what have you sent me? What is it you want to give me, to favor me with?

PRINCE. I will make you a present of a lofty mansion unfurnished. Just tell me the honest truth, are you living with my princess?

VANKA. O my Prince and father! I will tell you the entire truth—I am living with your princess, with darling little Annushka. Much have we drunk, much have we eaten, and much have we lain on downy mattresses.

PRINCE *(loudly)*. Vanka, oh Vanka, you contemptible wretch, how could you have dared to do this?

VANKA *(spitting)*. By mutual consent. I served you three full years, and I lived in faith and not in treachery. Surely I'm allowed to kiss a wench? That's what wenches are for.

PRINCE. Oh you, my faithful servants, exterminate this tempter Vanka.

VANKA. There should be something to exterminate me for! She fell for me, the dashing young gallant, she fell for me to no purpose.

PRINCE. Oh, my faithful servants, my merciless headsmen, my bold marshals! Tie the brave fellow's white hands with this silky twine, clamp the brave fellow's legs in these rough outlandish irons, cover his bright eye with black taffeta, grab the gallant by his yellow curls, lead him out to the open fields, to an open field of blood, to the place of execution, to that very white oaken block, and there chop off his wild head, and give him vain death—cut out his heart and liver. Let the young princess receive her punishment through him.

Vanka is led off. He bawls loudly.

In the chamber of the count. The count is sitting on a fretted oaken armchair. He is deep in thought. Enter Agobard, the old butler. He bows low to the count.

COUNT. Well, what do you want, you old fogy. I haven't got any time for you. If you've got something important, tell me, but if it's some nonsense that's brought you here, be off.

AGOBARD. Gracious Count, evil rumors have reached my ears. My allegiance will not let me hide them. The page Jehan, to whom you have bean so gracious, even beyond his deserts, sits in the Golden Hind drinking and bragging, alleging that our gracious lady, Countess Jehanne, forgetting her duty...

COUNT. Enough. Let gallows be set up behind the ditch, where the twisted birch leans over the swamp. Let Jehan be brought to me.

Agobard bows low and exits. Noise is heard outside. Voices can be heard: "Jehan is being led in! What did he do? They're taking him to the count. The count is angry with Jehan. The count is furious. But what happened? They're leading Jehan in, he's drunk. His clothes are torn. His eyes are red with weeping. Poor Jehan!"
The pages lead in Jehan. The menials look through the doorway.

JEHAN *(bowing low)*. Gracious Count, I have been brought to you for judgment. I am not aware of any guilt except that I have had too much to drink. Why are they dragging me like this? They should let me sleep it off.

COUNT. Jehan, answer me truthfully! Do you love Countess Jehanne?

JEHAN. I love her. Who could not but love such a gracious and kind mistress? All the servants love the countess and her gracious bearing.

COUNT. That's not what I'm asking you about. Have you had the effrontery to gaze lustfully upon Countess Jehanne?

JEHAN. Gracious Count, never! I have never forgotten my obligations to my mistress.

COUNT. In the drinking house you said that my spouse is being unfaithful to me with you.

JEHAN *(throws himself at the count's feet)*. I said that which has never been.

COUNT. How could you dare do such a thing?

JEHAN *(bowing again)*. From drunkenness and stupidity. People had the idea to outbrag each other, and I started making up all kinds of nonsense.

COUNT. What am I to do with you?

JEHAN. Forgive me for the sake of my loyal service, gracious Count.

COUNT. Agobard, let the boy be hanged.

JEHAN. Have pity on me, gracious Count! I'll die an innocent! *(Throws him - self to the count's feet, kisses his jack boots.)*

COUNT. Take him away, Agobard. Bind his arms and have him hanged on the double. Thus shall it be with anyone who dares to insult our honor and slander our beloved spouse. *(Jehan is led off. He weeps.)*

Scene 12

The Steward is caught up by his white arms and led out through the backyard.

VANKA. Oh, you evil headsmen! Don't take a dashing young gallant through the backyard. Lead this gallant past the stables, past that green garden and the chambers of the princess; yes, past her warm, brightly lighted bedchamber, where the princess and I slept together. I'll give you fifty rubles and fifty kopecks if you do it.

HEADSMEN. Let's do as the young gallant asks, it's all the same to us.

VANKA. Oh, hail to you, our fearsome friend, the headsman. Before he dies, let a dashing young gallant strum his psaltery.

HEADSMEN. Oh, you dashing young gallant! Take up your sounding psaltery and strum it, young gallant, before your death. But don't play too loudly—give us some nice tune.

VANKA *(plays soft tunes, sings, weeping the while)*.

> It was a goodly life this young gallant had,
> And my bright apparel was well worn,
> Fine drinking and eating this young man had well,
> All in beauty and goodness groomed
> And in the green garden he went roaming
> And under the apple tree he slumbered in his cot,
> And on Princess Annushka's white breast
> Did the dashing young gallant lie.

HEADSMEN. The brave young gallant has sung a new song, and a right touching one at that. He sings and the hot tears roll down his cheeks. Death will come—and you won't rejoice.

VANKA. Farewell, farewell, my father and mother. Farewell, farewell, my kith and kin! Farewell, my sweet princess! A time there was the prince did love and favor me. But swiftly was I smitten by his ire. And they're leading me off to a cruel death. *(The princess overhears the song and thrusts herself down to the waist from the window.)*

HEADSMEN. Oh, the princess has heard the new song. She has flung the lovely window open wide. Surely that's not a knife she's holding. What if she should cut her throat!

VANKA. Forgive me, Annushka, my sweet little Princess! They are taking me, the young gallant, to chop off my tempestuous head.

PRINCESS *(in the window)*. Oh, you evil headsmen, don't lead the young gallant out to the open fields, don't chop off his unruly head, but plunge your arms up to the elbow in these coffers of gold.

HEADSMEN. Let him go and the prince will chop our heads off! So what good will your gold do us?

PRINCESS *(in the window)*. Let the young gallant go, find some vile Tartar, even a dead one, and cut off his unruly head, and take that unruly head to the prince and tell him the unruly head was chopped off for his shameful deeds.

VILE TARTAR *(enters shouting)*. A rope, a rope!

HEADSMAN. We'll grab that one. *(They grab the Tartar, and let Vanka go.)*

PRINCESS. The headsmen's hearts have melted, Vanka, and they have let you go. Take this purse of gold and go home at once. And you, evil headsmen, take as much gold as you want.

HEADSMEN. Let's go, vile Tartar, we'll chop your head off for you.

VILE TARTAR. Why chop off my noddle? Without my head I can't live too well.

HEADSMEN. And so you'll just croak. *(Drag the vile Tartar off.)*

Jehan is led by the servants to the rear courtyard, to the bridge across the ditch, on the other side of which the gallows have already been set up.

JEHAN *(to the servants).* Friends, don't drag me off so soon. The gallows won't go away, and the angel of death isn't in any hurry. Lead me through the count's garden so that I can for the last time breathe my fill of the fragrance of the count's roses. Take me beneath the windows of our gracious lady; if I am fortunate, Countess Jehanne will glance from her window and I will see her bright eyes for the last time.

SERVANTS. Makes no difference to us. We'll take you wherever you want on your last journey.

JEHAN. Dear Agobard! Give me my lute—before death I'll play and sing, and take my leave of the wide world with a sad little song.

AGOBARD. Claude, bring him his lute—let him amuse himself. Sing and play before death, meet your fated end with good cheer. Only don't yell at the top of your voice, and don't strike all five strings at once—play softly and sing in a low voice.

JEHAN *(plays the lute and sings, at first softly, then louder)*:

> Not all is lasting in our life,
> Even love is sometimes evil.
> I've drunk a full cup of happiness,
> My life has been radiant,
>
> I've loved the countess more,
> Than is given to a page,
> And for this I'm to live no longer,
> But go off on my mortal journey.
>
> Often idleness is our undoing.
> You sing, and cheer your spirit,
> Then suddenly the gallows await
> And the shameful noose.
>
> Oh, if only I could for a moment be
> With my beloved before the end,
> To be with Countess Jehanne,
> Exchange but a little word!

SERVANTS. The fair Jehan has sung a touching song. He sings and cries like a girl. No one greets death gladly. And Jehan is still so young! It's enough to make you weep!

JEHAN *(sings)*:

> Before I start to swing
> In that tight fatal noose,

Let me press against you
With my curly head,
Let me glimpse the charm
Of her white neck, tender shoulders.
And hear in farewell,
Her sweetly ringing voice.
Allow me a farewell kiss,
And to shed a tear,
In that hour when the merciless
Headsman will bind my arms.
And then to bend my knees,
In prayer to the Holy Virgin,
So that I will not have excess suffering
From the noose.

The countess looks out her window. She listens to the song. Fear and sadness are in her face.

SERVANTS. The mistress is looking out the window. The countess has heard the song. She is weeping. She has pity for Jehan. Can it be true that she loves Jehan? What is that in her hands? The countess is playing with her dagger. Careful she doesn't cut her throat. With that little awe. You couldn't even kill a cat with it. Well, you can't be too careful.

COUNTESS *(from the window)*. Sweet Jehan, what has happened? There are tears on your cheeks, your clothes have been torn. And where are these good people leading you?

JEHAN. Forgive me, my gracious lady. Your counsels were wise, but I did not heed them, and now I am doomed to death. The Golden Hind lifted me up on his branching horns and has thrown me down at a fatal crossroad. *(Weeps.)*

AGOBARD *(bowing low)*. He's remembering the drinking house called the Golden Hind. In a fit of drunkenness he made up some cock-and-bull story so as to have something to brag about. That's why we're taking the boy away.

JEHAN. Beyond the ditch, over the swamp, there stand black gallows. They'll hang me from them.

COUNTESS. Poor Jehan, what did you say? Why are they leading you to the block?

JEHAN. Having drunk three deep goblets, I bragged about something that must remain for all in the realm of unrealizable dreams. I bragged about your love for me, dearest Jehanne. I foolishly betrayed my sweet dreams to the fury of insane ravings.

COUNTESS. Oh, foolish Jehan! You are deserving of punishment, but not such a terrible one. One of your years may be pardoned for dreaming of a beautiful lady's caresses. Good people, don't take him to the gallows, save the life of my faithful page. I will reward you generously.

SERVANTS. And if the count finds out? He'll execute us for such disobedience. What good will the generous gifts of our gracious mistress be then?

COUNTESS. Be not in so great haste; I'll go to my dear spouse, and beg him to spare this madman's life. You'll always have time to behead him if the count refuses to pardon him—the count's tardy pardon will be no good to a cold corpse on the gallows.

AGOBARD. We will carry out your command, mistress, we will wait. And in truth there's no cause to hurry. It's not for nothing old folks say: a man in a hurry can make people worry.

Scene 13

The prince's bedchamber. The prince is in a sweat from beating the princess; he sits panting, wiping himself with a kerchief. The princess is lying on the floor, begging for . giveness.

PRINCESS. The evil one led me astray, it wasn't I who sinned. Why would I deceive you, my bright falcon, of my own free will? The foe is strong, he shakes mountains, and sweeps people away like a broom.

PRINCE. I'll toss you about!

PRINCESS. Have pity, Prince. Never again shall this betide. All my life I shall repent.

PRINCE. You've had your beating, and now we have to live together. Arise and let us kiss.

Chamber in the count's palace. The countess on her knees is begging the count to spare Jehan. Agobard stands at the door.

COUNT. Arise, dear Jehanne. For the sake of your tears I'll give the insolent fellow his life. Agobard—take Jehan to the back courtyard, assemble the pages and all the servants, and let the boy be punished with a lashing. Then expel him from the castle: and may he never dare to show his face nearer than three days journey from the castle.

Exit Agobard.

COUNTESS. I thank you, my dear master.

COUNT. And you, Jehanne, pray long and fervently that in future the charms of your beauty will not tempt the weak. To the beauty given by God, Satan joins his temptations, which find a nest in a lovely body. We will pray to the benign Creator that he not give victory to the foe, the author of temptations; we shall expel Satan from your lovely body. And Satan is expelled, do you know how Jehanne?

COUNTESS. I know.

COUNT. How?

COUNTESS. With prayer.

COUNT. And what else?

COUNTESS. With fasting.

COUNT. And what else beside?

COUNTESS. Flagellation.

COUNT. The days of sadness will pass, and Satan will be expelled.

THE END